RUSSIANS IN BRITAIN

Ma
Te

Fror   arjevsky in the 1920s, to Cheek by Jowl's Russian 'sister
com   most a century later, Russian actor training has had a unique
influ   modern British theatre. *Russians in Britain*, edited by Jonathan
Pitcl   the first work of its type to identify a relationship between both
cour   theatrical traditions as continuous as it is complex.

U   eiling new strands of transmission and translation linking the great
Russ   émigré practitioners to the second- and third-generation artists who
resp   d to their ideas, *Russians in Britain* takes in:

- sarjevsky and the British theatre establishment
- slavsky in the British conservatoire
- hold in the academy
- el Chekhov in the private studio
- vood's Theatre Workshop and the Northern Stage Ensemble
- Mitchell, Declan Donnellan and Michael Boyd.

C   g a hitherto untold story with historical and contemporary
impl   ns, these nine essays present a compelling alternative history of
theat   practice in the UK.

Jona   **Pitches** is Professor of Theatre and Performance and Director
of R   in the School of Performance and Cultural Industries at Leeds
Univ   UK. He is the author of two books on Russian actor training,
Vsev   *Meyerhold* and *Science and the Stanislavsky Tradition of Acting.*
He h   ught masterclasses on Russian actor training at the RSC and in
Toky   alta and Shanghai, and is the founding co-editor of the Routledge
journ   *tre, Dance and Performance Training.*

RUSSIANS IN BRITAIN

British Theatre and the Russian Tradition of Actor Training

Edited by Jonathan Pitches

Routledge
Taylor & Francis Group

LONDON AND NEW YORK

First published 2012
by Routledge
2 Park Square, Milton Park, Abingdon, Oxon OX14 4RN

Simultaneously published in the USA and Canada
by Routledge
711 Third Avenue, New York, NY 10017

Routledge is an imprint of the Taylor & Francis Group, an informa business

British Library Cataloguing in Publication Data
A catalogue record for this book is available from the British Library

Library of Congress Cataloguing in Publication Data
Russians in Britain : British theatre and the Russian tradition of actor training / edited by Jonathan Pitches.
p. cm.
Includes bibliographical references and index.
1. Acting—Study and teaching—Great Britain—History—20th century. 2. Acting—Study and teaching—Russia (Federation)—History—20th century. 3. Theater—Great Britain—History—20th century. 4. Russians—Great Britain—History—20th century. 5. Great Britain—Civilization—Russian influences.
PN2078.G7R87 2012
792.02'80941–dc23
2011025867

ISBN: 978-0-415-59099-0 (hbk)
ISBN: 978-0-415-59100-3 (pbk)
ISBN: 978-0-203-14659-0 (ebk)

Typeset in Times New Roman by Prepress Projects Ltd, Perth, UK

MIX
Paper from
responsible sources
FSC
www.fsc.org
FSC® C004839

Printed and bound in Great Britain by
TJ International Ltd, Padstow, Cornwall

FOR GRANT

CONTENTS

FIGURES

CONTRIBUTORS

Jerri Daboo is a Senior Lecturer in Drama at the University of Exeter. She has worked professionally as a performer and director for fifteen years, drawing on her experience of training in bodymind practices including Buddhism, martial arts, Indian dance and body awareness. Her work is based in a psychophysical approach to performer training, with a particular focus on the work of Michael Chekhov, as well as ritual and cultural performance. She is the author of a monograph, *Ritual, Rapture and Remorse: A Study of Tarantism and Pizzica in Salento*, as well as a number of articles on Michael Chekhov and psychophysical acting. She is the co-author with Phillip Zarrilli and Rebecca Loukes of the forth-coming book *From Stanislavsky to Physical Theatre: Contemporary Psychophysical Approaches to Acting and Performance*.

Katya Kamotskaia trained at Vakhtangov's Shchukin Institute (Moscow). She taught at the State Institute of Cinematography, Moscow, where she met Bella Merlin in 1993, and is now based at the Royal Scottish Academy of Music and Drama in Glasgow. She has directed and led masterclasses all around the world, bringing together Russian heritages and British practices, deeply informed by Stanislavsky. Kamotskaia was the Russian language consultant to Jean Benedetti for his translation of Stanislavsky's *An Actor's Work*.

Robert Leach has taught at the universities of Birmingham, Edinburgh and Cumbria. His books include *Vsevolod Meyerhold*, *Revolutionary Theatre*, *A History of Russian Theatre* (edited, with Victor Borovsky), *Stanislavsky and Meyerhold* and *Makers of Modern Theatre*, as well as *Theatre Workshop: Joan Littlewood and the Making of Modern British Theatre*. His theatre work includes directing the Moscow premiere of the formerly banned *I Want a Baby* by Sergei Tretyakov at the Teatr u Nikitskikh Vorot in 1990, and founding the three-yearly Lichfield

Mysteries in 1994. His epic, *The Journey to Mount Kailash*, was published in 2010.

Bella Merlin is an actor, writer and actor trainer. She is Professor of Acting at the University of California, Davis. Her areas of research include practical acting processes, Stanislavsky and stage fright. Performance work includes *Tilly No-Body: Catastrophes of Love* (an original investigation into the lives and loves of Frank and Tilly Wedekind) and David Hare's *The Permanent Way* (Out-of-Joint/National Theatre). She has taught masterclasses at theatres and drama schools in Japan, Australia, Poland, France, and Colombia, and across the UK and America. Her publications include *Acting: The Basics*, *The Complete Stanislavsky Toolkit* and *Beyond Stanislavsky: The Psycho-Physical Approach to Actor-Training*. She is on the editorial board of *New Theatre Quarterly* and on the advisory panel for the Stanislavski Centre at Rose Bruford, UK.

Jonathan Pitches is Professor of Theatre and Performance in the School of Performance and Cultural Industries at Leeds University. His interests are in Russian, European and American performer training, as well as in intercultural performance. He has taught in many different countries, leading masterclasses in Tokyo, Shanghai, Malta and the UK – including the RSC's *Revolutions* season (in 2009). He is the author of two monographs – *Vsevolod Meyerhold* and *Science and the Stanislavsky Tradition of Acting* – and is co-founder and co-editor of the Routledge journal *Theatre, Dance and Performance Training*. In addition to *Russians in Britain*, he is co-editor of a new book, *Performance Perspectives: A Critical Introduction*, due to be published by Palgrave in September 2011.

Duška Radosavljević is a Lecturer in Drama and Theatre Studies at the University of Kent. Her research interests include dramaturgy, adaptation and the ensemble way of working, and she is currently working on a book-length publication on text and performance in contemporary theatre. Having started her career as the Dramaturg at Northern Stage, Duška went on to work at the Education Department of the RSC. As a freelance dramaturg, she has also worked for New Writing North, Dance City, NSDF and Circomedia, and she has written for *The Stage* newspaper since 1998.

David Shirley trained as an actor at the Arts Educational Schools and studied at RADA. He has extensive experience of performing in theatre, film and TV and is currently Course Leader of the BA (Hons) Acting programme and Director of Studies at the Manchester School of Theatre.

The founding Chair of the Conference of Drama Schools Research Forum and Co-convenor of the 20th/21st Century Performer Training group within TaPRA, he focuses his research interests on British and American actor training, Beckett's theatre and contemporary performance practice. His recent publications include articles and chapters on Sanford Meisner, Stanislavsky and post-dramatic theatre.

Amy Skinner is a Lecturer in Drama and Theatre Practice, currently based at the University of Hull. Her research interests include Russian and early Soviet theatre, theatre of the avant-garde, and connections between theatre and fine art. She also works extensively in creating theatre projects in community settings. She has contributed to the Prism, Palatine's distributed e-learning programme focused on theatre and art emerging in the modernist period, and to the journal *About Performance*. Her first monograph, *Collage and the Theatre: Games across Time and Space*, is due to be published by Intellect in 2012.

ACKNOWLEDGEMENTS

This book was conceived and mapped out in a swimming pool in Alsager, Cheshire, seven years ago, as my then very young sons were having their weekly swimming lessons. It began life as a single-authored book, but thankfully the review process persuaded me that there were colleagues far better placed than I to write on the practitioners featured here; my debt of gratitude is therefore first to the other contributors to this book, who have embraced the concept so enthusiastically and developed it in ways I could not have imagined. Contributors' own acknowledgements are detailed in the chapters that follow, so I will confine myself here to thanking those who offered personal support and encouragement along the way. Thanks to the team at Routledge and specifically Talia Rodgers, Ben Piggott and Niall Slater, for consistently seeing worth in the project and for detailed feedback in the last few weeks. Gratitude also must be extended to the University of Leeds and the School of Performance and Cultural Industries (specifically, as Heads of School, Susan Daniels and Sita Popat) for awarding me a semester's leave for the core research and writing time for Chapter 1 and for supporting an archival visit to Harvard. Many colleagues have looked at draft material and I am particularly indebted to Robert Leach, Bryan Brown and members of my Practitioner Processes Research Group (at Leeds University). Rob Elkington at the RSC and Grant Pitches have also read and commented very helpfully on the introduction and conclusion. For the archival research, Micah Hoggat at Harvard helped me plan my research trip carefully and Richard Thompson has been exceptionally generous in opening up his own private collection of Komisarjevsky-related materials and lending me unique sources for my research. My personal thanks are extended to Declan Donnellan and Katie Mitchell for being so generous with their time and thoughts on Russian theatre and to the two cohorts of second-year students who have taken my Russian Performer Training module at Leeds; their direct and honest responses as 'research users' have genuinely improved the material and moved it on. Finally, I would like to thank my wife, Ceri, and my now considerably older sons, Harri and George.

Every effort has been made to trace copyright holders for all copyright material in this book. The editor regrets if there has been an oversight and suggests the publisher should be contacted in such event.

Jonathan Pitches
Burley in Wharfedale, West Yorks

INTRODUCTION
The mechanics of tradition making

Jonathan Pitches

A coincidence of ideas

1936 was a busy year for the incorporation of Russian ideas into the British theatre tradition. In London, Theodore Komisarjevsky was directing *The Seagull* with a host of British luminaries including Edith Evans, John Gielgud and Peggy Ashcroft; 200 miles south west, Michael Chekhov was leading his first term at his newly inaugurated theatre studio near Totnes in Devon, with an altogether more international cast of students; back in London, Stanislavsky's much-awaited book, *An Actor Prepares*, was published by Geoffrey Bles, translated and adapted by Elizabeth Reynolds Hapgood; and Joan Littlewood and Ewan MacColl formed the Russian-inspired Theatre Union – the precursor to Theatre Workshop – having rigorously researched Russian ideas and practices in the Manchester Central Library.

Although such corresponding activities can, of course, be put down to mere coincidence (or equally to a particular construction of historical significances by the author), they are cited here for two important reasons. The first is to debunk one of the myths of theatre training history, still propagated in some circles today, that the Russian tradition of actor training bypassed Britain on its way to the United States; the second is to indicate in microcosm the many complexities which accompany the story of the Russians in Britain, particularly in terms of *how* these ideas infiltrated British culture.

In respect of the first point, Mel Gordon's recent *Stanislavsky in America* (2010) gives one indication of the kind of argument:

> Artistic chance, the persuasive power of individual personalities, social climate and even technological advances must be factored into the reasons why Russian breakthroughs in actor-training successfully migrated westward, leaping over central and Western Europe.
>
> (Gordon 2010: xiv)

Gordon's otherwise rich narrative, conceived as a long-awaited sequel to *The Stanislavsky Technique: Russia* (Gordon 1987), embellishes in chronological terms a well-documented story of Boleslavsky, Ouspenskaya, the Group Theatre, Strasberg, Adler and Meisner. One chapter is devoted to Russian émigré teachers, and in a short paragraph Michael Chekhov's work in Dartington is noted (Gordon 2010: 99), but the overwhelming belief inscribed in the book is that the soil in the USA was especially well suited to Russian seed, as the acknowledgements section confirms:

> To Slava Tskuerman and Nina V. Kerova, my dear friends and great artists. They were the first Russians to inform me that the true work of Stanislavsky could be found only in the studios and stages of New York City and the backlots of independent Hollywood.
>
> (Gordon 2010: v)

Phillip Zarrilli develops a similar line, more by implication than design, in *Psycho-physical Acting* (Zarrilli 2009). Noting that 'Stanislavski's legacy is profoundly diverse' (p. 14) and identifying a number of branches of his legacy including the Russian-based Maria Knebel and Vasily Toporkov, he nevertheless positions 'American versions of Stanislavski' (p. 15) as the main subheading of the 'Stanislavski Legacy' section before he briefly notes Bella Merlin's contribution in 'Moving beyond Stanislavsky' (p. 18). Boleslavsky, Strasberg, Adler and Meisner again dominate in this particular narrative and Sonia Moore is an addition to the history. Zarrilli's purpose in this section is different, to be fair: to reframe the word 'psyche' and to rid it of its (Western) connotations of the inner self. However, the implication is similar to Gordon's: that Stanislavsky's legacy is best measured in US practices (with one short diversion led by Chekhov in Dartington).

Such arguments are in the tradition of American Stanislavskian criticism begun by Christine Edwards and her seminal *The Stanislavsky Heritage* (Edwards 1965). It is roughly split into two main halves of material: the first deals with the Stanislavskian context in Russia, the second with its legacy or heritage, focusing solely on the United States. Here, Stanislavsky's star pupil, Michael Chekhov, and his formative years at the Theatre Studio in Dartington are reduced to a single sentence (Edwards 1965: 242). Theodore Komisarjevsky, a significant part of the Russian tradition, if not a direct disciple of Stanislavsky, is mentioned only as the son of Fyodor, Stanislavsky's teacher, and identified along with his sister as someone 'known in America' (Edwards 1965: 36). This is despite Theodore's twenty years in Britain (1919–39) and his internationally recognised work at the Shakespeare Memorial Theatre. Of similar significance as a book charting the spread of Russian ideas, Laurence Senelick's (1992) *Wandering Stars* goes some way to recognising a wider sphere of influences beyond the American context; it has separate essays on the splinter Moscow Arts Theatre company (the Prague Group), on Michael Chekhov in England and America and on Komisarjevsky in Stratford. However, even here there is a significant bias towards the US branch of the Stanislavsky tradition, even if Senelick's excellent introduction recognises the full European spread of Russian theatre exiles and their aesthetic impact (Senelick 1992: ix–xx).

There are clear and often justifiable reasons for this bias: the authors or editors in question are all American themselves, for one. In addition, there is a relatively clear and well-documented route to trace the Russian tradition of acting in the United States (from Boleslavsky's Laboratory Theatre onwards) and Stanislavsky himself visited the USA with his company (in 1923 and 1924) prompting a much more visible impact on the theatre (and film) culture there. However, whereas this particular history is now clearly understood and has been intelligently problematised by scholars such as Sharon Carnicke (2009), and David Krasner (2000), there are alternative routes to be carved out in the complex history of Russian actor training and its absorption outside its own borders. This book is designed to go some way to drawing such an alternative history, focusing on the shoots of activity that have flourished in the UK from 1919 to the present.

The second associated point embedded in the 1936 set of coincidences is the question of *transmission*. Any history of ideas that examines the influence of one practice on another has to address *how* these ideas are being transmitted or passed on, and this serendipitous moment in theatre history unmistakeably demonstrates the range of possibilities. These might be summarised into three broad mechanisms of transmission:

- training places: the studio-laboratory, the conservatoire, the academy;
- theatre spaces: stage productions and the spaces which housed them;
- documentation sources: acting publications, archival sources such as log books, transcripts of classes, photos, moving images, theatre reviews, actor/director testimonies.

In the case of Chekhov's studio, the *training place* as a mechanism for transmission is most prominent, although, as Jerri Daboo points out in her contribution (Chapter 3), this activity produced multiple *documentation* sources, thanks largely to Deirdre Hurst du Prey and her skills at shorthand. For Komisarjevsky, as I highlight in the first essay (Chapter 1), the *theatre space* was the main mode of transmission. This was partly because Komisarjevsky, without a training school, used the production's rehearsal period as a key training opportunity, and partly because his stage work became emblematic of a new emphasis on ensemble acting for an inter-war British audience. This, too, produced *documentation* sources as Komisarjevsky's actors and theatre critics were drawn to reflect on their experiences in writing, as was Komis himself. In the case of the publication of Stanislavsky's *An Actor Prepares* (the context of which is addressed in David Shirley's essay in Chapter 2), the transmission mechanism is clearly from a *documentation source* and this book, as well as the earlier *My Life in Art* (Stanislavsky 1924), was to become an important research resource for MacColl and Littlewood. Their deep study of all things Russian was aided by the Manchester Central Library's purchase of Leon Moussinac's tome, *The New Movement in the Theatre* (Moussinac 1931), but, as Robert Leach identifies in Chapter 5, the future Theatre Workshop was also to benefit from the embodied practice of Laban as 'transmitted' by Jean Newlove.

Beyond these examples, the other chapters in this book illustrate a similarly mixed mode of transmission in terms of the Russian acting tradition. Perhaps surprisingly, the academy as *training place* features quite visibly in the transmission of biomechanics into Britain in what Amy Skinner calls the second wave of interest in Meyerhold's practice (Chapter 4), but the history before that was fundamentally complicated by the limited range of *documents* associated with the training and, specifically, the lack of moving footage. Duška Radosavljević highlights the *theatre space* as a key platform for the dissemination of Dodin's ideas into the Northern Stage Ensemble (Chapter 6), as he, like Komis before him, used the rehearsal room as a training ground for the NSE cast, having set a high bar with his own stage productions with the Maly hosted by Alan Lyddiard in Newcastle. Finally, Kamotskaia and Merlin, in the penultimate chapter on Active Analysis and its use in the contemporary studio-laboratory (Chapter 7), illustrate the problems such fine transmission distinctions have in themselves. Their *training place* is within the academy, but the work is produced as a near-professional *stage production*, which again is analysed through the lens of associated *documentation* – in this case an actor's testimony (that is Merlin's). These different routes of influence are then mapped and organised in my final concluding chapter, which takes three case studies of Russian-inspired theatre practice today: Declan Donnellan, Katie Mitchell and Michael Boyd.

Broadly speaking, then, the book is divided into two: first-generation practitioners (Komisarjevsky, Stanislavsky Chekhov and Meyerhold) and second- or third-generation practitioners responding to the previous age in various ways (Littlewood, Lyddiard, Kamotskaia/Merlin and the triumvirate of Mitchell, Donnellan and Boyd). However, this neat patterning is recognised as a construct in itself and problematised in the conclusion. Indeed each chapter in its own way raises fundamental historiographical issues of lineage, of terminology and of history-as-storytelling (see Balme 2008: 111–17).

In summary, there are several reasons why this story of Russian theatrical influence in Britain should now be heard:

- It widens our understanding of the genesis and development of actor training methodologies in the UK.
- It helps examine the complex mechanics of tradition making and the politics of what might be called acting transmission.
- It offers a place to debate the often-unseen linkages between key British actor-directors and their Russian 'roots'.
- It provides a counterpoint to the oft-told narrative of Russian practitioners as progenitors of the modern *American* tradition of acting, and in doing so . . .
- . . . suggests an alternative mapping of theatre traditions in the UK from the 1920s to today.

Tradition and transmission: a few caveats

Although there seems to be a certain solidity around both 'tradition' and 'transmission' as terms, some caution is necessary before proceeding. Indeed, Raymond Williams was not overstating things when he called tradition 'a particularly difficult word' (Williams 1988: 318), even if the etymology cited in his micro-essay on tradition suggests a rather straightforward and simple process of linear transmission:

> Tradition from rw *tradere*, L – to hand over or deliver. The Latin noun had the senses of i) delivery, ii) handing down knowledge, iii) passing on a doctrine.
>
> (Williams 1988: 318–19)

It is not until you get to the fourth Latin definition, 'surrender or betrayal' (Williams 1988: 319) that an inkling is given of the term's complexity and of its inherent connection with issues of power, exclusion and intra-cultural exchange. In a sense, all tradition is about betrayal, as it entails specifying a particular set of practices, customs or beliefs that are deemed worthy of passing on; in doing so it inevitably excludes other possibilities. Eugenio Barba describes such a process in a foreword to the 1994 conference dedicated to acting traditions at the International School of Theatre Anthropology:

> Traditions stratify and refine the knowledge of successive generations of founders through their forms and allow each new artist to *begin* without being obliged to start from scratch.
>
> (Barba 1994: 197, emphasis in original)

The central dynamic of tradition is thus made clear: the knowledge of previous generations in tension with those practising within the tradition today. For this reason 'tradition' is very often juxtaposed with the term 'innovation', and the conflict within this dialectic is commonly described as keeping tradition alive. Barba again:

> Without such a struggle, artistic life collapses. The spark of life, in art, is the tension between the rigour of the form and the rebellious detail that shakes it from within.
>
> (Barba 1994: 197)

In effect the term 'tradition' swallows up the notion of 'innovation' at its source, suggesting that the two are perhaps better considered as a duality. This book chronicles the struggle associated with this duality, not only within a single tradition but *across* traditions, and in doing so brings to the fore the kinds of conflicts which typify the clash between 'rigour' and 'rebellion'. These include debates over the purity of a source, or the status of its original form; tensions in how far a technique may be adapted to accommodate a new trainee; considerations of the extent to which cultural conditions impose new readings on a training regime; arguments over the assimilation of other techniques into a single approach, or over whether an approach can be singular in the first place; and a related consideration of depth versus eclecticism. These tensions are discussed and rationalised in the concluding chapter, but this dialectic is to some degree at work in all of the book's chapters and is worth drawing out here.

'Transmission', too, is a term that merits some discussion. Closely associated with the term 'tradition', it connotes a linear passage of ideas, from source to target, a feeling enhanced by its use in broadcasting – 'to send out (signals) by means of radio waves or along a transmission line' – and in physics: 'to transfer (a force, motion, power etc.) from one part of a mechanical system to another' (Collins English Dictionary, 3rd Edition). In practice of course, and when the force or power transmitted is an acting pedagogy (not a billiard ball), transmission is seldom a straightforward process. The linearity of transmission is complicated by several factors, all of which feature in the chapters to follow in various guises, but which it might be helpful to summarise in advance:

- the practitioners' need to develop their ideas and thus a lack of fixity in respect of the source itself;
- the socio-political context of the ideas and its impact on how they may be communicated, in print or in practice;

- the receiver's own interpretation and embodiment of the ideas being transmitted;
- the extent to which a training regime is adapted to make it appropriate for the context and use of the receiver;
- the tendency of practice-based ideas to spread, mutate, and re-integrate into a culture in subtly different forms;
- the length of time the receiver is trained;
- mistakes, improvisations, misunderstandings, (wilful) misreadings.

This is by no means an exhaustive list but it does give an indication of the many factors which militate against a linear passage of ideas between trainer and trainee, and the extent to which the process of transmission is subject to many 'noise-related' interferences. These complications will all be in evidence in the chapters below.

Chapter summaries

It remains, then, to summarise the material of the book and to indicate the key ways in which all the contributors grapple with the unpredictable mechanics of tradition making.

Chapter 1 opens the book with an examination of Theodore Komisarjevsky's contribution to the British tradition. Already well documented as a director and a writer, Komisarjevsky's impact on training practices has not before been outlined and here I draw on a range of new and unpublished sources in an extended but informed speculation on Komisarjevsky's training methodology. Arriving in the UK in 1919, Komisarjevsky predates the publication of *My Life in Art* and the Prague Group's visit to London in 1928 and in many ways he constitutes a British-based Boleslavsky figure, being the first in the country to import the ideas of Russian acting. Although he was a (published) critic of many ideas of Stanislavsky, he nevertheless inculcated a belief in detailed and carefully researched ensemble work, spiced with a focus on musicality and image making. The chapter argues for a reappraisal of his contribution, not solely as a theatre maker of some notoriety but as a director-pedagogue whose ideas fell on fertile ground in a British theatre tradition in transition.

In Chapter 2 David Shirley charts the passage of Stanislavsky into the conservatoire sector in Britain. In comparison with the US story of Stanislavsky's absorption, Shirley argues, the UK history is far more piecemeal and difficult to trace. Here, the tendency of a tradition to bifurcate, travel and re-integrate into the culture is sketched in detail. The story details the early, 'direct' impact of Stanislavsky's writings via Michel Saint-Denis's

London Theatre Studio in the 1930s, alongside those already mediated by American-trained practitioners, such as Uta Hagen and her pupil Doreen Cannon, and introduced later in the 1960s. The genesis of the Drama Centre and its emergence from Central School of Speech and Drama is fundamental to the institutional landscape painted here, and Cannon is presented as a key interpreter of a Method-inflected Stanislavsky training spanning four decades, first at the Drama Centre, then at RADA (the Royal Academy of Dramatic Art). The chapter concludes with a survey of the range and diversity of training ideas in the British conservatoire sector, some of which have a clear relationship to the Russian tradition – Sanford Meisner, for instance – and some of which do not: Gardzienice and Laban.

Jerri Daboo's essay on Michael Chekhov is Chapter 3. As the focus for this book is on the UK, Daboo concentrates largely on the residential actor-training centre Chekhov established on the Dartington Estate in Devon for three years (1936–9) and only briefly examines his later work in the United States. She too identifies the work of Michel Saint-Denis, as an important counterpoint – as noted he was working in London contemporaneously with Chekhov's Theatre Studio – suggesting the Frenchman was more accepted by the British theatre establishment than an 'alien' Russian. Key to the new testimony here is Paul Rogers's description of Chekhov's work. Rogers became the only British-born inheritor of the tradition but kept silent about his training for fifty years: a measure of the extent to which there was suspicion at the heart of British culture (Rogers performed at the Royal Shakespeare Company) of foreign acting methodologies. Daboo ends with insights from current Chekhov practitioners, Graham Dixon, Sarah Kane, Franc Chamberlain and Martin Sharp, and with the conclusion that the Chekhov lineage represents a broken model of transmission with 'threads' of influence returning to the UK after the pivotal Emerson college conference dedicated to his practice was held in 1994.

For Amy Skinner, describing the transmission of Meyerhold's biomechanics into Britain in Chapter 4, the absorption of his ideas came in waves. These she examines in a reverse chronology, beginning with the third wave (post-2000), tracking back to the first biomechanics Masterclasses in the UK led by Russian practitioners (the second wave, in the 1990s) and further back again to the actual devising of biomechanical études by Nikola Kustov and others in the 1930s (the first wave). This examination reveals a significant weight of work being undertaken in the academy, with three universities leading research and practice in biomechanics; Skinner positions the practice-as-research movement (usually associated with contemporary performance) as a contributing factor in the teaching of Meyerhold in the higher education sector. Notable in this context is the adoption of a near-conservatoire training in biomechanics currently thriving at the

University of Central Lancashire. The common theme in this fluid history of biomechanics in Britain, as Skinner concludes, is a conflict between what she calls a purist urge (rigour in Barba's terminology above) and an interpretative one (rebellion). It is a central concern in the book as whole, as I have argued earlier, but for Skinner it defines Meyerhold's legacy as a practitioner.

Robert Leach documents how Russian practice inspired Joan Littlewood's Theatre Workshop in Chapter 5. In fact, Leach reveals that it was Littlewood's partner, Ewan MacColl, who first saw the currency of Russian theatrical ideas, and conceived of their relevance for British theatre in inter-war Britain. Central to this vision was the Blue Blouse movement in Russia and its model of a 'living newspaper' theatre, which MacColl adopted for his agit-prop group, the Red Megaphones. Later, as Leach chronicles, it was the dual influence of Stanislavsky and Meyerhold's practices, understood by virtue of a serious research imperative on behalf of Littlewood and MacColl. These ideas drove an intensive training regime, first at the Theatre Union and then at Theatre Workshop. Using archival sources of the workshop notes made by both MacColl and Littlewood, Leach captures the rich fusion of ideas underpinning their training and offers a close reading of the radical pedagogy inscribed within them. In this chapter, Theatre Workshop is revealed as a practice-led research laboratory sixty years before the term became recognised and its two main protagonists as dedicated practitioner-researchers, consuming Mordecai Gorelick's *New Theatres for Old* in the morning and exploring its ideas in the studio in the afternoon.

Chapter 6 focuses attention on the Northern Stage Ensemble (NSE) and its Artistic Director Alan Lyddiard. In this essay Duška Radosavljević draws on Jill Dolan's theory of utopian performatives to examine a significant window of Russian-inspired practice in the north east. Speaking from an eye-witness point of view, as the company's then Dramaturg, Radosavljević outlines the place the Maly theatre of St Petersburg had in Lyddiard's thinking about ensemble theatre and, specifically, its director Lev Dodin's acting methodology. In doing so, it is necessary to weave together several threads of commentary ranging from interviews with Lyddiard himself and other key players in the NSE at the time, to theatre critics and actors who witnessed at first hand the approach Dodin took to building an ensemble ethos. As the project ultimately came to an abrupt finish, it is a story coloured with what Radosavljević, drawing on Dolan, calls the 'inevitability of disappearance', but the aspiration to establish a European model of operation in an otherwise unreceptive British context pre-empts similar, more sustained, ensemble projects dealt with in the conclusion.

In Chapter 7, the only co-authored chapter of the book, Bella Merlin and Katya Kamotskaia analyse their artistic collaboration on a recent project to stage *The Seagull*. Given that this project was produced in the USA, it might appear anomalous in the current context but it draws heavily on Merlin's practice as an English actor trained in Russia and equally on the interpretation of Stanislavsky's Active Analysis by the Royal Scottish Academy's Kamotskaia. Thus, the focus in the opening section is mainly on the curriculum at the academy (RSAMD) and on how it re-interprets the System of Stanislavsky to develop what Kamotskaia calls 'the logic and sequence of the inner process'. This is then mapped onto Merlin's experience of performing the role of Arkadina under Kamotskaia's direction, so we are able to witness theory and its application in quick succession. In terms of the former, Kamotskaia reminds us of the three-sided, pyramidal structure of Stanislavsky's practice, drawing on Petr Ershov: not simply a psychotechnique but *ethics* and *aesthetics* braided together with *technique*. Merlin, in turn, takes us into the details of a rehearsal process, helpfully evidencing the different stages of Active Analysis and outlining the use of improvisation, to develop the all-important *experiencing* of a role according to the logic and sequencing of Kamotskaia's direction.

In my own Conclusion, some persistent themes of the book are drawn out and three short 'case studies' are presented to ground these themes in contemporary British practice: these are of Declan Donnellan and Cheek by Jowl, and of Katie Mitchell and Michael Boyd at the RSC. A simple dichotomy of *methodological* or *philosophical* influence is set up and the means by which Russian ideas have penetrated these directors' differing approaches are outlined. The last example of the RSC and its return to a conscious and explicit ensemble ethos helps return us to the theme of collective creativity begun by Komisarjevsky at the Barnes Theatre and later at the Shakespeare Memorial Theatre in Chapter 1.

Bibliography

Balme, C. (2008) *The Cambridge Introduction to Theatre Studies*, Cambridge: Cambridge University Press.

Barba, E. (1994) 'Traditions and the Founders of Tradition', *New Theatre Quarterly*, 38 (May), 197–8.

Carnicke, S. M. (2009) *Stanislavsky in Focus* (2nd edn), Oxon: Routledge.

Edwards, C. (1965) *The Stanislavsky Heritage*, London: Peter Owen.

Gordon, M. (1987) *The Stanislavsky Technique: Russia*, New York: Applause.

Gordon, M. (2010) *Stanislavsky in America*, Oxon: Routledge.

Krasner, D. (2000) *Method Acting Reconsidered: Theory, Practice, Future*, London: Macmillan.

Moussinac, L. (1931) *The New Movement in the Theatre*, London: B. T. Batsford.

Senelick, L. (ed.) (1992) *Wandering Stars: Russian Émigré Theatre 1905–1940*, Iowa City: University of Iowa Press.

Stanislavski, C. (1936) *An Actor Prepares*, trans. Hapgood, E. R., London: Geoffrey Bles.

Stanislavski, C. (1924) *My Life in Art*, trans. Robbins, J. J., London: Geoffrey Bles.

Williams, R. (1988) *Keywords: A Vocabulary of Culture and Society*, London: Fontana.

Zarrilli, P. (2009) *Psycho-physical Acting: An Intercultural Approach after Stanislavski*, Oxon: Routledge.

1

A TRADITION IN TRANSITION

Komisarjevsky's seduction of the British theatre

Jonathan Pitches

> To know how to direct acting one must know what acting is and how to teach acting.
>
> (Komisarjevsky, *Play Direction: Short Synopsis of Lectures*, Harvard Archive)[1]

Of the many influential Russian émigrés to have had a tangible impact on the British theatre tradition over the last century, Theodore Komisarjevsky (Figure 1.1) deserves special recognition. Whereas Michael Chekhov's legacy is built upon just three intensive years at Dartington from 1936 to 1939, Komisarjevsky worked for two decades in the UK (1919–39), directing scores of productions from London to Leeds to Glasgow, and culminating in a series of epoch-defining productions at Stratford's Shakespeare Memorial Theatre, before the Second World War. By the time Maria Germonova's splinter group of the Moscow Arts Theatre – the Prague Group – arrived in London in 1928, claiming to be continuing the Stanislavsky tradition and, according to Germanova's letter to *The Times*, 'interpret[ing] it to audiences in Western Europe',[2] Komisarjevsky had been practising as a director and teacher in Britain for almost ten years and had already earned a career-defining reputation for his own sensitive interpretations of Chekhov's plays. Whilst Meyerhold's purple period of theatrical work was appreciated from afar in the UK – and disseminated in publications such as Leon Moussinac's (1931) *The New Movement in the Theatre* – Komisarjevsky was producing *Le Cocu Magnifique* and *The Government Inspector* in the nation's capital, the latter with a young and impressionable

Figure 1.1 Portrait of Theodore Komisarjevsky in London. Source: Burra Moody
Archive.

Charles Laughton in the role of Osip, the servant. Komisarjevsky even beat
his Russian compatriots to the British bookshops, publishing his *Myself and
the Theatre* (Komisarjevsky 1929) with William Heinemann seven years
before *An Actor Prepares* appeared courtesy of Geoffrey Bles and four
years before Richard Boleslavsky's *Acting: the First Six Lessons* came out
in Theatre Arts Books.[3] Indeed, as the first Russian practitioner operating in
Britain, after the formation of the Moscow Art Theatre, Komisarjevsky can
profitably be thought of as the British-based equivalent of Boleslavsky in
the States,[4] at least for the many acting ensembles with which he worked in
the 1920s and 1930s.

From a number of angles, then, as a critic, a director and a teacher, Komis – as the British theatre establishment began to call him – had a demonstrable impact on the tradition of acting in the UK before the Second World War. His writing, and particularly *Myself,* infiltrated deep into British (and American)[5] theatre culture; his work as a director effectively initiated the British fascination with Chekhov before impacting decisively on the Shakespeare tradition thirty years before Peter Hall founded the Royal Shakespeare Company (RSC); his teaching was no less significant and influenced a generation of British theatre actors who were perhaps the first to perform on a truly international stage: John Gielgud, Peggy Ashcroft, Claude Rains, Charles Laughton, Anthony Quayle, George Devine, Alec Guinness.

However, whereas there is good evidence of his productions (mainly from prompt copies, reviews and associated correspondence), and his three books,[6] *Myself, The Costume of the Theatre* (Komisarjevsky 1932) and *The Theatre and a Changing Civilisation* (Komisarjevsky 1935) are still available for scrutiny, evidence of Komis's pedagogy is far more difficult to tie down. He founded a theatre school in Moscow in 1913 before he moved to Britain, taught at the Royal Academy of Dramatic Art (RADA)[7] and, after moving to the USA, taught again at Yale. His acting studio ran for nearly fifteen years once he settled in the United States and he spent much of his later life (1944–54) planning a fourth book, specifically on acting. Accounts of his approach to directing indicate that when he had time to devote to a production he also used the opportunity to develop the ensemble's skills. However, despite such a demonstrable and longstanding commitment to teaching, the evidence of what Komis actually *did* in the studio – his exercise regime, if not 'system' – is notable by its absence.

There are several reasons for this. One may simply have been the breadth of his vision. Komisarjevsky was a complete 'man of the theatre'. A trained architect, he designed the sets, costumes and lights as well as directing the actors. As Anthony Quayle put it in an interview for Michael Billington:

> He was a really remarkable man, a draughtsman and designer as well as a director. His was the entire and total concept. Even Peter Brook can't do everything . . . Komis could.
>
> (Billington 1988: 52)

Such theatrical polymathy meant that his priority or focus as a writer was never as clear-cut as was that of, say, Stanislavsky or Michael Chekhov, and this is reflected in his publication record, which includes writing on interior design, ballet, the history of costume and the socio-political context of theatre from the Greeks to the twentieth century.

A more significant reason for the lack of documentation of Komisarjevsky's studio work was the absence of a documenter or scribe to record his lessons. Meyerhold relied on prominent students such as Aleksandr Gladkov to keep records; Michael Chekhov had a dedicated transcriber in Deirdre Hurst du Prey, who recorded almost every lesson at Dartington for posterity. The formidable practitioner collective of the First Studio (Vakhtangov, Boleslavsky, Suerzhitsky and a young Chekhov) had a book permanently open in their studio to document the day's findings (Benedetti 1998: 15). Komis had no such system; he often led private one-to-one classes and when his collaborator and last wife Ernestine Stodelle was present she was likely to be co-presenting and therefore not best placed to record the sessions.

Another key factor in the lack of detail surrounding Komis's pedagogy seems to be his reluctance actually to commit his ideas to paper, beyond the important sections on training in *Myself and the Theatre* and snippets from *The Theatre*, both of which will be analysed later. The long-standing correspondence Komis had with the British actress Phyllada Sewell from 1930 to 1954 illustrates this resistance very tellingly. The idea of a book to complement his other theatre-related publications is first mentioned in a letter from Komis in December 1944:

> I have a few book projects in my mind. Probably they will remain in my mind forever, unless I win a couple of thousand in an imaginary lottery, and remove myself to an imaginary warm cottage in an imaginary land of quiet and dry warm weather.[8]

His pessimism proved to be accurate for, although Komis made reference to a book project in many other letters to Phyllada and engaged her partly in the brokering of a potential contract with the publishers of *The Theatre*, the Bodley Head, he remained stubbornly and strangely reticent when asked to expand on his ideas. The editor of the Bodley Head, C. J. Greenwood, for instance, received no reply when he asked the following (not unreasonable) question in a letter from 1950 pertaining to the project, now conceived as 'a handbook for professional students & amateurs':[9]

> All you have told me in your letter is that the length would be about 100,000 words or more and that it would be on producing plays and operas, and how to do it . . . Would it not be possible for you to write me in more detail on the plan of the book: say a couple of pages describing exactly what you propose doing, together with a list of chapter headings. I imagine this must be pretty clear in your mind.[10]

If the contents of the book had been clear in Komis's thinking four years before his death, then that is where they remained for they were never committed to paper. He did begin preliminary research for the study the following year, interestingly prioritising scientific research as his major source of inspiration: 'I am reading books on psychology to know more about modern theories for my book on acting. It's supposed to be the book for the Bodley Head man',[11] he wrote to Phyllada, capturing the acting zeitgeist in the United States at the time. However, the year after that, in September 1952, he was still promising to start it and professing to have forgotten all about Greenwood.[12] By the time he died, two years later, there was no significant progress made on the book, not even any drafts, and thus a considerable gap in the understanding of Komisarjevsky's contribution was created.

This chapter aims to address this gap, collating the significant circumstantial evidence relating to Komis's acting technique and re-assembling it from the perspective of *trainee* rather than spectator. In the case of the latter, there have already been several reconstructions of his directorial work which offer an excellent view of Komis's contribution from the audience's side of the fire curtain, both at the Barnes Theatre in West London (Tracy 1993; Bartosevich 1992) and, later, at Stratford (Berry 1983; Mullin 1974; Mennen 1979). There is also an extensive and highly scholarly biographical account of Komis conducted by Victor Borovsky and included in his *Triptych from the Russian Theatre* (Borovsky 2001).

Here the emphasis is different, even though it may at times be exploiting the same sources. In this chapter my aim is to reconstruct the pedagogy which underpinned the creation of those productions, insofar as this is possible. What follows, then, is perhaps best described as a piece of informed speculation using eye-witness accounts, actors' testimony, the snippets of training ideas inscribed in his three completed books and archival sources such as correspondence and lecture plans. All of these sources will be organised in pursuit of a simple question: what would Komisarjevsky's projected book on acting have looked like?

There are several reasons why this is a question worth asking: first, it promises to help uncover some of the pragmatics of Komis's contribution to the British theatre tradition, revealing his directorial successes in a different light and going some way to explaining how those successes were realised; second, it offers an alternative window onto a pivotal period in British theatre history, a period when nineteenth-century traditions of training based on ideas of restraint and individuality were giving way to European models of authenticity and ensemble; and third, it places in a different context statements made by many of the most notable British actors of the pre-war period concerning the craft of acting.

In sum, such a question should help offer a perspective on the pre-war British theatre tradition *in transition*, a period which Michael Billington describes in his excellent biography of one of those notable actors, Peggy Ashcroft, whose own career was very significantly 'entwined' with Komisarjevsky's, as we shall see later:

> [Peggy] talked engrossingly about the "family" of actors, directors and designers with whom her career has often been entwined: John Gielgud, Edith Evans, George Devine, Michael Redgrave, Anthony Quayle, Alec Guinness, Komisarjevsky, Michel St-Denis, Glen Byam Shaw, Motley . . . I began to understand the continuity that is part of the strength of British theatre: particularly the way in which from 1930 to 1968 a group of like-minded friends and associates created a classical tradition before the big institutions arrived. Even a single-minded visionary like Peter Hall was, in his foundation of the RSC, in many ways giving a practical form to dreams that had been entertained before him.
>
> (Billington 1988: 5)

Komisarjevsky was, for a period of some fifteen years, at the very centre of that family and, as such, must be seen as a pivotal figure in the important developments which ensued and which characterised the establishment, later in the last century, of many of 'the big institutions' – the National Theatre, the RSC and the Royal Court, to name three.

Background

Given the patchy evidence of Komisarjevsky's teaching, it should be instructive to outline, before any detailed analysis, the context within which the Russian émigré was working and to highlight the key historical moments in his career that have direct relevance to questions of training.

The name Komisarjevsky was in fact an anglicised version of his Russian name, Fyodor Fyodorovich Komissarzhevsky, and his patronymic – the middle name taken from his father – is an indicator of a lofty theatrical inheritance. He was the son of Fyodor Petrovich Komissarzhevsky (Stanislavsky's opera teacher and co-founder of the Society of Art and Literature), and the half-brother of Vera Fyodorovna Komissarzhevskaya (the world-famous actress at the Aleksandrinsky Imperial Theatre in St Petersburg). As such, Komisarjevsky was deeply immersed in the Russian theatre establishment from birth, even if he was denied full knowledge of his family ties until his mother died, and eclipsed for many years by the notoriety of his close relatives. He began working alongside his sister in

1903 at a formative moment in her career. Disillusioned with the Imperial Theatre treadmill and its lack of theatrical innovation, Komissarzhevskaya had determined to create her own independent theatre and signed up her half-brother as a shareholder in the venture the moment she met him in December 1902. (Hitherto, Komisarjevsky's mother had kept his theatrical inheritance a secret from him.) He was an immediate asset: fluent in several languages, training in architecture and blessed with what Victor Borovsky recounts was 'a great fanaticism and an almost sectarian faith in what he was doing' (Borovsky 2001: 153). Within three years, Komisarjevsky was working alongside Vera's newly appointed collaborator, Vsevolod Meyerhold, fresh from his own intense induction to the theatre, touring in the provinces and experimenting with Stanislavsky at his satellite Theatre Studio. Komisarjevsky worked as an assistant designer and *de facto* project manager on three of Meyerhold's most famous early productions:

> I had to supervise the making of the scenery and to design some of the costumes, props etc. The sketches for the dresses for 'Sister Beatrice', 'The Show Booth' and 'The Life of Man', together with settings for the latter play were my first work for the Theatre.
>
> (Komisarjevsky 1929: 76)

As is well documented, the collaborative relationship between Vera and Meyerhold was short-lived (just over a year in total) and was soon to explode in acrimony but the atmosphere in which Komisarjevsky was learning his craft must have been as instructive as it was intense. His sister, in reflective mode after Meyerhold had been asked to leave, described her own theatre at the time as 'a laboratory for a director's experiments' (Rudnitsky 1981: 126) and she was not using the term in any way positively. However, for Komisarjevsky, Meyerhold's experimental model was an important lesson in how to push forward an agenda of reform in the theatre – irrespective of its limited success in Komissarzhevskaya's theatre. Meyerhold later separated out his mainstream theatre practice from the innovations possible in studio work and from a designated teaching space or theatre school, and this became Komisarjevsky's intention, too, in 1913.

Reviving his sister's name, he formed the Vera Komissarzhevskaya Studio in Moscow, having moved to the city following Vera's early death from smallpox in 1910. The studio became the chief mechanism to develop actors with the skills he perceived as essential for a modern theatre; it ran in parallel, rather than in collaboration, with Stanislavsky's own studio developments (the First Studio was formed in 1912) and echoed in some important ways the training philosophy of Meyerhold, who also launched a studio in 1913. Both Komis and Meyerhold shared the belief that actors needed to be rounded cultural beings and thus their schooling had to include seminar discussion, history and philosophy as well as practical skills. Oliver Sayler witnessed this approach in action in 1918, in the fourth season of what Komis had called his Free School of Scenic Art:

> Development of diction and voice, with instruction in singing to assist the speaking voice; development of the body through plastic and rhythm exercises; study of the theory of theatrical art; wide acquaintanceship with literature of the theatre in all countries, improvisation on the stage for the development of emotional technique and imagination and finally experience on the stage of the theatre.
>
> (Sayler 1922: 182)

According to *Myself and the Theatre*, Komisarjevsky's belief in such a training space was first fuelled by his sister, who entertained (admittedly idealistic) aims of beginning a school herself: 'a place in the country, near the sea . . . where all of [her students] would find out for themselves their own way of acting' (Komisarjevsky 1929: 83). Far more influential on Komisarjevsky's thinking were his discussions with Vera, in the light of the Meyerhold debacle:

> In a conversation with me she said that she did not see the possibility of a Theatre as she had imagined it, unless she could have a company of actors, united by the same understanding of the art of acting, who would be able to *feel* each other when acting together . . . Every such Theatre must be like a community, following a 'master', something like what in the art of painting is called a 'school' in which all the disciples carry out freely and enthusiastically the ideas of their leader and are able to work all together on the same picture.
>
> (Komisarjevsky 1929: 82, emphasis in original)

It was this *felt* model of the ensemble (coupled, importantly, with the means by which to create it) that Komisarjevsky carried forward in his work in Britain. It was a feeling clearly evident in his signature productions and in his theoretical writing about the skills of the 'universal actor' (Komisarjevsky 1929: 143), as he envisaged them.

Komisarjevsky's plans to initiate a total training for the actor were unsettled by the Revolution and then, soon after, by his decision to leave the country; he did not ally himself with the new power structures and saw an opportunity to develop his craft abroad, in continental Europe and in Britain. In fact, it was not until he moved to the United States in 1939, twenty years after he had first arrived in Britain, that he was able again to establish a studio. Instead, the main outlets for his teaching in England were threefold: (i) teaching in established training institutions – for example RADA; (ii) private lessons often offered in his own house; and (iii) teaching through his direction of a specific play in production. On the latter point, often overlooked as a training mechanism, his last wife, Ernestine Stodelle, was emphatic: 'He directed like nobody teaches. He taught while he directed. It was absolutely extraordinary'.[13] In addition to these direct transmission routes for his ideas, there was the indirect impact of his writing, which, at least in one notable case, had a demonstrable impact on an actor's process: as Michael Redgrave's (1953) series of lectures *The Actor's Ways and Means* testifies. These outlets will form the focus of the analysis that follows this section.

Komisarjevsky's final stopping point, like that of many Russian émigrés, was the United States. He moved in 1939 and, although he spent much of his time after his second emigration claiming he would return – either to Russia or to England depending on the correspondent – he never lived permanently anywhere else. In teaching terms the outlets diversified in the States: he ran his own studio (The Komisarjevsky Drama Studio) based in New York, he taught in the Drama Department at Yale from 1940 to 1942,[14] he operated as an itinerant lecturer in and around New England, and he continued to induct actors into his theories through his directing projects. It is true, however, that the notoriety and relative stardom which he enjoyed in the last years in Britain – mainly through his Stratford seasons from 1932 to 1939 – were not a feature of his experience in America. This is perhaps best illustrated by his own recruitment advertisements for the Drama Studio, adverts which even many years after his time in the UK pointedly named actors and institutions from England as the chief enticement for students:

> Komisarjevsky: Director of John Gielgud, Elizabeth Bergner, Charles Laughton, Gertrude Lawrence, Akim Tamiroff etc., Shakespeare Memorial Theatre; Professor Royal Academy of Dramatic Art, London.[15]

With the exception of Tamiroff, who moved to the United States concurrently with Maria Ouspenskaya and Boleslavsky in 1923, all the references are to the British tradition.

Komisarjevsky had a reputation for being difficult to work with and anyone who has reviewed the extensive correspondence in the Houghton Library, Harvard, will get a strong sense of this, with several extended and internecine disputes immortalised in handwritten script. However, he was equally known for developing deep-seated connections with his actors. This, on the one hand, led him to his oft-quoted nickname, 'come-and-seduce-me', and set him on a course of repeated dysfunctional and short-lived relationships – including his brief marriage to Peggy Ashcroft (1933–35). On the other, it was a measure of Komisarjevsky's seductive skills as a teacher, to which several leading actors and actresses give testimony and which will now be analysed. In this context, it is particularly poignant to consider his relationship with Phyllada Sewell. Whether romantically inclined or not, the twenty-four years of their correspondence evidences that, in just one or two short lessons in the early 1930s with the 'Master', Sewell's understanding of the craft of acting was transformed. It was this experience which helped develop a bond which was strong enough not to be compromised either by Komis's often unnecessary demands for secretarial support at a distance, or by the gulf of the Atlantic which lay between them from 1939 onwards. She was one of his very last correspondents in 1954 when he finally succumbed to the heart condition he had suffered from for many years and her reaction to the first lessons he taught a quarter of century earlier is indicative of his uncanny influence:

> Last term a simply wonderful thing happened. I had a lesson from Komisarjevsky! Then another lesson and then a third!!! . . . I studied the part of Anna in Ivanoff with him but never got as far as acting it. Everything Anna says – I must know why she says it – I must find out all her thoughts and know all her past. Komi's brain seems to work about ten times quicker than anyone else's – and the queer thing about him is that you can follow his thoughts quite easily and know what he is feeling at once – in fact his is a wonderful example of his own theories of acting. If he will have me I want to go on learning from him in the Autumn – I feel that if he cannot teach me to act then nobody will.[16]

Looking beyond the love-struck and naïve tone of this diary entry, one can detect a number of important guiding principles to preface the discussion in the next section: the belief in the need for detailed interrogation of a character, the commitment to analysis before action, the implicit idea of an emotional connectedness necessary for creative work – that 'group feeling' Komissarzhevskaya first sought – and the strong sense that this was a man whose 'theories of acting' were already well developed.

Acting and the Régisseur: the book for the Bodley Head man

Although, as we have seen, Komis never provided C. J. Greenwood with as much as a contents page for his proposed book on acting, there is sufficient evidence available to suggest several themes to his thinking about the discipline. To give these themes particular emphasis and clarity, I am going to present them here as chapter titles for a book, the title of which, I will argue below, might have been *Acting and the Régisseur*:

Introduction: *Three Kinds of Acting*
Chapter 1:   *Training for a Synthetic Theatre: The Universal Actor*
Chapter 2:   *Analysis and Preparation*
Chapter 3:   *Images and Imagination*
Chapter 4:   *The Production as Composition: Music and Musicality*
Chapter 5:   *Developing Ensemble*
Chapter 6:   *The Role of the Régisseur*

Granted, to express this as a 'missing contents' page is at one level just a rhetorical device and, of course, there is a level of speculation involved in its construction. However, as will be seen, it is in the spirit of Komisarjevsky's approach to draw on the creative imagination and to *assimilate* it to the available evidence (Komisarjevsky 1935: 20), and this 'ideal' book structure also has the advantage of keeping us focused on the matter in hand: *acting training*. Doubtless, Komis would have spent considerable time in this unwritten tome sketching the historical context of many of these ideas – given the range of references in evidence in his other three books and the repeated histories which emerge across them. However, in using this approach, we are forced to stay on message and can concentrate firmly and consistently on the question of acting! What emerges is a vision of an artist whose ideas are very much part of the early twentieth-century evolution of training ideas attributed now to the Stanislavsky tradition but who, unlike Stanislavsky himself, was able *directly* to influence the work of British actors as this tradition was first developing.

Acting and the régisseur

Komis was very scathing of the British word 'producer': '[it] means farmer, a husbandman, an agriculturalist and *not* an artist', he opined (Komisarjevsky 1935: 15). He preferred to use the French word, also used in Russia: *régisseur* or *rezhisseur*. However, although he clearly spoke from the perspective of what we would now call a theatre director, his understanding of the role was not confined to the theatre function; it was, in fact, intimately connected to the ideal pedagogical model of training he had developed with his sister Vera. In *The Theatre and a Changing Civilisation*, Komisarjevsky defines the régisseur's role, reiterating its connection to a training 'School':

Rehearsing a play, the régisseur forms an interpretative unity of the individualities of all the performers – i.e., a synthesis of their thoughts and feelings and of their expressive methods . . . The régisseur is a spiritual leader, a kind of magician, psychologist and technical master. It is also necessary that his company should have worked with him and lived in the same idealistic atmosphere for quite a long time and formed what in art is called a 'School'.

(Komisarjevsky 1935: 19)

Although many who worked with him would have recognised something in his notion of the régisseur-as-magician, the model of a long-standing ensemble steeped in his own methods was never, unfortunately, realised during his twenty years in the UK. However, it is worthy of note that here Komisarjevsky is speaking over fifteen years after he left Russia and yet his ideals had not shifted from the blend of laboratory, school and theatre studio he had conceived in Moscow before the Revolution. The régisseur was the prime mechanism for delivering his vision of a theatrical unity or 'whole', what Ernestine Stodelle identified as his directorial signature:

I think it is this grasping of the elements which fused the [theatrical components] together and weaved out of the strands . . . a whole. That's it, it's a whole, it's an entirety.[17]

For this reason it is fitting to consider the term as an overarching title for his book, as an expression of the specific kind of actor trainer he was in Moscow and should have been in inter-war Britain.

Three kinds of acting

For Komisarjevsky there were three broad categories of actor: the naturalistic actor, the stagey actor and the imaginative actor. The first, he argued in *Myself*, was 'almost a tradition', the proponents of which were inclined to 'mumble monotonously, to "throw away" lines, to avoid gestures . . . to speak while chewing, etc' (Komisarjevsky 1929: 131). The second, what he called a 'degenerate form of the romantic or "Shakespearean" school of acting', involved *simulation* as opposed to felt actions:

Such actors – let us call them 'stagey' actors – start working on a part at what should be its final stage, *i.e. the outer expressions*. Working on a part in this way usually consists of evolving and producing 'rubber stamps'.

(pp. 131–2)

The imaginative actor, by contrast 'builds up his part and acts it from the "inside"' (p. 132), thus implying that the overall process for the latter is to develop an inner life before moving to fix the external score of the role, the final stage of 'outer expressions', as he puts it.

Needless to say, of these three categories, it is the imaginative actor which Komisarjevsky particularly valued. However, before we ascribe too much importance to these rather blunt distinctions it is important to separate out what is instructive here from Komisarjevsky's other agenda: 'the imaginative actor' is a term coined to criticise Stanislavsky's ideas as much as it is to define the ideal performer. Later in this section in *Myself*, he moves to a direct attack on the System, characterising it as a process which denies the imaginative input of the actor and, at its worst, creates the monotonous mumbling he considered to be part of the naturalistic tradition:

> The idea of Stanislavsky's system can be summarised in one sentence which I once heard from his own lips, when he came to my Theatre to persuade me to become a producer at his own: 'The people who breathe the air of Miaznitskaya . . . cannot express sincerely any feelings other than those of Miaznitskaya and those are the feelings they must revive on the stage in order to be "natural"'.
>
> (p. 138)

However, although Stanislavsky was an easy target, and many have levelled similar criticisms – particularly in relation to the American strain of Stanislavskianism led by Lee Strasberg – there is little in this analysis of any weight. Imagination is one of the first lessons in Year 1 of Stanislavsky's *An Actor's Work on Himself* (Stanislavsky 2008: 60–85) and figures significantly in the overall thinking of the System, linking the 'magic if' with 'given circumstances', for instance. Even though this book was not published formally by this time, Komisarjevsky was well aware of this and had already been castigated by Stanislavsky for saying something very similar in his published summary, *The Actor's Creative Work and Stanislavsky's Theory* (1916).[18] In actual fact, it was he who sought out Stanislavsky for a role in the Moscow Art Theatre, not the other way round; he was never accepted, though,[19] and seemed not to be able to resist the temptation to criticise the Stanislavsky system when he could, despite the close affinities with his own approach.

Far more interesting than the anti-System rhetoric is the manner in which Komisarjevsky's imaginative actor approaches a role. Using the imagination as the creative agent, the actor, he says, 'puts himself into the power of the interrupted sequence of images he has created beforehand' (Komisarjevsky 1929: 133), and this important idea will be analysed later, in the section on 'images'.

Training for a Synthetic Theatre: the Universal Actor

As early as 1913 Komisarjevsky's work was driven by one overriding aim, as Oliver Sayler reports:

> To achieve a harmony between the interpretation of the actors, the ensemble, the forms and the colours of the scenery and costumes, the music and the light – the harmony between all these and the idea and the style of the dramatic author.
>
> (Sayler 1922: 182)

Later, in his own writing, Komisarjevsky called the realisation of this idea Synthetic Theatre, the training for which created his fourth category of actor: the Universal Actor. This ideal model of the modern performer provides a centrepiece for his ideas on training. Rather like Wagner's *Gesamtkunstwerk*, it is a totalising vision of performance which draws all theatre's constituent elements together. Viewed as a whole, the demands for such a multi-talented performer seem rather ambitious:

> An actor who played in such a synthetic show would have to possess a knowledge and practice of music, poetry, singing and dancing and would have to be master of every means of theatrical expression and, therefore, a perfect performer, a universal actor, as I call him. After all, a perfect actor of the drama, even if he is not required to sing, must also be a universal actor. He must be able to combine all the forms of expression he has to use, create a synthesis of them, subordinating all of them to his conception of the part and to the single rhythm of his emotions.
>
> (Komisarjevsky 1929: 143–4)

However, broken down, this exacting model of acting calls for a number of core skills which are far more achievable. These might be summarised as musical sensibility, plastic and vocal dexterity, emotional sensitivity and range, and scenographic awareness, all underpinned by a strong knowledge of the play and its context. As the final sentence in the quotation suggests, there is no doubt in Komisarjevsky's theatre that all these elements are organised by the actor primarily to service the needs of the play, not to indulge purely aesthetic aims. It followed that the *analysis* of the play by the actor was, a pivotal mechanism in the overall realisation of the production.

Preparation and analysis

As Phyllada Sewell's above-quoted diary-entry indicates, analysis of character was very important in Komisarjevsky's approach: 'Everything Anna
says – I must know why she says it', she faithfully reported, 'I must find out
all her thoughts and know all her past.'[20] There are several other indications,
from more established actors in the British tradition, that such preparatory
analysis was a prerequisite when working with Komis. Charles Laughton,
for instance, who first met him at RADA working on *commedia dell'arte*
scenes, began his approach to his part as a pickpocket in Komisarjevsky's
production of *Lilliom* (Duke of York Theatre, 1926) using what we would
now understand as a typical Method approach. As the actor-biographer
Simon Callow records: 'to get the part right, [Laughton] went down to the
docks and studied pickpockets, for hours on end' (Callow 1987: 15).

Peggy Aschroft identifies a similar influence:

> I always felt that I was the pupil and he was the master and he was very
> inspiring. I learned from him how to approach a part, how to analyse a
> role, how important it was to understand the director's whole concep-
> tion of a play.
>
> (Billington 1988: 53)

John Gielgud, too:

> I played in some Chekhov plays under Komisarjevsky in 1924. He was
> an enormous influence in teaching me not to act from outside . . . I
> recall how the force of this struck me for the first time. It was when I
> played Trofimov, the student in *The Cherry Orchard* . . . I have looked
> into a glass, as it were, and suddenly seen and understood how this man
> would speak and move and behave. I found that this picture remained
> in my mind and I was able to lose myself completely in the role.
>
> (Funke and Booth 1961: 6–7)

In his period working at the Barnes, Komis would rehearse at first in
his own flat in Bloomsbury, which he shared briefly with Peggy Ashcroft.
Here, as Gielgud recounts in *Early Stages*, they would prepare meticulously
before going near the stage:

> There we all sat, crowded round the table at first, reading the play for
> many days on end . . . Some five weeks later, when we reached a more

advanced stage of rehearsals and arrived at the Barnes Theatre, we realised why so much care had been taken in dealing with the limited space at our disposal.

(Gielgud 1987: 64)

Reading this, it is hard not to think of the famous picture of Anton Chekhov, Stanislavsky, Meyerhold and all the rest of the *Seagull* cast, gathered round the table reading the play at the Moscow Arts in 1898. Indeed, buried in this passage, describing events almost thirty years after that photograph, is the evidence of a commitment to Russian-based 'table work' or 'cognitive analysis' (Carnicke 2010: 13) thriving in England, an approach which ultimately had a similar impact on the London audiences of Chekhov as it had done on the Moscow spectatorship. Interestingly, though, the transmission vehicle for this analytical approach was not first and foremost Stanislavsky, even though much of the ensuing history has suggested as much. Instead, actors who ultimately helped define the inter-war generation of British theatre were learning their analytical craft from an arch-critic of the Moscow Arts director: Komisarjevsky.

Images and imagination

As we have seen, the notion of imagination was central to Komisarjevsky's thoughts on training: 'the first essential is imagination', he says in *Myself* (Komisarjevsky 1929: 112). This emphasis in 1929 put him significantly ahead of Michael Chekhov, who is more readily recognised for his integration of imagination into actor training. Surprisingly, Komisarjevsky never met Chekhov, despite their overlapping in the UK for some three years at the end of the 1930s and for fifteen years in the States; nor did Komisarjevsky refer to Chekhov in any of his books, even though there is much shared ground. Komis has many interesting things to say on the actor's use of imagination and the attendant issue of what he called 'images' but, for clarity and brevity, there is nothing more explicit than an annotated lecture plan he prepared for Hollander Concert and Lecture Bureau to help advertise his first US lecture series:

> Imagination. Creation of images. Projection of images in body action, sounds and speech. Chains of images and continuity of action. Desire to produce action.[21]

The process is clear: the imagination is called upon to produce images in the actor's mind, stimulated by the play and by provocations from the director: this is an essential element Komis called 'assimilation' (Komisarjevsky

1929: 113). These images are related both to the character itself (a mental facsimile of the role) and to things which prompt action from the actor: thus the images created in the actor's mind's eye are designed to elicit clear actions in the real world. These actions then lead to emotional content, which, as the images are arranged with 'continuity' in the mental process, also has a logic and a thread of consistency:

> The 'image' of the character, as well as the 'images' prompting his actions, must be sufficiently definite and clear and the emotions roused sufficiently rich (of an assimilative creative order) to stimulate the actor to sincere outer expression.
>
> (p. 113)

With the benefit of hindsight, after *An Actor Prepares* (1936) and *To the Actor* (Chekhov 1953) were first published in English, Komis's ideas look to be a fusion of Stanislavsky and Michael Chekhov: a combination of creative image production (Chekhov's Imaginary Body) organised logically and consistently (Stanislavsky's Throughaction[22]). However, it is important to remember that these ideas were first introduced to Britain before either book was published or, in the case of Chekhov, well before he arrived to teach in Dartington in 1936. Komis should, then, be credited with developing a radical approach to character development, in keeping with the Russian tradition but with a demonstrable identity all his own, which, on the evidence available, worked very effectively in practice. Peggy Ashcroft explained her approach to the emotional rollercoaster Chekhov created in *The Seagull*, in her last production with Komis at the New Theatre:

> For a while, I never had the confidence that I could do what I wanted in the last act . . . What I came to realise is that Nina identifies with the Seagull. In the second act Konstantin kills a seagull and Trigorin weaves it into a subject for a story about a girl who lives by the lake and then is casually destroyed just like the seagull. That is why Nina, who in the final act is in a state of exhaustion and hysteria, goes back to the lake where they did the play . . . The difficulty is that you have to come in at such a pitch of exhaustion and despair. Then you have to recover sufficiently to play the scene with Konstantin. Then you have the shock of hearing Trigorin's voice. But all through the scene is the idea of a seagull. I kept that visual image in my mind throughout and I felt, in the end, I achieved what I was after.
>
> (Billington 1988: 82)

As Komisarjevsky's teaching suggested, it was the *image* which provided the key for Ashcroft, an image to hold onto throughout the performance and which ultimately made sense of the emotional demands of the final act.

The production as composition: music and musicality

The work of the régisseur, was, for Komisarjevsky, 'a matter of composition just as in any other work of art' (Komisarjevsky 1929: 164). His vision of a Synthetic Theatre, with its unified elements of costume,[23] scenery, lighting, sound and acting, was underpinned by a profound musical sensibility – music was in essence the organising force behind his theatre. This musical emphasis was not confined to his opera work or to the comedies he directed. 'Every play', he argued, 'even the most naturalistic one, has music concealed in it' (Slonim 1963: 208). Norman Marshall, who compiled the Komisarjevsky entry for the *Oxford Dictionary of National Biography*, asked him to expand on the idea in an interview he conducted. Sitting at a grand piano he first bashed out a repetitive rhythm. 'It is an English theatre', he said:

> 'But in the theatre it should not be so. It should be like this'. Then he played his improvised little tune again with innumerable variations of tone and tempo. It was exactly what Komisarjevsky did in his own productions, giving them intricate patterns of rhythm.
>
> (Billington 1988: 84)

This was a technique he echoed in the rehearsal room, too, according to the actor Warren Jenkins, who directly experienced Komisarjevsky evoking the mood of the scene for the ensemble by 'playing it' on a piano (Allen 2000: 167).

As a master interpreter of Chekhov, it is perhaps not surprising that he was so inclined to a musical understanding of the play text – this was something Meyerhold had written about as early as 1906 in the *Naturalistic Theatre and the Theatre of Mood*. However, Komisarjevsky worked this way in all his productions, most notably perhaps in the Shakespeare Memorial Theatre productions (1932–9), summarised by Ralph Berry as exemplars of his 'unfailing musical and rhythmic sense' and of 'the pictorial quality of his compositions' (Berry 1983: 84). Of most interest in this context is the notion of musicality as a way of facilitating an actor's work, and Berry's connection of music with scenography is important here. For it is music's temporal discipline, as well as its innate abstraction, that allows it to bridge the range of elements at work in the theatre. Lighting can be thought of in musical terms – and often was in Komis's productions – as much as the emotional content of a scene. From the actor's point of view,

Komisarjevsky's musical stimuli allowed him to operate in the way he was most comfortable: non-invasively and by suggestion. Musical prompts can be internalised and interpreted individually but they can also be used to marshal the skills of an ensemble, a point recognised with quite exceptional sensitivity by one of the very early interviewers of Komis in the UK, the drama critic of *The Observer* in 1920:

> M. Comesarjevsky's [sic] method of 'extempore' training is to induce the actor, through the use of his own imagination, to find out his special way. Then comes the further problem of fitting the company together which can no longer be done by the use of the moulds, nor through the old familiarity of people who know each other's tricks. It must be the joint expression of various individualities: it must grow out of the psychological interplay of various natures and when it is achieved it has genuine 'naturalism', a truth which is not easily exhausted.[24]

As a prescient evaluation of the contribution Komisarjevsky was to make in Britain, as well as a snapshot of a tradition in transition, the drama critic's article, written just weeks after Komis moved to England, is an important piece of evidence.

Developing ensemble

In harmony with Komisarjevsky's ideas on music and musicality is his very clear position on the importance of ensemble. Here, perhaps more than any other area of his practice, is he demonstrably (and happily) part of the Russian tradition – although Duke Georg of Meiningen is arguably the absolute root of these ideas. The creation of an ensemble was, of course, a prime motivator for Nemirovich-Danchenko and Stanislavsky in forming the Moscow Arts Theatre (and Komis points out their debt to Meiningen in *The Costume of the Theatre*; Komisarjevsky 1932: 147); it forms a central plank in Chekhov's Technique as a separate chapter alongside improvisation, in *To the Actor* (Chekhov 2002: 35–46); and it has been a strong theme in Russo-English theatre collaborations since, with companies such as Cheek by Jowl, and most recently the RSC under Michael Boyd, demonstrably inspired by the Russian ensemble tradition.

For Komisarjevsky the question of ensemble was indisputably a pedagogical one and he saw the context of the debate in characteristically polarised terms. There were two kinds of theatre: what he called the Star theatre, on the one hand, and the Ensemble or Team, theatre on the other. The latter 'cannot succeed unless the actors not only work but are trained together',[25] he emphasised in a *Manchester Guardian* interview in 1932.

Ironically, as has been indicated, this is something he did not manage to achieve in the UK, despite promising to develop a training school in 1920 and again in the early 1930s and in the face of his own protestations against the instability of the British system.[24]

The feeling of ensemble, Komis argues, is possible 'only if the players are innerly connected with each other' (Komisarjevsky 1929: 123) and this understanding – *complicité* it might be called now – can be generated by specific exercises. In this instance, unusually for Komisarjevsky, whose natural urge was to historicise, he names specific ways to develop such connectedness in *Myself*:

> Exercises should consist of improvisations of short scenes . . . with or without words. Scenes without words, or 'mimes', should sometimes be acted with music . . . The actor chooses a piece of music, invents a story to fit the form of the music and then acts it.
>
> (p. 126)

Silent etudes are part of Stanislavsky's later 'active analysis' period, associated with the period 1935–8 and later disseminated by Maria Knebel, but ultimately their genesis and use as a training tool lie with Meyerhold, before the Revolution, and as early as 1909. Meyerhold, in turn, derived the practice from *commedia* (Braun 1991: 114). It is not surprising, given Komisarjevsky's own fascination for *commedia* and his early 'training' with Meyerhold at his sister's theatre, that he should look to such a form. Here, Komisarjevsky is explicitly drawing on music, suggesting an improvisation-based approach using short scenes or what he calls 'mimes' (acting 'just as in a play' but with no words). The principal aim of these exercises was to develop an intuitive music-inspired sense of understanding amongst the players, working first to develop an individual responsiveness and then to work collectively.

There may not have been a School to measure the success of this ensemble approach, but the reviews of his productions during this period testify to a hitherto unseen quality of togetherness in the companies with which he worked. Two contemporary reviews will have to suffice to exemplify what was clearly a tangible phenomenon. From the *Manchester Guardian*, 18 February 1926:

> The work that Mr Komisarjevsky is doing in London now is to bring us the Moscow tradition of production, which goes back to the time of Chekhov's actual companionship with Stanislavsky . . . Mr Komisarjevsky has an able team at Barnes now, but he gets more than ability out of them. He stirs the sparks in their English bodies and translates them . . . to the Russian world.

And from the same paper, 8 December 1925:

> It is unjust to make selections from a cast which the producer had
> schooled into a model exercise of team-work, and the Stage Society
> is to be congratulated on opening the new season with one of the best
> performances in recent years.

For the latter reviewer, describing Komis's production of *Ivanov* at the Duke
of York, the work of the director embraces not just the simple staging of a
piece but the inculcation of an entirely new approach, a fresh understanding
of ensemble to which the newly 'schooled' cast clearly responded well. It
is a view consistent with the tenor of this chapter: that, notwithstanding
the lack of a formal pedagogical infrastructure to help deliver his training
system, Komis still managed to develop a teaching philosophy in the UK
which had demonstrable impact.

The role of the régisseur (by way of conclusion)

It should be clear by now that Komisarjevsky's interpretation of the role
of the régisseur was far beyond the contemporary English function of a
producer; when he moved reluctantly from using the latter term in *Myself*
to criticising it directly in *The Theatre* six years later, it was not just an
exercise in semantics. For, without a specialised outlet for his teaching in
Britain, Komis redefined the role of the theatre director to allow him to
continue subtly and without fanfare to reform the British tradition of actor
training. This was not possible in all of his productions. Indeed many of
his extravagant Shakespeare pieces at the Memorial Theatre were done in
remarkably short preparation periods – just six rehearsals for *King Lear*
(1936). However, where he was able to commit more time – and the Barnes
theatre is an ideal example of this – he could effect that magical transformation of understanding which Phyllada Sewell captured in her diary entry.
Phillip Ridgeway, the manager of the Barnes project, was in no doubt about
the significance of this change, calling for it to be a model for a new Civic
Theatre in Manchester:

> At Barnes we used to rehearse our Chekhov productions for six weeks
> and it was only after we had our players in hand for two or three weeks
> that we could set to work to create the atmosphere which, I think I may
> say, was generally admitted to be brilliantly achieved. This history of
> the Moscow Arts Theatre, in which Komisarjevsky was trained, is the
> history of limitless patience. The history of English repertory has been
> a record of gallant struggles in the midst of a scramble . . . Thus the
> originators of a civic theatre would have to take long views.[27]

Ridgeway had of course got Komisarjevsky's lineage confused – either that or he was consciously appropriating the more famous name of Stanislavsky's Moscow Arts to make his point about a privately funded, long-term commitment to ensemble theatre. Still, the point remains: Komisarjevsky's Chekhov productions became trailblazers for a newly considered and painstakingly crafted Art Theatre, which had its roots in the Russian model. This was not simply because they were well directed, or that the orchestration of the elements was 'synthesised' with great skill by the régisseur – although both it seems were true. It was also because Komis had *internalised* a system of training which he was using with this actors, a system which, as we have seen, had a remarkable impact on some of the inter-war 'greats' of the British tradition. He did not properly organise this system in published form and so the evidence for it has had to be drawn together from a range of sources in this essay.

However, one nagging question remains: had he written his planned study on acting, and had he used it with his students in America, where he *was* able to establish a training studio, would it have been as potent as the rather surreptitious inculcation of his ideas into the British tradition?

My answer to this final speculation of the chapter is to suggest: no. Whether he had already 'peaked' as a director after leaving Britain, or he simply did not work with as many gifted actors in the United States as he did in the UK, the evidence suggests that the ad hoc manner in which he worked, coupled with the professional testing grounds he encountered in England, resulted in his defining a Russian-tinted modus operandi for the imaginative actor, which he was never truly able to establish in the United States. In the USA, his classes were small, his student cohorts were inconsistent and he was forced to advertise for more throughout his time there. As Stodelle confirmed in an interview with Victor Borovsky: 'the teaching he did and the acting and teaching I did and dancing helped us survive'.[28] More importantly, there was already established a growing Russian industry of Stanislavsky-trained or associated practitioners. Komisarjevsky's sometimes subtle but important innovations in this industry tended to be lost in the complexity of Russian-based schools of acting. In the year Komisarjevsky arrived, there were 11 'Stanislavsky-based' acting studios out of 25 operating in the States and three 'anti-Stanislavsky', including his own, according to Mel Gordon's estimate (Gordon 2010: xiv). This evaluation is as misleading as the many British commentators, including Ridgeway, who labelled Komis 'a student of Stanislavsky'. The truth is that Komisarjevsky's teaching approach was – like his theory of directing – a creative synthesis of Russian ideas from the early twentieth century, peppered with some important singular innovations, such as his notion of image-chains. He was not able to make this visible enough in the United

States amongst all the other contenders, but in Britain he defined the legacy of Russian-inspired acting technique and, with or without his own version of *An Actor Prepares*, should now be credited for doing so.

Notes

1 Unpublished lecture notes from Houghton Library, Harvard, HTC bMS Th 490, folder 68.
2 *The Times*, 17 April 1928.
3 It is of course true that Stanislavsky's *My Life in Art* had been published before Komis's *Myself* in 1924, but this did not include precise details of the director's specific acting system.
4 Boleslavsky, a Pole who had worked with Stanislavsky on some of his early signature productions, including A *Month in the Country* in 1909, moved to the USA in 1922. There he founded the American Laboratory Theatre. According to Mel Gordon's (2010) *Stanislavsky in America* 'it was through the American Laboratory Theatre that the Stanislavsky System . . . finally came to the New World' (p. 16).
5 For the American impact of *Myself*, see Letter dated 2 August 1945 from Henry Schnitzler, Dept of Dramatic Art, Berkeley, California: 'I have read all the books you wrote . . . With particular interest I studied your discussion of Stanislavsky's "System" in your book *Myself and the Theatre* . . . In fact, I shall use the last three chapters of this fascinating account as "Required Reading" on one of my classes in acting'. Houghton Library, Harvard, HTC bMS Th 490, folder 153.
6 Komisarjevsky is also credited with a fourth book, co-written with Lee Simonson and titled *Settings and Costumes of the Modern Age* (Komisarjevsky and Simonson 1933) but, since his contribution amounts to a seven-page introductory essay, I am not counting this in his major output.
7 There is very little evidence on Komis's teaching at RADA partly because archival records were lost in a fire. Jacqueline Lyons, however, in an unpublished MA by Research thesis for Newcastle University, New South Wales states: 'Komisarjevsky introduced pantomime and commedia training for actors at R.A.D.A. in 1925 offering himself as a teacher. The courses ran part time until 1928. As a result of these classes, a number of public performances were given by R.A.D.A. students. Both Charles Laughton and George Devine were taught mime by Komisarjevsky' (Lyons 1991: 37). The source of this information was the RADA administrator Richard O'Donaghue.
8 Burra Moody archive: from a letter dated 15 December 1944. I am indebted to Richard Thompson for making these materials available to me.
9 Burra Moody archive: from a letter dated 20 November 1949.
10 Letter dated 28 March 1950, Houghton Library, Harvard, HTC bMS Th 490, folder 15.
11 Burra Moody archive: from a letter dated 15 July 1951.
12 'I am going to write that book on acting now. What is the name and address of that Bodley Head man?' Komisarjevsky: in a letter dated 25 September 1952, Burra Moody archive.
13 From an interview with Ernestine Komissarzhevsky-Chamberlain (née Stodelle) by Victor Borovsky, 21 March 1993, Burra Moody archive.
14 There are documents from Allardyce Nicoll, the then Chair of Drama at Yale, confirming this (HTC bMS Th 490, folder 122), and the dates 1940–2 are

verified by the Yale archive. Komis directed *The Cherry Orchard* there with Yale students.

15 This advertisement is from 1939–40, Houghton Library, Harvard, HTC bMS Th 490, folder 87, but advertisements as late as 2 January 1949 in the *New York Times* are worded almost identically.

16 Diary entry dated 10 August 1930, Burra Moody archive.

17 From an interview with Ernestine Komissarzhevsky-Chamberlain (née Stodelle) by Victor Borovsky, 21 March 1993, Burra Moody archive.

18 Extracts from this book are reprinted in translation in Sayler (1922: 250–4). A typical example of Komisarjevsky's critique of Stanislavsky would be: 'while stage exercises which favour the development of fantasy and the imagination of the actor enrich his consciousness, those exercises which consist in recollecting the worldly experiences of the actor limit the activity of his consciousness' (p. 251).

19 'Komissarzhevsky . . . made several attempts to join his company' but Stanislavsky 'warned him that he would not promise immediate independence' (Borovsky 2001: 270).

20 Diary entry dated 10 August 1930, Burra Moody archive.

21 Play Direction, Synopsis of Lectures: Houghton Library, Harvard, HTC bMS Th 490, folder 68.

22 Benedetti, in his latest translations of *An Actor's Work*, reclassifies the Hapgood term, Through line of action, as Throughaction; in Russian, *Skvosnoe Deistvie* (Stanislavsky 2008: 684).

23 Costume was an equal part of the acting process as far as Komis was concerned, and was connected to the actor's psychic mentality: 'The second requirement of any stage costume is to assist the actor in his interpretation of the part and accentuate the expressiveness of his movements to reflect the rhythm of his creative mind' (Komisarjevsky 1932: 169).

24 'The Play and the Actor: A Russian Producer and His Ideas', *The Observer*, 18 January 1920.

25 'A Producer on His Art: Komisarjevsky and British Theatres', *Manchester Guardian*, 27 December 1932.

26 See Komis's interviews in *The Observer*, 18 January 1920, and in the *Manchester Guardian*, 27 December 1932.

27 'Civic Theatre: What Might Be Done', *Manchester Guardian*, 14 June 1926.

28 From an interview with Ernestine Komissarzhevsky-Chamberlain (née Stodelle) by Victor Borovsky, 21 March 1993, Burra Moody archive.

Bibliography

Allen, D. (2000) *Performing Chekhov*, London: Routledge.

Bartosevich, A. (1992) 'Theodore Komisarjevsky, Chekhov and Shakespeare', in Senelick, L. (ed.), *Wandering Stars, Russian Emigre Theatre 1905–1940*, Iowa City: University of Iowa Press, pp. 102–15.

Benedetti, J. (1998) *Stanislavski and the Actor*, London: Methuen.

Berry, R. (1983) 'Komisarjevsky at Stratford-upon-Avon', in Wells, S. (ed.), *Shakespeare Survey, Volume 36: Shakespeare in the Twentieth Century*, Cambridge: Cambridge University Press, pp. 73–85.

Billington, M. (1988) *Peggy Ashcroft*, London: John Murray.

Borovsky, V. (2001) *A Triptych from the Russian Theatre: An Artistic Biography of the Komissarzhevskys*, London: Hurst.

Braun, E. (ed.) (1991) *Meyerhold on Theatre*, London: Methuen.

Callow, S. (1987) *Charles Laughton: A Difficult Actor*, London: Methuen.

Carnicke, S. (2010) 'Stanislavsky's System: Pathways for the Actor', in Hodge, A. (ed.), *Actor Training*, Oxon: Routledge, pp. 1–25.

Chekhov, M. (2002) *To the Actor*, Oxon: Routledge.

Emeljanov, V. (ed.) (1981) *Chekhov the Critical Heritage*, London: Routledge and Kegan Paul, pp. 295–312.

Funke, L. and Booth, J. E. (1961) *Actors Talk about Acting: Nine Interviews with Stars of the Theatre*, London: Thames & Hudson.

Gielgud, J. (1987) *Early Stages*, London: Hodder & Stoughton.

Gordon, M. (2010) *Stanislavsky in America*, Oxon: Routledge.

Komisarjevsky, T. (1929) *Myself and the Theatre*, London: Heinemann.

Komisarjevsky, T. (1932) *The Costume of the Theatre*, New York: Henry Holt.

Komisarjevsky, T. (1935) *The Theatre and a Changing Civilisation*, London: Bodley Head.

Komisarjevsky, T. and Simonson, L. (1933) *Settings and Costumes of the Modern Age*, London: Studio Publications.

Lyons, J. (1991) *Theodore Komisarjevsky in the British Theatre*, unpublished MA by Research Thesis, University of Newcastle, New South Wales.

Mennen, R. (1979) 'Theodore Komisarjevsky's Production of "Merchant of Venice"', *Theatre Journal*, 31 (3): 386–397.

Moussinac, L. (1931) *The New Movement in the Theatre*, London: B. T. Batsford.

Mullin, M. (1974) 'Augures and Understood Relations: Theodore Komisarjevsky's "Macbeth"', *Educational Theatre Journal*, 26 (1): 20–30.

Redgrave, M. (1953) *The Actor's Ways and Means*, London: Heinemann.

Rudnitsky, K. (1981) *Meyerhold the Director*, trans. Petrov, G., Ann Arbor, MI: Ardis.

Sayler, O. M. (1922) *The Russian Theatre*, New York: Brentanos.

Senelick, L. (1999) *The Chekhov Theatre*, Cambridge: Cambridge University Press.

Slonim, M. (1963) *Russian Theatre from the Empire to the Soviets*, London: Methuen.

Stanislavsky, K. (2008) *An Actor's Work*, trans. Benedetti, J., Oxon: Routledge.

Tracy, R. (1993) 'Komisarjevsky's 1926 Three Sisters', in Miles, P. (ed.), *Chekhov on the British Stage*, Cambridge: Cambridge University Press, pp. 65–77.

2

STANISLAVSKY'S PASSAGE INTO THE BRITISH CONSERVATOIRE

David Shirley

As the previous chapter has established, it is evident that Theodore Komisarjevsky's arrival in London in 1919, followed by his landmark productions of Chekhov at the Barnes Theatre during the 1920s and Shakespeare at Stratford-upon-Avon in the 1930s, provides the foundations from which to begin tracing the early influence of Stanislavskian thinking in Britain. The introduction of new ways of thinking about 'character' and alternative approaches to rehearsal enthralled this country's theatre community and clearly had a lasting impact on many of the period's most celebrated actors including Peggy Ashcroft, John Gielgud, Rachel Kempson, Charles Laughton and Michael Redgrave.

Although we know that Komisarjevsky spent some time teaching at RADA (the Royal Academy of Dramatic Art) during the mid 1920s – where he first encountered John Gielgud and Charles Laughton – very little is known about the content of his classes or indeed about his approach to teaching, beyond the fact that he taught *commedia* techniques. Did he also begin to articulate and put into practice some of the ideas pioneered by Stanislavsky and, if so, how were they received by the students and staff with whom he worked? Although it would be inappropriately simplistic to claim that Komisarjevsky served as a conduit through which Stanislavsky's theories were initially disseminated in the UK, the realisation that he published *The Actor's Creativity and Stanislavsky's Theory* two years before he emigrated to Britain suggests that he was certainly influenced by Stanislavsky's reputation and work, if only as a spur to his own thinking about acting and authenticity.

Writing about Claude Rains's experience of teaching at RADA in the 1920s during exactly the same period in which Komisarjevsky taught there,[1] David Skal offers a telling account of what both men are likely to have encountered:

> When Rains began his association with RADA, it was based in a pair of old houses in London's Gower Street. The school's curriculum was heavily weighted with the disciplines inherited from the era of Tree and Irving – gesture, elocution, fencing, and movement. The more deeply psychological influence of Stanislavski was barely noted by the British theatre establishment. . . . The British theatre had no government subsidies at the time. Because of this, it was a market-driven industry and therefore embraced techniques that were proven commercially.
>
> (Skal 2008: 45)

The idea that RADA's training regime was shaped by commercial rather than artistic-driven imperatives is further reinforced by the discovery that a number of the students seemed anything but motivated:

> Rains was immediately struck, and forever frustrated, by the unevenness of talent, much less professional aspiration . . . 'These young students, what were they there for? Fun, having larks, some of them . . . They'd laugh. I used to get livid'.
>
> (Skal 2008: 46)

In a conventionalised theatre culture where actors' performances tended to be driven by a preoccupation with the external manifestations of 'gesture' and 'manners', the insistence on an 'inner reality' – the source of which springs from the imagination – must have appeared extraordinarily innovative and radical. With the added excitement that ensued as a result of the publication in Britain and the USA of Stanislavsky's *My Life in Art* in 1924,[2] it must have seemed like the beginning of a new era for British actor training – and to a large extent it was. But in what ways did this period serve to generate new ways of thinking about actor training in the UK and how can we begin to track and account for the establishment of Stanislavsky's theories as the mainstay of British conservatoire training?

The attempt to outline a history of the appropriation of Stanislavskian methodologies in British training establishments is fraught with difficulty. Although Komisarjevsky's period at RADA certainly provides a good starting point, the absence of any clear account of his work there makes it difficult to offer anything more than a speculative approach to the construction of this history. Moreover, unlike the situation in the United States, where the work of Richard Boleslavsky together with the much publicised US tours of Stanislavsky himself prompted the emergence of The Group

Theater (1931–40) and the subsequent development of a series of actors' 'studios' led by the likes of Stella Adler, Lee Strasberg, Harold Clurman and Sanford Meisner, the passage of Stanislavsky's work into Britain is much more erratic and piecemeal.

As we will discover, part of the issue here is that many, many acting teachers in the UK who are likely to have taught aspects of the System would not necessarily have acknowledged Stanislavsky or any of his followers as their source. Claude Rains is a perfect example of a teacher who intuitively recognised the value of Stanislavsky's techniques, but who may not have labelled them as such for his students:

> Rains would never have a formal introduction to Stanislavski's 'method', though he would later express considerable appreciation for the technique. In fact, he clearly took a similar approach to building his characters, instinctively grounding them in solid psychological motivation.
>
> (Skal 2008: 45)

The reference to 'instinct' here is important; much of Stanislavsky's methodology developed as a result of the careful observations of the highly accomplished actors with whom he worked. For many experienced practitioners it was not the working methods themselves that proved revelatory, but rather the fact that, for the first time, they had been documented and ordered into a formalised 'system'. Like Rains, various British actor trainers would have relied on their own professional instincts or encouraged a process of learning through 'imitation' as the means through which to guide and instruct their students. John Gielgud, who trained at RADA during the years when Rains taught there, recalls his own efforts to emulate his master's technique:

> I worked as hard as I could and imitated Rains' acting until I became extremely mannered . . . I strained every fibre in my efforts to appear violent and emotional and only succeeded in straining my voice and striking strange attitudes with my body.
>
> (Skal 2008: 47)

Despite the undoubted challenges confronting an attempt to chart the growth of Stanislavskian methodology in this country, it is important to outline the different stages in its progression if we are to begin to acquire a clear understanding of the inter-relationship between professional theatre practice and performer training in twentieth-century British theatre. The evolution of realist/kitchen-sink drama in the 1950s, for instance – most notably at the English Stage Company under the directorship of George Devine – marks an important moment in the history of British theatre, the influence of which would later help to fuel the advancement of realist TV and film drama. Aside from being a celebrated actor and director in his own right, Devine was also actively involved in the training of actors at the London Theatre Studio (1935–9) and the Old Vic Theatre School (1947–52). One of the more obvious advantages, therefore, of unearthing the roots of Stanislavsky's work in the UK is that it might reveal new ways of accounting for and reflecting on the growth of social realism in British drama during the 1950s and 1960s.

Beyond elements of what might be called Stanislavskian practice in Komisarjevsky's work at the Barnes Theatre, we have very little information about the development of Stanislavsky's work at other British drama schools. Perhaps the next phase in which to track more precisely the development of Stanislavsky's work in Britain is through the work of Michel Saint-Denis and the two schools he established in London between the 1930s and 1940s. Heavily influenced by the work of his uncle, Jacques Copeau, with whom he trained and worked during the mid to late 1920s in France, Saint-Denis sought to foster an approach to actor training that combined advanced levels of physical skill and expressiveness with an acute sensitivity to the internal impulses that fuel complex and psychologically convincing characterisations. Like Komisarjevsky, Saint-Denis was a gifted director and during the 1930s his frequent visits to London with the Compagnie de Quinze[3] attracted much attention:

> the public's reaction, the tone of the press, the daily visits we received from leading members of the acting profession, made us feel that the impact of our performances was something more than just an ordinary theatrical success. People of all sorts wanted us to know that they were refreshed by our plays and by our way of acting. They found us direct, real, devoid of artificial brilliance.
>
> (Saint-Denis 1982: 42)

Feeling that the British understood his work and having attracted support from admirers that included Peggy Ashcroft, John Gielgud, Alec Guinness, Tyrone Guthrie and Laurence Olivier, Saint-Denis dissolved the Compagnie de Quinze in 1935 and moved to London, where he opened the London Theatre Studio (LTS).

In establishing his new school, Saint-Denis's aims were clear:

> We wanted to equip our young acting students with all the means of expression we used at the Compagnie des Quinze, but we wanted to

extend the imaginative, the creative basis of the Quinze's training. It had been a wonderful training but it had, nevertheless, made us specialists of a particular kind. I realised that the L.T.S. had to go beyond that specialization if it wanted to be in a position to face the problems of interpreting classical and modern plays in all their variety. There were problems I had previously hardly touched upon: among them the technical and artistic development of voice and speech, and, especially, imaginative expression through language.

(Saint-Denis 1982: 45–6)

Although Saint-Denis had 'a tremendous suspicion of any "method", whether old or new, which stops questions or discourages change' (Saint-Denis 1982: 80), it is clearly evident from all of his writings that the curriculum he designed at his new London school was greatly inspired by Stanislavsky's work:

Stanislavsky reached these shores in 1937 through a book called *An Actor Prepares*, and . . . many of us at that time paid great attention to it . . . and we put into practice quite an amount of Stanislavsky in 1937 in a school which was called the London Theatre Studio.

(Brook et al. 1963: 28)

The two men first met each other in Paris in 1922 when the Moscow Arts Theatre Company (MAT) brought a production of *The Cherry Orchard* to the Théâtre des Champs Elysées. Initially cynical about the company's reputation, on that occasion Saint-Denis witnessed a performance that was to leave a profound impression on him:

This visit of Stanislavsky and his company was of incalculable importance to me. For the first time our classical attitude towards the theatre, our efforts to bring a new reality to acting, a reality transposed from life, were confronted by a superior form of modern realism, the realism of Chekhov.

(Saint-Denis 1960: 42)

Elsewhere in his writings, Saint-Denis pinpoints important aspects of the performance that were to shape his work in the future:

in the domain of interpretation, the actors of the Moscow Art Theatre Company succeeded in achieving a profound truth. Through his work Stanislavski found a perfect balance between the actors' subjective introspection, their objective study of the characters and their technique of physical action and spoken expression. They arrived at a freedom in acting which I have never seen equalled.

(Saint-Denis 1982: 36)

What became immediately apparent to Saint-Denis was that despite the obvious differences between the physically stylised and highly experimental work he had been exposed to with Copeau and the more psychologically motivated work of Stanislavsky, the strengths of each artist

grew out of their rejection of all theatrical artifice. The impression of perfect authenticity generated a feeling of great liveness which reached across the footlights to the audience.

(Saint-Denis 1982: 36)

In addition to highlighting his admiration of Stanislavsky and the MAT, Saint-Denis's description of the actors' performances in *The Cherry Orchard* also draws attention to the values he would later subscribe to as a teacher: the fluidity of their inner impulses, the spontaneity and improvisational quality they brought both to the text and to the use of gesture, the sense of a world that existed beyond the immediate life of the stage, their relationships to the objects and furniture around them, and the complexity and variation they brought to the use of emotion.[4]

Although it is evident that Saint-Denis recognised the value of Stanislavsky's theories, he was by no means convinced that they could be applied to all forms of drama – especially the classics. Reflecting on his experience of having seen the MAT production of *The Cherry Orchard,* he later asked:

would these actors, performing so marvellously the poetic realism of Chekhov, be equally convincing if they were to play the great 'classics' – the Greek, the Spanish, the French, the Elizabethan? What of Shakespeare, that prototype of non-naturalistic dramatists?

(Saint-Denis 1982: 37)

Recalling Stanislavsky's own description in *My Life in Art* of the difficulties he encountered when working on his 1911 production of *Hamlet*, Saint-Denis argued that a preoccupation with naturalistic detail or with the psychological motivations of actors will ultimately prove reductive when applied to Shakespeare and, by implication, most other forms of classical drama. Pointing to the text of *Othello*, he suggested that the world created by Shakespeare is highly poetic and unique and as such calls for a difference of approach. Rather than viewing the play as an imitation of life, he contended that its 'essence is expressed by rhythmic images in a musical language with which a realistic performance based on rational details, will come into conflict' (Saint-Denis 1982: 38). Plays of this kind he asserted, do not merely imitate life; instead they are nourished by a reality that they will ultimately move beyond. Such a consideration prompted Saint-Denis to examine the question of how an actor might begin to 'live a part that is beyond the natural world?' (Saint-Denis 1982: 38).

In part, it was the desire to find solutions to the challenges raised by this question that served to shape and inform the philosophical and pedagogical ideas on which Saint-Denis would later base his approach to actor training. Importantly, at the heart of this approach was a very particular understanding of the notion of realism. Distinguishing between 'deep realism, which studies and expresses . . . the meaning of human life' and 'superficial realism . . . that is satisfied with the representation of the external' (Saint-Denis 1960: 51), Saint-Denis believed that training in the classical theatre was of immense importance if the realistic approaches of modern theatre were to avoid the 'danger of becoming sensational, sentimental or merely empty' (Saint-Denis 1960: 52). Of crucial significance here was an unapologetic affirmation of the importance of *style*:

> To have its meaning revealed a classical play must be acted in the reality of its style so far as we can understand and achieve it . . . The deeper modern realism becomes in its expression as well as in its subject matter, the more it is possible to say that a modern actor, if he is brought up in a classical tradition which he has properly understood, will be better equipped to bite on modern forms of theatre.
>
> (Saint-Denis 1960: 51)

Although it is very clear throughout his writings that Saint-Denis was a great admirer of Stanislavsky's work, he did not import the System wholesale into his new school, preferring instead to adapt and re-invent many of the exercises and techniques in accordance with the demands of individual genres and traditions.

> If Stanislavski's system is applied literally, it leads merely to realism, but applied selectively, with discrimination, it can be made 'the grammar of all styles'.
>
> (Saint-Denis 1982: 38)

Interestingly, despite his reservations and the suspicions he harboured in relation to organised 'systems' of training, when he came to write about his work and the schools he founded, there is no mistaking the striking similarities between the training techniques deployed by Saint-Denis and those advocated by Stanislavsky. These include the 'representation of actions taken from . . . daily life like waking up, eating a meal . . . dressing and undressing' as well as exercises designed to promote 'the need for concentration and observation . . . the importance of emotional memory . . . the use of space, of rhythm, of the continuity of action' (Saint-Denis 1960: 103). As Jane Baldwin (2010: 88) has indicated and as Saint-Denis himself has acknowledged, the inaugural year of the LTS coincided with the first publication of Elizabeth Hapgood's translation of Stanislavsky's *An Actor Prepares* in 1936 – a fact which perhaps accounts for the unmistakable similarity between the descriptive terminology used by Saint-Denis and that developed by Stanislavsky.

Although, like Stanislavsky, Saint-Denis was committed to the view that acting is essentially an art of transformation, he remained wary of those approaches to training that are overly dependent on introspection or intense subjective analysis:

> I once saw a naturalistic play where the actors applied strictly the teachings of the 'Method': they were not concerned so much with the presentation of the play, the 'cloth', as with the 'lining'. Their faces, their gestures and words, were far less important to them than their nervous systems, their secret 'stirrings', the meaning behind the words. Though a photograph of life was intended, only the negative was being shown, not the finished print.
>
> (Saint-Denis 1982: 189)

Although the reference to the 'Method'[5] is not a direct attack on Stanislavsky's 'System', it does suggest that Saint-Denis was sceptical about training techniques that foreground interior, psychological or naturalistic approaches to performance. Though fundamentally a realist, Saint-Denis was also profoundly influenced by the highly experimental and theatrical work he had undertaken in the 1920s with Jacques Copeau and later with his own company, the Compagnie des Quinze. Always resistant to the limitations of naturalism – especially those forms which disavowed *theatricality, reflexivity* and *playfulness* – he was determined to ensure that the training methods he adopted served to 'enlarge the actor's field of expression' and to 'put each technique that he learned to the service of his acting without falling into the trap of specialisation in any of them' (Saint-Denis 1982: 46).

Of all the training techniques that Saint-Denis introduced to his schools, perhaps the most significant was mask work. Commencing with the need to develop sensitivity to the economies and precision demanded by the use of neutral mask, students would eventually progress to character mask work. Whereas the former involved no costume or dialogue of any kind and only the simplest of props (a blank page, for instance, to symbolise a letter) the latter gradually introduced performed scenarios featuring a number of actors aided by the use of costumes, props and sometimes even small-scale sets. Careful to resist the drive to become overly dependent on the use of pure psychology or emotion in the training of his students, Saint-Denis's use of mask provides the perfect illustration of a methodology that (a) nurtured the development of emotional sensitivity from within a profoundly physical, yet depersonalised, form of signification, (b) highlighted the importance of style by providing a framework in which to amplify and moderate the means through which emotional impulses are experienced and communicated by individual actors and (c) provided maximum opportunity for theatrical invention, improvisation and play in the creation of dramatic personas. By allowing for a fluid, two-way exchange between the emotional and physical realms of experience, mask work sessions provided the perfect vehicle through which Saint-Denis could begin to combine the best elements of his work at the Compagnie des Quinze with the techniques developed by Stanislavsky. Revealingly, as Jane Baldwin (2010: 87) makes clear, George Devine also taught mask work at the Studio, a skill he acquired directly from Saint-Denis, who suggested that such work permits the student actor 'to experience, in its most startling form, the chemistry of acting' (Saint-Denis 1960: 170). Devine would subsequently take this work to the Royal Court Theatre, where he introduced it to William Gaskill, John Dexter and Keith Johnstone (see Harrop 1992: 68).

At one level, the techniques developed by Saint-Denis chime with those of Stanislavsky's *Method of Physical Actions.* There is, for instance, a clear acknowledgement of the importance of using physical activity as a means of stimulating inner impulse. Unlike the situation in the USA, where teachers such as Lee Strasberg encouraged acting students to establish a character's 'inner life' before moving to external realities, Saint-Denis's approach developed and adapted Stanislavsky's work in such a way as to enable actors to reach beyond the immediacy of their own subjective experiences to achieve genuinely convincing physical and emotional transformations that were appropriate to the dramatic worlds they were called upon to inhabit. In a very real sense, therefore, it can be argued that Saint-Denis both embraced and extended Stanislavsky's work in a manner that allowed it to be used as a universal 'morphology of acting' rather than as an individual performance style that is most closely associated with naturalism. Indeed, Saint-Denis was convinced that usage of the latter kind was far from what Stanislavsky had intended:

I think that Stanislavski would have been the first to hate the idea that his way of working and of training people should be called a system . . . He was a great master of the theatre of his own time and never confined himself to the narrow limits of 'naturalism'.

(Saint-Denis 1960: 52)

With the outbreak of the Second World War in 1939, the LTS was forced to close and Saint-Denis returned, for a brief period, to his native France. In 1945, however, he was invited by Laurence Olivier to form the second of his two British drama schools, which was to be based at the Old Vic Theatre. The Old Vic Theatre School, as it became known, was conceived as part of a much larger organisation that included the Old Vic Theatre Company, a small-scale touring company known as the Young Vic and an experimental company to be led by Saint-Denis, George Devine and Glen Byam Shaw.

The formal liaison with an established company that was much acclaimed for both classical and contemporary work was, for Saint-Denis, indispensable to what he would later describe as a 'total school' (Saint-Denis 1982: 51). His absolute commitment to the classics and belief in the importance of style as a springboard from which to enable students to access deeper levels of reality served to refine and extend the teaching methodologies he originally introduced at the LTS. Unfortunately, despite a public outcry, the Old Vic Theatre School was forced to close in 1952 following serious funding problems and various acrimonious exchanges between members of the governing body.[6]

There is no doubt that a close analysis of Saint-Denis's writings about each of the schools he established in Britain reveals that an important aspect of his work as a teacher addressed the need to resolve the apparent conflict between the psychological imperatives informing Stanislavsky's early theories and the stylistic demands of other forms of classical and contemporary realism. In Saint-Denis's view Stanislavsky never actually resolved this problem[7] and, as a consequence, his appropriation of the System was measured and selective:

if we welcomed Stanislavsky it is because we thought that if we put ourselves at that school we might find a basic way of working which, if we looked at it very carefully, so as not to let it overstep towards realism, or put us in a prison of concentration out of which it would be very difficult to find a sort of freedom which is necessary for big style,[8] that might be good.

(Brook et al. 1963: 28)

Before moving on to examine the next phase of Stanislavsky's journey into the British conservatoire, it is worth considering the degree to which many of those with whom Saint-Denis worked both at the LTS and at the Old Vic Theatre School would later go on to play very significant roles in helping to shape the ongoing development of British actor training as well as that of British theatre in the 1950s and 1960s. Amongst the many teachers and practitioners that worked alongside him, perhaps the most influential were John Blatchley, Glen Byam Shaw, George Devine, Marius Goring and Litz Pisk. Whereas Glen Byam Shaw went on to become the director of Stratford-upon-Avon's Shakespeare Memorial Theatre, George Devine would play an instrumental role in establishing the English Stage Company at the Royal Court Theatre, of which he would also become the first Artistic Director between 1956 and 1965. With a reputation for defining new forms of writing and performance, this company, alongside Joan Littlewood's Theatre Workshop Group, played a crucial role in helping to redefine the aesthetics of British acting technique. The following, which is taken from the recorded text of a discussion held at the Royal Court Theatre in 1963 between Peter Brook, Kenneth Haigh, Charles Marowitz and Michel Saint-Denis, offers a glimpse into the kinds of concerns that were being raised by some of Company's leading practitioners:

> Before 1956 English acting was mostly genteel and external . . . After 1956 it was proletarian and external. I think that the New Wave acting . . . is of course a terribly important development in the theatre. And . . . this new style of acting, the acting required by these plays came about – was called into being – not by the drama schools but by the writers themselves. They were putting out new kinds of work and the actors had to find the means to express it. And it was the actor grappling with the text and being tutored by the writer, who in a sense discovered the style in which these plays had to be performed. The true drama teachers of this period were people like Osborne, Pinter, Wesker, Behan, Owen and Delaney – these were the people who actually taught the actors.
> (Brook et al. 1963: 21–2)

Tempting though it may be, it would, of course, be an exaggeration to suggest that the pioneering work of the Royal Court can be directly attributed to Saint-Denis's influence on Devine when the two worked together at the LTS and the Old Vic Theatre School. This said, the unmistakable reference to the importance of 'style' and the suggestion that it was through 'grappling with the text' that the actors began to find new forms of expression suggests that the long partnership between the two men and Saint-Denis's modified and adapted versions of Stanislavskian methodology were to play a significant role in fostering the experimentalism and creativity that proved indispensable in helping to shape the alternative forms of realism that became the hallmark of the English Stage Company. Clearly sensing that the drama schools were not actually enabling actors to meet the demands of this new kind of theatre, Marowitz went on to call for a review of training practices:

> what is needed is (a) new systems of training as a sort of antidote to the drama school education. (b) an awareness of craft problems, which is to say problems apart from those of external technique – where do I move, how do I get there? (c) a new relationship between the actor and the producer which is based on a creative collaboration, not simply a matter of moves and voice production, and (d) *aware* criticism which is essentially aesthetic, theatrically orientated and not merely journalistic.
>
> (Brook et al. 1963: 23)

Marowitz's lack of faith in the effectiveness of British conservatoire training for actors is echoed in John Elsom's *Post-War British Theatre*:

> After the war – and despite the acclaimed performances of Olivier, Richardson and others . . . English acting was associated with a particular type of elegance, a natural 'upper-classness' which so prevailed that the Royal Academy of Dramatic Art was used as a finishing school when the other finishing schools were closed.
>
> (Elsom 1976: 24)

Despite the early influence of Theodore Komisarjevsky and the developmental work of Saint-Denis in both of his London schools, the testimonies of both Marowitz and Elsom suggest that by the late 1950s and early 1960s many leading British drama schools were failing to furnish students with the kinds of skill that were being demanded by the profession[9] – a realisation that leads us to the next stage in attempting to trace the progression of Stanislavskian methodology into the British conservatoire.

Although it may well have been the case that a number of drama schools taught unaccredited versions of Stanislavskian methodology, very few, if any, taught acting as a discrete discipline. They preferred instead to build training regimes around the skills of movement and voice and the rehearsal/performance of scene study projects and public productions which, as the earlier commentary from Charles Marowitz implies, were largely concerned with 'external technique'.[10]

In 1960, the British director John Blatchley – who had worked alongside Michel Saint-Denis and George Devine at the Old Vic Theatre School – joined the staff at Central School of Speech and Drama. Following the demise of the Old Vic School, Blatchley maintained close links with George Devine, for whom he often deputised at the English Stage Company. Clearly conscious of the inadequacies of actor training at many British drama schools, Blatchley set out to improve the situation. One of his first appointments was that of Harold Lang, a celebrated actor and gifted teacher known for his Stanislavskian work. Before accepting the new appointment, however, Lang insisted that Blatchley appoint Swedish dancer and choreographer, Yat Malmgren, as the School's movement director. Before long Blatchley's new team – which also included Christopher Fettes – established something of a reputation for their radical teaching methods – especially those of Yat Malmgren. Whereas many staff were intrigued and clearly welcomed Blatchley's innovations, a significant number did not, including the then principal of Central School of Speech and Drama, Gwyneth Thorburn. Apparently concerned that his movement work was compromising the vocal training by producing unhelpful 'neck tension' (Fettes 2002), Thorburn dismissed Malmgren. Before long Malmgren's departure was followed by that of Christopher Fettes, John Blatchley and several other tutors – all of whom objected to the, in their view, partisan attitudes of Central's principal. Equally important here is the realisation that members of staff were also joined by a large percentage of second-year students who were about to embark on the final year of their course.

Devoted to their teachers and inspired by the techniques to which they were being introduced, a core group of these students secured the lease of an old Methodist church in nearby Chalk Farm, where they persuaded Blatchley and his team to deliver the final year of their training. This building would later become the permanent premises of the London Drama Centre, a school that was to prove particularly instrumental in helping to ensure the continued development of Stanislavsky's work in Britain.

Until the early 1960s, the transition of Stanislavsky's methods into British theatre and training had been shaped initially by the influences of European practitioners such as Theodore Komisarjevsky and Michel Saint-Denis and subsequently by the publication of Elizabeth Hapgood's English translations of Stanislavsky's works including *An Actor Prepares* (1936), *Building a Character* (1949) and *Creating a Role* (1961). Although well established in the United States, the various versions of the American 'Method' system of training had not really managed to gain a foothold in Britain. In part, this may be because of a degree of antipathy on the part of British practitioners towards the advocates of the Method:[11]

> English actors not only felt that they had been better trained in Stanislavski's methods, but also that the Method actors misunderstood them. The Method actors were too introverted in their approach, and

confused by the attempt to reconcile Freud, psychoanalysis and group therapy with the business of acting. 'The Method-ists', wrote Tyrone Guthrie . . . 'over-prize the search for truth as opposed to the revelation of Truth'.

(Elsom 1976: 24)

It must have come as something as a surprise, therefore, when having established their new drama school at Chalk Farm, Blatchley, Malmgren and Fettes agreed to invite Method-trained Doreen Cannon, a former pupil of Uta Hagen's, to become the Drama Centre's first Head of Acting. Having trained at New York's HB Studio,[12] Cannon spent a number of years working as a professional actress in the United States before coming to Britain in 1959. In the early days of the English Stage Company, George Devine invited her to give a series of masterclasses at the Royal Court Theatre[13] for actors in company, and it is likely to have been at this point that Blatchley first encountered her. Interestingly, at around the same time Uta Hagen herself came to London to appear as Martha in the West End production of Edward Albee's *Who's Afraid of Virginia Woolf*.[14] Whilst in London she hosted series of acting workshops for British professionals – something that Doreen Cannon would later continue when Hagen returned to the United States.

Although her approach, both as a teacher and as a professional, was essentially derived from the teachings of a series of Method practitioners that included Stella Adler, Lee Strasberg, Harold Clurman and Sanford Meisner, Hagen was fundamentally a pragmatist and approached both Stanislavsky and the Method with an open mind:

Today the Method is taught or referred to in . . . schools and universities throughout the country. It seems to be more open to a variety of interpretations and misinterpretations than the Holy Bible. As we know, Stanislavsky's discoveries were based on *his* understanding of how the great realistic actors applied the psychology of human struggles and drives, their response to emotional, physical, and mental stimuli and to their consequent actions. Sticking slavishly to his doctrines is an injustice to Stanislavski himself.

(Hagen 1991:46)

Alongside a remarkable career on stage and in film, in which she worked with Marlon Brando, Jose Ferrer, Laurence Olivier, Anthony Quinn and Paul Robeson, Hagen also maintained a close association with the HB Studio in New York, where she taught with her husband, Herbert Berghof. Possibly the most acclaimed actor of all of the period's Method teachers,

Hagen in her approach to training seemed acutely aware of the realities of the profession itself:

> There was a balance in her approach, which was method acting, but not taken to the self-immolating extremes of some of its practitioners. Though she demanded respect, she eschewed pretension. 'I teach acting as I approach it – from the human and technical problems I have experienced through living and practice,' she said.
>
> (Stearns 2004)

Given her work with Blatchley and his colleagues at the Royal Court, who, as we have seen, were keen to establish a new approach to actor training, together with her association with Uta Hagen, who won a Tony Award in 1963 for her performance in *Who's Afraid of Virginia Woolf?*, Cannon must have seemed the perfect teacher for a school that was determined to break the mould of British actor training.

Hagen's approach to training is well documented in her two books *Respect for Acting* (Hagen 1973) and *A Challenge for the Actor* (Hagen 1991). Although neither book had been published when Doreen Cannon arrived in Britain, it is from the experiences of having been taught the exercises and techniques described in these works by Hagen herself that Cannon developed her teaching practice at the Drama Centre in the 1960s and 1970s and at RADA in the 1980s and 1990s.

Although it is unnecessary to record the Hagen/Cannon approach in full detail here, it is worth noting those aspects of the methodology which are directly influenced by the Stanislavsky 'System'. Importantly, like Saint-Denis before them, both of these teachers sought to adapt Stanislavsky's work in such a way as to harness the psychological/inner impulses of the actor to the physical/external stimuli that result from environmental factors. Unlike earlier versions of the Method, this approach acknowledges the importance of emotional *and* physical transformation and stresses the need for technical virtuosity and skill (Hagen 1991: 37–41). Distilling the main tenets of Stanislavsky's work into a series of 'Object Exercises', the training begins with a rigorous process of self-observation that is conducted through various solitary and small group scenarios designed to stimulate and enhance sensitivity to environment, objects, inner and outer impulses, personality traits, relationships and given circumstances. Each scenario is carefully monitored by the tutor, and students – who are discouraged from playing 'characters' – are required to undertake extremely detailed preparation prior to each presentation. The actor and writer Simon Callow, who trained at the Drama Centre in the early 1970s, neatly summarises the initial stages of the training:

The early work, in every class, was simplicity itself. Stanislavsky is based squarely on the concept of Action: that everything in a play is done *in order* to achieve a want of some kind. This resolves into the formula: OBJECTIVE (What do I want?); ACTION (What do I do to get it?); OBSTACLE (What stands in my way?). The ACTION subdivides into ACTIVITIES, the separate means that I use to get what I want. There are INNER ACTIONS (which I use on myself) and OUTER ACTIONS (on other people), INNER OBSTACLES (my problems) and OUTER OBSTACLES (the problem of other people). The whole sequence of actions in a play adds up to the character's SUPER OBJECTIVE (their whole thrust in the world of the play).

(Callow 1984: 33)

The search for artistic integrity and emotional truthfulness in this work is of paramount importance, and many students, including Callow, initially resisted the possibility of appearing vulnerable. As a way of encouraging students to work more freely with emotion, Cannon also used the Emotion Memory Exercise – a Method-based technique through which the tutor leads a student to re-experience intense and often traumatising events from the past. Admitting that it did not work for him, Callow nevertheless recalls some of the remarkable results he witnessed in fellow students:

Girls with tiny Minnie Mouse voices suddenly bellow like oxen; stoics weep hysterically; po-faced people laugh till the tears run down their faces. My own flat-mate reconstructed his expulsion from monastery school. As the memory took hold, he fell out of his chair on to the floor, dragging himself along the ground with his bare hands, his fingernails digging into the floorboards, emitting a terrifying growl from the pit of his stomach. He crawled behind the piano, panting, eyes flashing. The teacher was visibly rattled, and so were we all. It was hot stuff.

(Callow 1984: 34)

What makes this interpretation of Stanislavskian theory especially interesting is the extent to which it combines an emphasis on emotional expressiveness with an understanding of the demands of classical text. Alive to accusations that early Method approaches tended to fetishise emotional engagement at the expense of stylistic considerations, Hagen developed a whole series of exercises that focused on the need for actors to develop what she referred to as a 'Historical Imagination':

We must find our way into a playwright's particular world by exploring its content and meaning, by looking for identification with the human

struggles in that world. When we succeed in doing so, we may shame-
lessly accept a critical judgment that we have arrived at a perfect style
for the play. If, on the other hand, in a mistaken hunt for reality or for
lack of skill, we fail to identify with the dramatist's vision of reality,
or if we wilfully ignore it or simply bend it to suit our limited vision
of reality, we may be rightly accused by the viewer of having no style.

(Hagen 1991: 214)

The emphasis on 'skill' and 'style' in this extract recalls similar concerns
that were expressed by Michel Saint-Denis. The thing that all of these
teachers – including Doreen Cannon – appear to have had in common
was a desire to find ways of adapting Stanislavskian technique in a way
that enabled it to respond to different forms of realism across a variety of
dramatic genres and theatrical styles. Indeed, one of the most distinguishing features of the Drama Centre's provision – which continues to be the
case today – is its emphasis on a classical training across a wide range of
British and European texts. Although the school may well have adopted a
Method-based approach to the training of actors, the application of such
methods was very much concerned with addressing not just the importance
of working truthfully with emotion, but also the interpretative demands of
an extremely diverse repertoire.

The influence of Yat Malgren's work at the Drama Centre is also of considerable importance when considering the development of Stanislavskian
methodology in British actor training. Prior to his involvement with Central
School of Speech and Drama and later the London Drama Centre, Malmgren,
like Doreen Cannon, had also taught at the English Stage Company at the
Royal Court Theatre. Having worked very closely with the German movement specialist Rudolf Laban in the 1950s, Malmgren went on to develop a
system that has now become known as Movement Psychology. Combining
C. G. Jung's theories of *Character Psychology*, Rudolf's Laban's *Movement
Analysis* and Stanislavsky's *Method of Physical Actions*, this approach to
actor training strives for the embodiment of inner impulses in the physical
actions and gestures of a dramatic character. An understanding of the role
of *sensation* is of primary importance to this work, as Simon Callow makes
clear:

It can't be demonstrated and imitated, like dancing, because its essence
is experience. One learns what a sensation *is*, not what it looks like; and
sensation is at the heart of acting. Emotional, intuitive, physical, and
intellectual sensation; quick sensations and sustained ones; direct and
flexible, bound and free, strong and light.

(Callow 1984: 39)

Elsewhere in his writings, Callow is unequivocal about the connections between Malmgren's work and that of Stanislavsky:

> Yat was particularly enthusiastic about Stanislavsky's work because he valued logic so strongly and he co-opted Stanislavsky's theory of actions – the idea that everything said or done in a play has a specific objective which governs the characters – as the underpinnings of his own work on physical expression.
>
> (Callow 2010: 91)

Complementing Malmgren's movement work and Cannon's interpretative classes, Callow also acknowledges the Drama Centre's 'intensely theoretical' (Callow 2010: 91) approach to the training – especially in relation to Christopher Fettes's classes in 'Analysis' from which he acquired 'a rigorous account of the Stanislavsky work' (Callow 1984: 31). Interestingly, it is also worth noting that mask work at the school was taught by John Blatchley, who, like George Devine, had worked with Michel Saint-Denis at the Old Vic School in developing an approach to mask which, as has previously been stated, sought to promote a dynamic interaction between a performer's inner impulses and their outward expression.

In common with both of the schools founded by Michel Saint-Denis, the establishment of the London Drama Centre sought to develop an approach to teaching that embraced Stanislavsky's methods without compromising the interpretative demands of a wide range of classical and contemporary texts. Whereas Doreen Cannon's work and its focus on psychological motivation provided a perfect platform from which to consider the inner dimensions of character development, the highly physical work of teachers such as Yat Malmgren and John Blatchley helped to ensure that the focus of such training did not become unduly dependent on what Charles Marowitz described as a 'a manic insistence on psychological reality' (Brook et al. 1963: 22). Although it is impossible to deny the influence of the American Method in the formation of the school's work, the emphasis on the need to train students for a richly varied classical repertoire coupled with intensive exposure to the techniques of classical ballet, Laban and Mask helped to ensure a continued focus on the importance of physical expressiveness and the use of gesture.

In an interview with Professor Kathy Dacre in *Teaching Stanislavski* Dee Cannon, an acting teacher at RADA and the daughter of the late Doreen Cannon, suggests that 'it wasn't until Drama Centre was formed in 1963 that the influence of Stanislavski really began to take hold'. Prior to this moment, she argues, the teaching in British drama schools tended to adopt a 'literary approach' to training in which 'the teaching had been based principally on

rehearsal and the performance results sometimes lacked veracity and depth'
(Dacre 2009: 64–5). A possible explanation for the relatively late adoption
of Stanislavsky's work in British training institutions can be garnered from
the following comment by John Gielgud that was included in his review of
An Actor Prepares for *Theatre Arts Monthly*:

> In Russia and on the continent the theatre is taken seriously as an art.
> In Anglo-Saxon countries it is, if you generalise, a business. Alas the
> modern commercial theatre is bound to be a bitter disappointment to
> those trained in Stanislavsky's theories. But it is our theatre which is
> wrong, and not the training.
>
> (Croall 2001: 250)

Although there are records at Rose Bruford College indicating that,
when the college was first established in the 1950s, there were classes that
focussed specifically on Stanislavsky's methods, very little is known about
what these classes actually entailed (Dacre 2009: 7). By the mid 1980s,
however, when a graduate of the Drama Centre was appointed to lead the
acting curriculum, the training evolved in such a way as to incorporate
Doreen Cannon's work and the use of 'Object Exercises'.

Although it is impossible to deny the fact that many acting teachers were
influenced by Stanislavsky's techniques, there is no doubt that the establishment of the London Drama Centre marks a very important stage in the
evolution of his work in British conservatoire institutions. Since 1963, the
Drama Centre's appropriation of Stanislavskian methodology – especially
as reflected in the work of Doreen Cannon – has, through the influence of
former staff and graduating students, migrated to many, many British drama
schools including the Arts Educational Schools (where John Blatchley
also taught), Central School of Speech and Drama, East 15, Italia Conti,
Guildford School of Acting, LAMDA (the London Academy of Music and
Dramatic Art), the Manchester Metropolitan University School of Theatre,
Mountview Academy of Theatre Arts, RADA, Rose Bruford College
and the Royal Scottish Academy of Music and Drama (now the Royal
Conservatoire of Scotland). Whereas the training at each of these institutions varies in accordance with the philosophy and aims of each course,
the interpretation of Stanislavskian methodology remains strikingly similar.

Revealingly, as RADA's improvisation tutor Chris Heimann's comparison between modern British and Russian interpretations of Stanislavskian
methodology makes clear, one of the distinguishing features of British
interpretations of Stanislavskian methodology has, until very recently, been
a tendency to prioritise the text over the importance of physical behaviour

(Dacre 2009: 66). Although, in part, this may well be a legacy of the 'literary' approaches referred to earlier, there is clear evidence to suggest that many schools continue to adapt and reshape Stanislavsky's work in accordance with different training contexts. At Rose Bruford College, for instance, the influence of Gardzienice and an emphasis on musicality are combined in the training to encourage enhanced degrees of fusion between the body, the voice and the text. By circumventing solely intellectual responses to text, this approach seeks to foster stronger connections to inner impulses (accessed through the use of music and rhythm based exercises) and thereby to the subconscious.

At RADA, Brigid Panet has increased physical awareness and expressiveness in her students by developing a fusion between the work of the nineteenth-century American psychologist William James and the Hungarian dancer Rudolf Laban. Though somewhat different in emphasis from the work of the Drama Centre's Yat Malmgren, the result offers an alternative psychophysical approach to performance that is designed to redirect the student actor's 'entire attention from the truth of daily life to the truth of imagination' (Dacre 2009: 66). By contrast, the work of Dee Cannon, also at RADA, utilises animal-based exercises in order to move students 'beyond normalisation towards something exciting and visceral' (Dacre 2009: 69).

A preoccupation with the need to move beyond literary or text-based approaches to training is also reflected in the enthusiasm with which the work of the American Method practitioner Sanford Meisner has been incorporated into the training regimes of many British conservatoires. Developed more than sixty years ago in New York's Neighbourhood Playhouse School, the Meisner Technique stresses the importance of physical *behaviour* as a means of accessing the emotional life of a given character. By encouraging sensitivity and responsiveness to the 'liveness' of each dramatic moment, this approach fosters increased spontaneity and interpretative freedom. In recent years Meisner's work has been adopted at variety of schools including Bristol Old Vic Theatre School, Central School of Speech and Drama, Italia Conti, Mountview, RADA and Rose Bruford College.

It is important to recognise at this point that, despite recent developments in how British drama schools have begun to reshape and re-apply Stanislavsky's work, the importance of physical training was central to the ethos informing the development of each of the London schools established by Michel Saint-Denis. Moreover, Stanislavsky's own writings and his development of the Method of Physical Actions bear testimony to the view that the need for physical expressiveness is a key tenet of his entire System. Given this observation, any residual tendency to revert to a methodology that prioritises literary qualities over the physical ones possibly reveals more about antique British attitudes to performance training than it does about Stanislavsky's.

In tracing the emergence of Stanislavsky's work in the British conserva-toire tradition there are a number of important considerations that seem especially relevant. First, there is the discovery that at each stage of its transition there have been extremely strong links between developments at individual drama schools and the actual profession itself. Komisarjevky's work at RADA, for instance, was closely linked with his work at the Barnes Theatre and at Stratford's Shakespeare Memorial Theatre; Michel Saint-Denis's work at the LTS and the Old Vic Theatre School ran parallel to his involvement initially in his own company the Compagnie des Quinze and subsequently with London's Old Vic Theatre Company; and the emer-gence of the London Drama Centre owes much to the development of the English Stage Company at the Royal Court Theatre in the 1950s, where John Blatchley assisted George Devine, and Yat Malmgren and Doreen Cannon are known to have run workshops for the professional company. In direct contrast to the establishment of the Method in the United States, the progression of Stanislavskian teaching methodology in Britain has largely been shaped by the desire to respond to the interpretative demands of live *theatrical* performance as opposed to those of the *screen*.

Second, rather than focus almost exclusively on the need to nurture psychological motivation, British interpretations of Stanislavsky's methods have tended to stress the importance of 'style' as a means of connecting with and inhabiting alternative forms of realism to those which are most com-monly associated with naturalism. Although it is true that Stanislavsky's development of the Method of Physical Actions contradicts the claim that his System privileges psychological rather than physical impulses, the emphasis on language, style, movement, gesture and rhythm at each of the schools we have considered has helped to refine and particularise Stanislavskian technique to enable the integration of realism with a classi-cal performance tradition. The aim was to ensure that actors trained in this way were as adept at responding to the interpretative demands of Greek, Jacobean and Restoration drama as they were to those of classic naturalism and the experimental theatres of Brecht, Beckett, Ionesco and Pinter.

Finally, each of the schools we have examined developed training regimes in which the actor's art was defined essentially in terms that stressed the need for a transformation – physical, psychological and emotional – from the persona of the performer to that of the dramatic character. Authenticity in performances was directed not so much towards the real-life experiences of the actor as to the *imagined* personality of a fictitious character. In this way, Stanislavskian teaching practice in British drama schools tended to limit a propensity towards the psychological subjectivism that was often a feature of early Method-based approaches to interpretation.

Rather than absorb Stanislavsky's principles wholesale, it seems that British actor trainers have consistently sought new ways of adapting and applying his techniques to a diverse range teaching and rehearsal situations. Moreover, instead of allowing the aesthetics of naturalism to dilute the richness of its own theatrical traditions, early British drama schools pioneered an approach to training that adopted Stanislavsky's System not merely as a workable lexicon for an individual performance style, but rather as a kind of 'grammar of all styles', which, according to Michel Saint-Denis, is actually what 'it aspires to be' (Saint-Denis 1982: 38).

These days Stanislavsky's methods feature prominently in the curricula of most British drama schools and there is no doubt that his influence of his work has helped to shape contemporary performance practice. This said, it is also important to acknowledge that, just as Komisarjevsky, Saint-Denis, Devine, Blatchley and others refused to approach Stanislavsky's work as a closed system, neither do many of the teachers and practitioners working in drama schools today. The emergence of new forms of writing coupled with the growing influence of mediatised and live-art performance practice – both of which frequently challenge stable and knowable conceptions of selfhood – pose very particular challenges for a training system that is heavily dependent on coherence and unity for its effect. Whether or not Stanislavsky's System continues to exert its current influence in the future remains to be seen, but perhaps one thing is certain:

> even if the system is . . . surpassed, Stanislavski remains a sure master. He will provide the young with a point of departure towards new discoveries.
>
> (Saint-Denis 1959: 29)

Notes

1 John Gielgud enrolled as a student at RADA in 1923 and Charles Laughton enrolled in 1925. Both actors were taught by Komisarjevsky and Rains during their time there.
2 Michael Billington's 1988 biography of Peggy Ashcroft offers a clear sense of the enormous influence of *My Life in Art*. The publication quickly became Peggy's 'bible' (Billington 1988: 19).
3 Saint-Denis formed the Compagnie de Quinze in 1930. Many of the original performers in this troupe had previously been members of the Copiaus, Copeau's own company, which was based in Burgundy and disbanded in 1929.
4 For detailed accounts of Saint-Denis's responses to this production of *The Cherry Orchard* see Saint-Denis (1982: 35–7) and Saint-Denis (1960: 41–2).

5 For a clear example of how Saint-Denis distinguished between the American 'Method' and Stanislavsky's 'System' see 'Who Alienated Konstantin Stanislavski?', a discussion at the Royal Court Theatre on the state of English acting between Peter Brook, Kenneth Haigh, Charles Marowitz and Michel Saint-Denis (Brook et al. 1963).

6 A detailed account of the events leading up to the closure of the Old Vic Theatre Centre can be found in Philip Roberts (1999: 1–5).

7 A very clear statement about what Saint-Denis believed to be the shortcomings of Stanislavsky's 'System' can be found in Saint-Denis (1959).

8 The reference to 'big style' in this context can be taken to mean 'the written styles of old theatre like Shakespeare or even like Restoration comedy' (Roberts 1999: 3)

9 Additional evidence pointing to deficiencies in the training offered at leading institutions can be found in biographical accounts of the early careers of figures such as Joan Littlewood, Harold Pinter and Joe Orton – all of whom trained at RADA.

10 Further evidence to support this view can be found in Dacre (2009: 64).

11 Further evidence to support the view that the Method was resisted in Britain can be seen in Charles Marowitz's attack on Lee Strasberg (Brook et al. 1963: 20–3).

12 The HB Studio, founded by Hagen's husband, Herbert Berghof, where she taught for many years, was founded in accordance with the same principles as the Actor's Studio, of which Berghof was a charter member (see Hagen 1991: 18).

13 Confirmed in personal communication to the author by Dee Cannon dated 16 August 2010.

14 Revealingly, Hagen spent some time training at RADA in 1936 and would later write 'It didn't matter that the training wasn't great. I learned much more about living like a "cosmopolitan"' (Hagen 1983: 82). Elsewhere she suggests that RADA's training was 'At best academic, stressing the training of voice, speech and movement, but I knew there was something wrong with being lined up against the barre to recite the speeches of Rosalind or Gertrude in unison with twenty others, with the same inflections and gestures' (Hagen 1991: xviii–xix) Her opinion of RADA's training corresponds with similar views expressed by Claude Rains and John Elsom.

Bibliography

Baldwin, J. (2010) 'Michel Saint-Denis: Training the Complete Actor', in Hodge, A. (ed.), *Actor Training*, London: Routledge.

Billington, M. (1988) *Peggy Ashcroft*, London: John Murray.

Brook, P., Haigh, K., Marowitz, C. and Saint-Denis, M. (1963) 'Who Alienated Konstantin Stanislavski?: A Discussion at the Royal Court Theatre on the State of English Acting', *Encore*, 10 (3) (May–June): 18–34.

Callow, S. (1984) *Being an Actor*, London: Methuen.

Callow, S. (2010) *My Life in Pieces*, London: Nick Hern Books.

Croall, J. (2001) *Gielgud: A Theatrical Life*, London: Methuen.

Dacre, K. (2009) *Teaching Stanislavski: An Investigation into How Stanislavski Is Taught to Students in the UK*, London: Rose Bruford and Palatine Research Publication.

Elsom, J. (1976) *Post-War British Theatre*, London: Routledge and Kegan Paul.

Fettes, C. (2002) 'Yat Malmgren: An Obituary', *The Guardian*, 13 June.

Hagen, U. (1973) *Respect for Acting*, New York: Macmillan Publishing.

Hagen, U. (1983) *Sources: A Memoir*, New York: Performing Arts Journal Publications.

Hagen, U. (1991) *A Challenge for the Actor*, New York: Scribner Publishing.

Harrop, J. (1992) *Acting*, London: Routledge.

Lacey, S. (1995) *British Realist Theatre: The New Wave in Its Context*, London: Routledge.

Roberts, P. (1999) *The Royal Court Theatre and the Modern Stage*, Cambridge: Cambridge University Press.

Skal, D. J. (2008) *Claude Rains: An Actor's Voice*, Lexington: University of Kentucky Press.

Saint-Denis, M. (1959) 'Stanislavsky and the Teaching of Dramatic Art', *World Theatre*, 8 (Spring): 23–9.

Saint-Denis, M. (1960) *Theatre: The Rediscovery of Style*, New York: Theatre Arts Books.

Saint-Denis, M. (1982) *Training for the Theatre*, Saint-Denis, S. (ed.), New York: Theatre Arts Books.

Stearns, D. P. (2004) 'Uta Hagen Obituary', *The Guardian*, 17 January.

Whyman, R. (2008) *The Stanislavsky System of Acting*, Cambridge: Cambridge University Press.

3

MICHAEL CHEKHOV AND THE STUDIO IN DARTINGTON

The re-membering of a tradition

Jerri Daboo

Michael Chekhov, nephew of the playwright Anton, and student of Stanislavsky, brought his version of the Russian tradition of acting to Britain, where he ran a theatre studio for training actors in his methods for two years (1936–8). The Chekhov Theatre Studio, situated in Dartington Hall near Totnes in Devon, is a remarkable and virtually unique example of an attempt at establishing a residential actor-training centre in Britain. This chapter will explore how the Studio was established; the particular approaches to training which were undertaken; and the reasons for the eventual relocation of the Studio to America. Despite Chekhov's having lived in England for three years, there was no continuous transmission of his work in Britain in the aftermath of the Studio. In fact, there is a fifty-year gap from the end of the Studio until a resurgence of interest in his work in 1989 as a result of the effort of one of his past students. As such, this chapter will also examine the notion of a broken transmission, assessing how the lineage of Chekhov's teaching can be traced through a range of both 'routes' and 'roots'[1] from different parts of the world. These are now consolidated within teachers in Britain but they show that there has been no direct or continual thread of transmission within Britain itself from the time of the Dartington Studio. Thus the notion of the revival of a tradition is also significant, along with the ways in which adaptation and the tracing back of a lineage to the original Russian master play a part for those who use his methods in drama schools and universities, and professionally, in contemporary Britain.

Background

Michael Chekhov was born in St Petersburg in 1891. In 1911 he met Stanislavsky, who, after auditioning Chekhov, immediately invited him to join the First Studio of the Moscow Arts Theatre (MAT), where he was taught by and worked with Stanislavsky, Sulerzhitsky and Vakhtangov. Chekhov subsequently became director of the Second Studio of the MAT in 1924. Throughout this period of working with the MAT, he emerged as an actor of great skill, most particularly in the creation and embodiment of characters. What also occurred was Chekhov's deepening interest in spirituality. The First Studio explored exercises from yoga, and Chekhov additionally read books on Hindu philosophy (Gordon 1983: 8). However, it was while he was suffering from a personal crisis and breakdown in 1921 that Chekhov discovered the work of Rudolf Steiner and his system of Anthroposophy, which had a profound and lasting impact on the rest of his life. Chekhov was very drawn to these ideas, and found that they helped him personally to deal with his own crisis, and gave him a sense of joy and fulfilment, noted in his autobiography when he says that '[t]his 'encounter' with Anthroposophy was the happiest period of my life' (Chekhov 2005: 135). He also began to attempt to use some of the ideas and aesthetics within his own theatrical work,[2] but, in the climate in the 1920s under the influence of the Soviet regime, anything perceived as spiritual or mystical was not acceptable; having been warned of his imminent arrest Chekhov left Russia in 1928, and lived in exile for the rest of his life.

Chekhov spent the next seven years moving from Germany, to France, to Latvia, to Lithuania, acting and teaching. He joined Solomon Hurok's Moscow Arts Players, a company of Russian émigré actors that toured to the United States in 1935. Chekhov played the part of Khlestakov in Dostoyevsky's *The Inspector General* in Russian to great acclaim, and it was whilst the production was playing at the Majestic Theatre in New York that he was seen in the performance by Beatrice Straight. She decided that Chekhov was the very acting teacher she had been searching for, and it was from this encounter that he was invited to form a Studio in Dartington Hall, which was owned by Beatrice's mother and step-father, Dorothy and Leonard Elmhirst.

Both the Elmhirsts were committed philanthropists, with the personal funds to make their ideas realisable. Leonard was born in 1893. In 1921, he met the Indian writer, artist and thinker Rabindranath Tagore, who proved to be a major influence on Leonard's approach to agriculture, the arts and social reform. Leonard became director at the Institute of Rural Reconstruction, named as Sriniketan by Tagore, which was situated in the village of Surul, four kilometres away from Tagore's ashram in Shantiniketan, West Bengal.

Tagore impressed on Leonard the importance of agricultural and community development and regeneration, as well as the value of the arts. He suggested that Leonard should form a community in Devon as an experiment in education, agricultural traditions, rural regeneration and the arts. This experiment was realised in partnership with Leonard's wife, whom he had met whilst in college in America. Dorothy Whitney Straight, born in 1887, was an heiress to the Whitney fortune inherited from her father, and also to that of her first husband, Willard Straight, who had been a prominent philanthropist, and with whom she had three children, including Beatrice. Leonard and Dorothy joined together not only in marriage, but also in their desire to create a community along the lines suggested by Tagore. After searching in Devon they found Dartington Hall just outside Totnes, and in 1925, the same year that they were married, began their philanthropic venture.

Dorothy's daughter by Willard Straight, Beatrice, was very keen on acting and this, combined with Dorothy's own strong love of the arts and Leonard's encouragement from Tagore, prompted them to decide to host a theatre training school within Dartington. Beatrice wanted to learn from the best teacher available, and so began searching for the right person to bring to Devon. It was during this search that she and her travelling companion, Deirdre Hurst du Prey, saw Chekhov performing in New York, and decided that she had found the most appropriate actor and teacher. They persuaded Dorothy and Leonard to see him perform in America, after which they invited him to form the Studio. Despite his very limited English at the time, Chekhov agreed to relocate to Devon to set up the school of acting, with the intention of this leading to the establishment of a touring company. He arrived in England with his wife Xenia in October 1935, a year before the Studio opened, in order to learn English, which he did in a remarkably short time, and prepare for the realisation of his dream to lead a school of actor training.

In order to publicise the Studio, the Elmhirsts produced a booklet and pamphlet describing its purpose and aims as well as the particular focus of Chekhov's work, to attract actors to come to Dartington. As well as emphasising Chekhov's Russian heritage and lineage, the booklet also explicitly states the influence of Steiner with the teaching of Speech Formation and Eurythmy at the Studio. The emphasis on the use of exercises developed from a 'spiritual' system such as Steiner's, as well as the type of language used to explain the 'ideals' of the Studio, may go some way to explaining why Chekhov found difficulties in recruiting the type and quality of actor with which he wanted to work. According to the booklet:

> In all its work the Studio will struggle against the absence of an ideal in the contemporary naturalistic theatre. Modern problems are so

serious, so intricate, and so tortuous that if a solution is to be offered in the theatre, the theatre must leave the ways of mere imitation and naturalism and probe beneath the surface. [. . .] All technique must be re-scrutinized and re-vitalized; external technique must be permeated by the power of a living spirit; inner technique must be developed until the capacity for receiving creative inspiration is acquired.[3]

This use of idealistic language infused with spiritual overtones partly contributed to the reasons why the Studio in Dartington was closed after two years and relocated to America, which will be discussed more fully later in this chapter. In some respects, there was a contradiction in what Chekhov said he was looking for in the students he wanted at the Studio. According to the Chekhov teacher Graham Dixon, he wanted young, untrained actors whom he could shape through his work: '[Chekhov] did stipulate he didn't want anyone who'd done a normal theatre training. He wanted naive young people that were untouched, and he could form them'.[4] However, Chekhov also lamented that some of the great actors of the time working in London, such as John Gielgud and Peggy Ashcroft, did not come to work with him in Dartington. This was particularly in view of his desire to form a professional touring company at the end of two years, but at that stage it was felt that there were not enough actors of a sufficient calibre in the Studio to undertake the quality of performance Chekhov wanted for the company.

One of the main reasons why there may have been difficulty in recruiting high-quality actors to the Studio may lie in its location and the nature of the training programme. A young actor wanting to establish a successful career in Britain would be drawn to being based in London, at the heart of the theatre scene. Spending three years in an isolated village in a remote part of Devon, working with a teacher they did not know, may not have been an attractive proposition to an ambitious actor. Additionally, Chekhov was not very well known in Britain. Deirdre Hurst du Prey believed that 'if young artists really knew more about Mr. Chekhov and what he has to offer any actor they would flock to him'.[5] However, Chekhov himself decided that he did not want either to travel through Britain searching and auditioning for good actors, preferring instead to rely on the booklet for publicity, or else to raise his public profile through interviews with the press. As du Prey noted: 'he has found from the past that much harm can be done by ill-informed reporters, and statements can be imputed which were never made'.[6] Linda Jackson, the Secretary to the Studio, raised some further questions in 1938 concerning the lack of established actors applying to join. She suggests that in part this is due to the way in which the Studio was publicised, in that it might have given the impression that it was not a serious actor training centre, but rather a 'dilettante "arty" Rural Theatre Group'.[7]

All these factors point towards the reasons for the lack of British actors in particular who applied to attend the Studio. Only a small proportion of the students in Dartington actually came from Britain, the majority instead coming from America, where auditions were also held, as well as Canada, Australia, New Zealand and other parts of Europe. Another factor which may have contributed to the problems in this respect was the culture of actor training and theatre aesthetics in Britain at the time. The training in drama schools tended to be very conventional, and geared towards producing a good solo actor, rather than an ensemble. Theatre during the 1930s was, likewise, very traditional, and so Chekhov's ideals of creating a new type of theatre, as well as actor, may not have been seen to be useful for the types of opportunities available for a young actor at the time. There was also no tradition in Britain of a residential actor training school or centre focused around one teacher or form of practice. However, in addition to Chekhov's Studio in Dartington, one other School opened in the same period to challenge the emphasis on the solo actor: the London Theatre School, which opened in 1935, and was run by Michel Saint-Denis. Both centres were dedicated to teaching actors a new way of working in order to create different forms of theatre, and both worked in a tradition of improvisation, movement, and ensemble playing.

Saint-Denis and Actor Training in London

Saint-Denis (1897–1971) trained and worked with his uncle, Jacques Copeau, at the Théâtre du Vieux-Colombier, before developing his own approach with his company, the Quinze. When they performed in London in 1931, their new style and approach to performance inspired many of the leading young actors of the day, including Olivier, Gielgud, Ashcroft and Tyrone Guthrie. Despite being schooled in the established British conventions of the time, many of these actors desired to find a new way of working, and Saint-Denis's approach, with an emphasis on developing a sense of the ensemble as opposed to the solo 'star' actor, as well as on movement and improvisation, was seen as offering not only a new way for actors to perform on stage, but also new types of production aesthetics. He was invited to form the London Theatre School in 1935 and, from that point until his death, played a part in some of the most significant theatrical ventures in Britain,[8] such as the Old Vic Theatre Centre and the Royal Shakespeare Company (RSC); he was invited by Peter Hall to become a director of the latter in 1961. Hall states that Saint-Denis 'was a Frenchman whose influence on British theatre directly changed the way most of us work' and that venues and companies such as the Royal Court, the Royal National Theatre, the English National Opera and the RSC 'have all been influenced by his beliefs and inspired by his passions' (Hall 2009: vii).

While Saint-Denis was at the heart of the theatre scene in London, working with some of the great actors of the time, Michael Chekhov was in Dartington, also attempting to establish an actor-training centre with new approaches to performance. That there were two European directors, both nephews of famous theatre practitioners, both schooled in a specific tradition of training but moving away from their teachers to develop their own style, and both founding schools of actor training in Britain at the same time, marks a significant shift in attitude towards an understanding of the need for training beyond what was being offered in drama schools. However, Chekhov did not have the lasting impact and legacy that Saint-Denis had on British theatre. Part of the reason for this may be attributed to points raised earlier both in terms of location and also reputation, as Saint-Denis's work had been seen on the London stage, whereas Chekhov was still relatively unknown in Britain. Additionally, the Dartington Studio was residential and required three years of commitment, whereas actors could study with Saint-Denis and work professionally at the same time. However, Hall also points out that even Saint-Denis's approach was seen with some suspicion by British actors, for whom a systematic and sustained training was not part of their experience. He suggests that it was perhaps a sense of 'English pragmatism' or 'openness' that:

> Encouraged us to distrust theory, perhaps as an excuse for avoiding craft. This was a danger which Michel never failed to point out to us. What he did for the Royal Shakespeare Company and for me is quite incalculable. He spoke to a new generation of young actors and directors about our European heritage – about Stanislavsky, Copeau and Brecht. He had known these men.
>
> (Hall 2009: viii)

Certainly the idea of 'avoiding craft' in terms of the intense forms of training that were happening in the 'European heritage' in mainland Europe rather than Britain, is an indication both of the difference in approach to the notion of training, and also of the cultural distance that was felt in Britain from traditions in 'Europe' such as Stanislavsky and Copeau. Hall's statement establishes Saint-Denis as a direct player in, and inheritor of, this European lineage, and therefore able to instruct British actors in this approach to performance that was unfamiliar to them.

The 'English pragmatism' stated by Hall may also account for the reluctance to accept and embrace the work of Chekhov. The actor Paul Rogers suggests that the reason for the lack of British students in the Dartington Studio was that:

> The English, particularly at the time, were very much stick-in-the-mud. They had actually got as far as accepting Michel Saint-Denis. [. . .] But somebody called Michael Chekhov working, as far as they were concerned in the depths of the country down in Dartington Hall, it meant little or nothing. One had to be particularly alert to realise that anything was going on at all. The disinterest was overwhelming.[9]

This was despite the name of Stanislavsky, and the works of Anton Chekhov, becoming more well-known and accepted in London at the time.[10]

Chekhov's training at Dartington

Despite the problems with recruitment, the Dartington Studio opened in 1936 with a group of twenty to twenty-five students (the number is variable according to different lists). This included a few students from Britain, such as Paul Rogers, Daphne Moore, Jocelyn Wynne and Alan Harkness, who was originally from Australia but living in Britain at the time; some from America, including Eleanor Faison, Hurd Hatfield and Mary Louise Taylor; Blair Cutting from Canada; Terence Morgan from New Zealand; and Kester Baruch from Australia, where he had previously worked with Harkness. In addition, there were two students who had worked with Chekhov in Latvia, Joseph Gustaitus and Edward Kostaunas. Other students included those closely connected with Dartington: Beatrice Straight, Deirdre Hurst du Prey, and even Dorothy Elmhirst herself started taking classes with Chekhov. Several of the students were given a full scholarship to attend the Studio, including Mary Haynsworth, Blair Cutting, Alan Harkness, Hurd Hatfield, Terence Morgan and Paul Rogers. Other students had to pay the fees, which were £150 or $750 per year for tuition and board.[11]

Auditions were held in both Dartington and America. Paul Rogers, at the time a local school boy, had been spotted acting in a play to help raise money for the monks in Buckfastleigh. He was invited to audition for Chekhov, who 'saw the raw material'[12] and potential in Rogers, and invited him to the join the Studio. Rogers explains that the Studio 'started with huge advantages',[13] mainly thanks to the money invested in it by the Elmhirsts. The Barn Theatre had been constructed in 1934, and the rehearsal rooms for the Studio were custom-made with sprung sycamore wooden floors. All students had to wear a 'uniform' consisting of a stockinet practice dress, and simple sandals with a calf-skin sole, to allow complete contact with the floor. For Rogers, the uniform was important because it 'eliminates difference. [. . .] It does not iron out your personality at all. If anything, it gives your personality the chance to shine though unhindered by extraneous rubbish'.[14] The practice dress also allowed for a free range of movement during the exercises (Figure 3.1).

Students were trained by Chekhov in his exercises, which were all designed to help develop the inner and outer life of both actor and character through body and speech. This is what Chekhov described as the 'psychophysical' approach to actor training and performance. This aspect of the psychophysical was present in all the work that Chekhov did with the students. However, in addition to studying with Chekhov, the students were also introduced to other techniques and teachers to complement and supplement their work in acting. Some of these classes were given by other artists who were also being given refuge in their exile from parts of Europe. The Elmhirsts invited a number of prominent figures in the arts to live and work in Dartington during the 1930s, including the dancer and choreographer Kurt Jooss, director of the Ballets Jooss and co-founder with Sigurd Leeder of the Jooss–Leeder School of Dance in Dartington; the artist

Figure 3.1 Students in their practice dress performing the 'wrestling without muscles' exercise with Michael Chekhov observing, in the Studio in Dartington, 1938. Photograph by Fritz Henle, courtesy of The Dartington Hall Trust Archive.

Hein Heckroth, who worked with Jooss as a designer; Rudolf Laban, whose approach was also based in Steiner's principles; the potter Bernard Leach; the American painter Mark Tobey; and a range of musicians including Hans Oppenheim, with whom the Elmhirsts wanted to establish a Music Theatre Studio alongside Chekhov's Studio. In this rich and unique artistic atmosphere, Chekhov invited some of these fellow residents of Dartington to work with his acting students. Lisa Ullmann, who had been born in Britain and trained with Laban in Berlin before working with Jooss in his dance company and moving with him to Dartington, taught dance to Chekhov's students. They also had classes with the artist Mark Tobey, not to learn how to paint, but according to Paul Rogers 'to experience the whole being making marks with chalk to music on great acreages of paper stuck to his walls'; and likewise practising sculpture was in order to experience moulding clay 'with the consciousness of the whole being'.[15] Chekhov was using these different art forms to help students use their whole body and mind in a creative activity, and the use of clay can be related to the 'Moulding' exercise found in the Four Qualities of Movement (Moulding, Floating, Flying, Radiating; see Chekhov 2002: 8–10). The Indian dancer and choreographer Uday Shankar and his company were also frequent visitors in Dartington, and gave a performance on 6 October 1936 to celebrate the opening of the Chekhov Studio Theatre (Figure 3.2). In *Art Is Higher Activity Than Life*, Chekhov pointed out the particular quality present in Shankar's dancing as an example of how to perform with the whole being:

> What does it mean to do something with our whole being? Shankar can lift one eyebrow and we say – how beautifully he dances. Words are so clever but movement is simpler. Therefore we can begin our work with movement, with psychological gesture, and let the words come on the movement. [. . .] We see so many actors today who stand with their hands in their pockets and say 'I love you' – No relation between words and movement. Your body must say the words.[16]

In order to develop this connection between body and words, Chekhov invited Alice Crowther to teach Steiner's forms of Eurythmy and Speech Formation to his students. Crowther had trained with Steiner at the Rudolf Steiner Centre in Dornach, Switzerland, and was about to return to her native Australia when she received the invitation from Chekhov. Crowther's classes in Eurythmy and Speech Formation became a fundamental part of the training in the Studio. Chekhov had previously utilised Eurythmy with actors in his Second Studio at the MAT (Whyman 2008: 192). Franc Chamberlain defines Eurythmy as being:

Figure 3.2 The first class on the opening day of the Chekhov Theatre Studio with Michael Chekhov (far right), Uday Shankar and his company, on 6 October 1936. Photograph by Yishnudass Shirali, courtesy of The Dartington Hall Trust Archive.

> A system of movement developed by Steiner in which sounds are given specific physical postures. In this way, sounds are 'made visible' and poems, for example could be turned into movement sequences. [. . .] Steiner's work on speech as invisible gesture is this process in reverse, where the performer in the act of speaking is making an inner gesture.
>
> (Chamberlain 2004: 15)

It is clear from this description why Eurythmy would have been important to Chekhov beyond the fact of the association with Steiner, owing to the connection between gesture and sound, as well as the importance of rhythm, which is so significant in his exercises. He told his students that '[t]hrough Eurhythmy you will be able to discover the Archetypal feelings'.[17] Figure 3.3, showing a Eurythmy class at the Studio, illustrates both the use of strong gestures, in this case using rods, as well as the unity of the ensemble even with the split between the men and women.

Figure 3.3 'Get the Right Feeling Through the Right Means', Eurythmy class in
the Chekhov Theatre Studio, Dartington Hall, 1937–8. Dancers include:
John Schoepperle, Alan Harkness, Paul Rogers, Eleanor Faison, Cartio
Gabrialson and Anna de Goquel. Photograph by Fritz Henle, courtesy of
The Dartington Hall Trust Archive.

The influence of Steiner and spirituality continued to be significant for
Chekhov in his work and ideas. In addition to occasionally mentioning
Steiner within the Studio sessions, Chekhov also held a weekly class in
which he would talk on Anthroposophy. Through this, some of the students
became interested in Steiner. Dorothy Elmhirst formed a close friendship
with Chekhov, and developed a keen interest in Anthroposophy to the extent
that she kept a copy of Steiner's *Esoteric Science* beside her bed. Students
such as Alan Harkness, Kester Baruch and Dennis Glenny were similarly
drawn to Steiner, and continued the involvement with Anthroposophy after
leaving the Studio. However, the inclusion of Steiner and the emphasis on
spirituality also led to a sense of suspicion of Chekhov's training within
Dartington. In relation to Peter Hall's statement earlier about English pragmatism, this connection to the esoteric may well have contributed to the
fifty-year gap of knowledge and practice of Chekhov's work within Britain,
and is still a point of debate for contemporary practitioners using and teaching his work (see Chamberlain 2003).

   The Studio went on to perform a number of plays in Dartington in 1938,
including *Peer Gynt*, *The Lower Depths* and *A Midsummer Night's Dream*

(Figure 3.4). However, events during 1938 led to the eventual closure of the Studio in Dartington, and its relocation to America. One reason for this, discussed earlier, was the concern with creating a professional touring company with the standard of actors in the Studio. Paul Rogers, one of the most talented young actors, left the Studio, as had other students such as Kester Baruch, for personal or professional reasons. Deirdre Hurst du Prey wondered if America might prove a more fertile ground for attracting actors to work with Chekhov: 'Whether there is more talented material there than in this country is a moot point, but at least there would be enthusiasm for Mr. Chekhov and his work, whereas here there is apathy to be overcome'.[18] This potential for greater interest in America may have been due to the integration and renown of the work of Stanislavsky and other Russian teachers into actor training programmes, even if in a distorted manner. With the Elmhirst and Straight connections in America, this seemed to offer greater opportunity for the development of the Studio and touring company.

Figure 3.4   Mary Haynsworth as Titania and Paul Rogers as Bottom in *A Midsummer Night's Dream*, Dartington 1938. Photograph courtesy of The Dartington Hall Trust Archive.

The other main reason for leaving Britain was the imminent onset of the Second World War. Chekhov appears to have been deeply affected by the trouble in Europe during the late 1930s. Graham Dixon states that according to Dennis Glenny, an Australian actor who was part of the Studio in Dartington, Chekhov 'would disappear for days at a time in Dartington in a depressed state knowing what was happening in Europe', and Alan Harkness would take over his classes.[19] A letter from Deirdre Hurst du Prey in October 1938 confirms Chekhov's difficulties in coping with the situation:

> Evidently the 'crisis' was the most awful experience here at Dartington. What with all the foreigners not knowing from one moment to the next whether they would be sent to concentration camps or shot as deserters if they didn't go back . . . everyone fitted for gas masks and volunteering for war work [. . .] Well, it must have been a horrible nightmare here . . . everyone looks worn from it . . . Mrs. Elmhirst looks years older and Mr. Chekhov went through a bad time although he startled everyone by declaring that he was going to do what he could to fight Hitler![20]

Chekhov's own experience of war, exile and fear of imprisonment, and his sensitive nature, were clearly making his life and work very difficult. The threat of war was being felt in Britain and this, along with the strong possibility of the British students being conscripted, and the families of American students being concerned for their safety, resulted in the decision to relocate the Studio to Ridgefield, Connecticut. Some of the Dartington students decided to move to the new Studio with Chekhov to continue their training, and in December 1938 this group sailed on two ships to America. The new Studio, with George Shdanoff (who had been in Dartington since 1937) as its Associate Director, was immediately established along similar lines to the one in Dartington, as it was a continuation of the three-year training programme which had begun in Britain. However, the Ridgefield Studio encountered problems with funds, and finally closed on account of the War. Chekhov moved first to New York, establishing a touring theatre company, and then to Hollywood, working with some of the most famous film actors of the day, before dying there in 1955.

After Dartington: the threads of Chekhov's transmission into British actor training

If Chekhov had a low profile in Britain while he was living there, his name virtually disappeared from the British theatre scene after his departure in 1938, until a workshop in London set up by one of his former students,

Felicity Mason, in 1989. One of the reasons for this gap of fifty years is that there was only one actor working professionally in Britain at the time who had worked with Chekhov: Paul Rogers. Rogers became a very successful stage actor, with renowned performances including Lear, Macbeth and Shylock at the Old Vic, and creating the role of Max in Pinter's *The Homecoming*, for which he won a Tony on Broadway. However, Rogers had left the Studio in Dartington before completing the training, and did not discuss his connection with Chekhov for almost fifty years. He was invited to speak at the Chekhov conference in London in 1989, and subsequently interviewed for the documentary film *Michael Chekhov: The Dartington Years*, made by Martin Sharp in 2002. In this interview, he stated that he struggled to understand much of the training he had done with Chekhov in Dartington. He felt he was 'tagging along, with great enthusiasm, but I wasn't sure I was catching up'.[21] However, it was in an interview with Sheridan Morley for *The Times* in 1982 that he explained his reasons for not mentioning Chekhov during the height of his acting career:

> Chekhov moved his whole company on to America [. . .] but I'd decided to stay in England because I wanted to get married,[22] and we moved to London where I kept very quiet about my Moscow Art training. In those days it was regarded in the West End with some suspicion: Michel St. Denis was doing quite enough foreign work already and nobody else wanted to know.
>
> (Morley 1982)

This reinforces the points made previously about the way in which Chekhov was regarded with suspicion by the mainstream theatre world in London, and also the distrust of 'foreign' teachers and approaches to acting, whilst contradictorily revering the Russian masters.

Although it is difficult to assess the impact that Chekhov's training had on Rogers's acting in the long term, Rogers himself has hinted at the importance that it played. When touring as Hamlet in Australia in the 1950s, he stated in an interview that the training he had done with Alice Crowther, herself an Australian, had been very important in his work an actor (Kane 2010). In his interview with Martin Sharp, as well as stating that he found the work difficult to understand and that 'the stuff was cranky and took an enormous amount of swallowing', he also acknowledged the skill of Chekhov's teaching:

> All I'm left with is the sensation of having been taught by a man who was extraordinarily articulate. All these various things, of atmosphere, of the creation of character, of the growth of the imagination, were

all taught to us by him in terms of speech, and then translated into movement.[23]

Even though he did not feel comfortable discussing his experience of working with Chekhov in public due to the 'foreignness' and suspicion with which it might be regarded, he states that Chekhov was 'a father to us all', and that 'I wish to God he could have seen some of my later work'.[24]

With Rogers, as the only direct connection to Chekhov still in Britain after the closure of the Dartington Studio, not speaking about his time there, the name and work of Michael Chekhov were virtually forgotten in the British professional theatre world. As the Chekhov teacher Sarah Kane explains, 'there's Paul Rogers, and then there's a great hole in this country'.[25] The way in which the revival or revitalisation of interest in Chekhov and his work occurred in Britain is one of drawing together threads from different parts of the world, and raises questions about the notions of 'lineage' and 'tradition' within forms of actor training.

One of these threads comes from Australia. As noted above, several of the student actors in the Dartington Studio originated in Australia, including Alan Harkness and Dennis Glenny, as well as the Eurythmy and Speech Formation teacher, Alice Crowther. Harkness went to America with Chekhov and worked as his assistant in Ridgefield, but later left and continued his interest in Anthroposophy by travelling to the Rudolf Steiner Centre in Dornach. He was killed in a car accident in 1952, and Graham Dixon questions whether there might have been a greater continuity and awareness of Chekhov's work if he had lived longer.[26] Alice Crowther returned to Australia, and taught Speech Formation in Sydney. One of her students there was Dixon, who wanted to do some extra speech work to help with his acting, and was recommended to work with Crowther by Brian Barnes. Through these lessons with her, Dixon became interested in Steiner and Anthroposophy, which has continued to play a major part in his teaching of Chekhov, and his own theatre work with his company Dionysia, which has been presenting fairy tales and devised productions of Shakespeare in Australia and Europe since 1980. He met Sarah Kane in Stuttgart, and both came to England in 1988, where they are currently two of the principal teachers of Chekhov's techniques in Britain. Kane had been introduced to Chekhov's work through the European thread, working in Germany and Switzerland on voice and actor training. There was also a thread from Russia, though a more covert one initially because Chekhov and his work were discredited in Soviet Russia until his 'rehabilitation' on the curriculum after 1969 (Chamberlain 2004: 20). Maria Knebel had worked with Chekhov at the Second Studio of the MAT, as well as with Stanislavsky towards the end of his life, and continued to teach in Soviet Russia. This lineage continued in the teaching of Active Analysis at the All Russian State Institute of Cinematography (VGIK). It was here in 1993–4 that the British actress Bella Merlin[27] came to study for ten months with Katya Kamotskaia, Albert Filozov and Vladimir Ananyev, which further developed her interest in Michael Chekhov, which she took back to Britain, using the methods in both her acting and teaching.

Another thread came from America, where former students from Dartington, as well as those who subsequently worked with Chekhov or his students, made various attempts at sustaining the teaching of his work. However, his name never gained the popularity or currency that Stanislavsky's did, and, even though there were actors such as Beatrice Straight, Jack Colvin, Mala Powers and Joanna Merlin who were using his methods in their professional work, there was a gap in training during the 1960s and 1970s. According to Atay Citron writing in 1983:

> Of the three teachers whom Chekhov certified in 1938, only Blair Cutting has been teaching continuously for 30 years. The other two, Deirdre du Prey and Beatrice Straight, returned to teaching in 1980, when Straight founded the Studio on the upper-east side of Manhattan. [. . .] But from Chekhov's death in 1955 until the opening of the New York Studio in 1980, there has been no systematic teaching of the Chekhov Technique.
>
> (Citron 1983: 91)

The New York Studio started by Beatrice closed in 1990. The Michael Chekhov Association (MICHA) was founded in New York in 1999, and continues to hold classes, workshops and teacher training programmes in Chekhov's work in America and Europe.

Another significant factor from the American thread was the publication of Chekhov's work in English. However, like translations of Stanislavsky's work, these were often modified for an American audience, which included the cutting of much of the material related to Steiner.[28] Mala Powers produced a new version of *To the Actor* in 2002 which included previously unpublished material. These publications of Chekhov were important in introducing his work to practitioners in Britain. Both Bella Merlin and Franc Chamberlain encountered Chekhov's work in the 1980s through reading the available edition of *To the Actor*. For Chamberlain, currently a lecturer at the University College Cork, '*To the Actor* spoke to me as an actor in a way that the writings of Stanislavsky, Brecht, Artaud, Grotowski, Craig, Copeau, or Boleslavsky didn't'.[29] He also states that the special issue on Chekhov published in *The Drama Review* in 1983, as well as the *Theatre Paper* by Deirdre Hurst du Prey published in 1981–2, were part of his development of interest in Chekhov, along with his own previous contact with Anthroposophy. Although these texts by Chekhov were available in English, it was not until 2005 that Chekhov's autobiographies were published in English as *The Path of the Actor*, co-edited by Andrei Kirillov and Bella Merlin.

Important as these publications were, it was the decision of Felicity Mason, also known as the writer Anne Cumming, to hold a workshop on Chekhov in London in 1989 which truly began the revitalisation of interest in Chekhov's work in Britain, fifty-one years after he had left Dartington. For this workshop she gathered together actors who had worked with Chekhov in Dartington, including Deirdre Hurst du Prey, Eleanor Faison, Hurd Hatfield and Paul Rogers. This led to a further such event at the Steiner-based Emerson College in Forest Row, Sussex, in 1994. Graham Dixon points out that, despite being held in Britain, this International Workshop did not attract many British participants,[30] but two of these were Bella Merlin and Franc Chamberlain, who both played an important part in the continuation of Chekhov's work in Britain. Chamberlain describes the workshop as being:

> A very intense and rich experience. There were very few British academics/practitioners there – or British students. [. . .] Over the month I had my teaching scrutinised by Jack [Colvin], Deirdre Hurst du Prey, Mala Powers, Mary Lou [Taylor], Sarah Kane and others. [. . .] There was a seminar which met every morning which basically consisted of me, Lendley Black, Andrei Kirillov, Marina Ivanova, and Vladislav Ivanov together with an interpreter (Oleg Yefremov came once or twice, I think). Occasionally people would drop by for a few minutes and join in, but it was mostly the five of us discussing/debating the work and its significance. [. . .] It was during a class with Jack that I suggested the name 3 Sisters for the set of 3 exercises that [Chekhov] taught to Jack and which, until that point, had no name.[31]

Sarah Kane and Martin Sharp founded the Michael Chekhov Centre UK in 1995 as a result of the 1994 workshop, and Graham Dixon began the Michael Chekhov Studio London in 2003.

Conclusion: lineage, revitalisation and the question of authenticity

It is this drawing together of different threads from Australia, Europe and America that led to the re-ignition of Chekhov's work in Britain. In this way, there was no continuous transmission or legacy of Chekhov's teaching within Britain after the Dartington Studio, but instead a re-emerging or revitalisation as a result of different factors and sources merging together to create a new movement. Thus there was a flow of direction which started in Dartington, then left and moved out to different places along various routes, before flowing back again to Britain to re-establish the teaching of Chekhov's work, but in a very different way from how it had been taught in Dartington. The term 'revitalisation' is particularly useful in this context. The anthropologist Karen Lüdtke uses this expression following the work of Hermann Tak 'to avoid the term "revival", which may be misread as a return to a previously existing situation, discounting the impact of changes in the political economy' (Lüdtke 2009: 22 n5).

This certainly applies in the case of Chekhov's work, as what is being taught in Britain now is adapted and translated through different teachers and practices in order to be useful for actors working in the contemporary theatre world. What may be seen in Britain today are a number of teachers using aspects of Chekhov's work in different ways, with some having more experience of learning and teaching the techniques than others. This can also be observed in the lineage of transmission that has occurred in Britain from the late 1980s starting with Sarah Kane and Graham Dixon, then during the 1990s others such as Franc Chamberlain, Bella Merlin, Jonathan Pitches, Martin Sharp and John Wright (co-founder of Trestle Theatre Company and Told By An Idiot). A combination of their students and others who have studied with teachers in America and Europe are now also working professionally and teaching in drama schools and universities in Britain today, including Cass Fleming (Goldsmiths), Christopher Heimann (RADA, and Co-Artistic Director of The Imaginary Body), Philip Weaver (East 15, and Associate Director of The Spinning Wheel Theatre Company), Amanda Brennan (Central School of Speech and Drama) and Sinéad Rushe (Central and Director of Out of Inc). Katya Kamotskaia is currently teaching at the Royal Conservatoire of Scotland. Another practitioner in Britain who explicitly speaks of the influence of Chekhov on his work is Phelim McDermott, joint Artistic Director of Improbable.

It is not surprising that Chekhov's work is being used in so many different ways within Britain, particularly considering the broken line of transmission that occurred, and the revitalisation of his work through many different threads. Martin Sharp suggests that:

> There has been a mass appropriation of the work that's leaked out of the lineage. Because there's not been a training to hold the lineage, the leakage has occurred, and different people have absorbed the leakage and created their own practice.[32]

Lineage, in this sense, is about being inspired by a practitioner's work, and feeling an affinity with it that informs and expands what the actor is doing. Sharp explains that Phelim McDermott may not be 'doing' Chekhov's work as such, but rather has 'a great resonance with the principles',[33] and it is these principles that form the lineage. For Graham Dixon, 'it's a living lineage, of people who were very important in my life',[34] whereas Sarah Kane, commenting on the need for some performers and teachers to speak of a lineage back to the Russian source, states: 'I can understand that an individual feels that need. It's a justification, a sense of "I know where I'm coming from" '.[35] Even if the reality of that lineage is one of fracturing, divergence and re-making, there is a justifiable desire to sense and articulate a transmission directly back to Chekhov himself.

However, this range of approaches to Chekhov's work can lead to disagreements between practitioners as to ideas of 'authenticity', 'purity' and the 'correct' way to do his exercises. In a similar way to Stanislavsky, this is in part due to the different contexts in which Chekhov worked, and how the students in those contexts chose to develop that work in their own way. Citron points out:

> When a master dies, other problems arise: which disciple can transmit the method to future generations, and what does it mean to transmit a method? Since Western cultures perceive teaching, learning and acting as highly individual processes, a particular student's personal understanding of a method is paramount. The different American interpretations of the Stanislavsky system, for example, have created several distinctive, rival schools.
>
> (Citron 1983: 92)

The term 'Chekhov technique' or 'method' is being used by many different teachers in different ways, so it is perhaps inevitable that these problematic issues may arise in examining the notion of lineage and transmission. A potential danger is that Chekhov's name and work may become 'commodified' as a label for an actor or teacher wanting to promote themselves as having a direct heritage in the Russian tradition, yet the label alone does not necessarily guarantee any real evidence of this in their work. The notion of 'tradition' is likewise problematic as this tends to imply a fixed object, rather than a fluid and changing form. This can also be applied to the sense of 'authenticity' in a practice. Erik Cohen suggests that authenticity is 'not a primitive given, but negotiable' (Cohen 1988: 379) and Theresa Buckland, writing in relation to forms of traditional dance and folk culture, states that authenticity is 'more often than not a speculation' (Buckland 2001: 1). The idea of 'authenticity' can create a conflict between the belief in a fixed and unchanging way of doing an exercise, and the process of fluidity and change which tends to be the experience of those who are actually working with or teaching the exercise.

This debate between authenticity and adaptation can be seen when examining how Chekhov's techniques are being used today. Within drama schools and universities, his work is generally taught as part of a course, rather than as a separate training on his methods alone. His work is also being used in teaching physical theatre and movement, as well as acting for theatre, television and film. Although his techniques appear to be adaptable for these other forms, Graham Dixon questions if there might be a danger that:

> Chekhov gets sidelined as a method for physical theatre performances only. There's so much more to it that you can train actors using Chekhov who can become the greatest classical actors, who really deal with text.[36]

The actor Simon Callow, in discussing acting styles, also suggests that the 'dimension of imaginative fantasy in acting, so stressed by the great Russian teacher Michael Chekhov, has been sidelined into what is absurdly called "physical theatre"' (Callow 2009). With the different forms of performance which contemporary actors may be involved with, perhaps Chekhov's methods being used in a more flexible way is appropriate as a means of training. Martin Sharp suggests that a potential problem with teaching Chekhov's work is to do with style, in that Chekhov developed his exercises within a very particular aesthetic, and this was reflected in the type of acting seen within the Studio in Dartington:

> Chekhov's aesthetic was rooted in turn-of-the-century Russia, and quite quickly he got absorbed in twentieth century naturalistic performance and working with film actors, but this left him cold. [. . .] The kind of acting that Dartington stood for was very symbolic, very Expressionistic. [. . .] We would understand it very differently now.[37]

In this sense, it is perhaps to be expected that approaches to teaching his work would be adapted for a contemporary theatre, as well as being used in conjunction with the work of other practitioners. Bella Merlin explains that for both her acting and teaching:

> I think Michael Chekhov's ideas and practices are in many ways as unavoidable as Stanislavsky's. So even if their respective techniques are not being consciously used, they are there as part of the fabric of

what an actor is doing. With all these trainings, I honestly believe that
they can be applied to different degrees to any role or medium – from
Macbeth to Macleans Toothpaste commercials, depending on the actor
and the imaginative approach. I am very eclectic and maverick in my
use of actor-training. I don't adhere to any one theorist or practitioner,
I use whatever might provoke my imagination at the time – Meisner,
Chekhov, Stanislavsky, Knebel, Adler, Hagen, Brecht, Grotowski.[38]

Sarah Kane, with her training in Steiner speech work, has a particular
focus on using the Chekhov work with speaking text, which is highly valuable for actors. Her teaching of Chekhov is flexible depending on the context
and the students. She never starts in the same way, and feels that having
a set pattern of doing the exercises is 'not very Chekhovian. Chekhovian
is going in, looking, listening, sensing, asking where's the door in for this
particular individual, this group of people, this particular time, and this
particular place'.[39] For Graham Dixon:

> You do have to adapt according to the particular group of people that
> are in front of you, but at the same time, what I try to do is work with
> the principles, and see with the basic techniques, the chapters of *To The
> Actor* are the basic techniques, where does that come from? What are
> the principles behind that? The whole thing of the space of inspired
> acting, that once you're there, you have access to all the other doors
> that come into that space. So it's holistic, there's no separation between
> movement and speech and acting in Chekhov's work.[40]

The sense of tradition and lineage can be continued, but in a changed way,
and perhaps this is also what Chekhov himself intended.

This chapter on Chekhov has demonstrated that, despite his being a
Russian in Britain, the teaching and practice of his work has not come down
in an unbroken line from Dartington, but rather is an amalgam of threads
and sources from other parts of the world converging back in Britain. Yet
there is still a connection to the teaching that Chekhov undertook in the
unique setting of the Studio in Dartington, as it is through some of those
students who travelled elsewhere that the heritage of Chekhov's work is
again being taught in Britain. The flow of the lineage out of Britain eventually flowed back in again, even if in a changed form. The extraordinary
story of the Elmhirsts' experiment in Devon has resulted in a legacy of
Chekhov's work, and a wealth of documentation in the archives from the
Studio. However, owing to the recent closure of the College in Dartington,
and the relocation of the Studio archives to Exeter, this particular chapter
in Dartington's story is now also closed. Perhaps the work of both Chekhov

and Dartington were in some ways ahead of their time. Chekhov gave a lecture entitled 'The Theatre of the Future' in 1935, and it could be said that this 'future' is present now in today's actors and theatre, with an emphasis on the psychophysical, the imagination, and the creative individuality of the performer. Martin Sharp suggests that the 'lineage has been carried as an imaginative future, a projected image',[41] and there is an opportunity to see glimpses of this lineage embodied in its own terms in British theatre today.

Acknowledgements

With thanks to Graham Dixon; Sarah Kane; Martin Sharp; Heather McIntyre and Yvonne Widger at the Dartington Hall Trust; and John Draisey at the Devon Records Office, Exeter.

Notes

1 Jatinder Verma makes an interesting distinction between these two words: 'Roots lead backwards. Routes are more progressive, leading you to make connections with others' (Arnot 2002). In this sense, this chapter looks both ways: backwards to the roots and origins of Chekhov's work, and forwards to the routes of transmission that have led to the different strands of the teaching and practice of his work in Britain today.

2 See Byckling (2006), Whyman (2008), Chamberlain (2003, 2004) for further information.

3 The Dartington Hall Trust Archive: 'Chekhov Theatre Studio, Dartington Hall' booklet, written by Christopher Martin, Leonard Elmhirst, Dorothy Elmhirst, Deirdre Hurst du Prey and Michael Chekhov, 1936, MC/S4/17/A.

4 Interview with Graham Dixon, 7 July 2010.

5 The Dartington Hall Trust Archive: Deirdre Hurst du Prey, Notes, 1938, MC/S4/14.

6 The Dartington Hall Trust Archive: Deirdre Hurst du Prey, 'Problems discussed with Mr Chekhov', Spring 1936, MC/S4/14.

7 The Dartington Hall Trust Archive: Linda Jackson to Deirdre Hurst du Prey, Spring/Summer 1938, MC/S4/14.

8 His influence was also seen internationally, with his founding of the National Theatre School of Canada in Montreal (1960), and the co-founding with John Houseman of the Drama Division of the Juilliard School in New York (1968).

9 Interview with Paul Rogers by Martin Sharp, 1 August 2000.

10 Saint-Denis became renowned for his productions of Anton Chekhov's plays in London. He drew on Stanislavsky's exercises by working through *An Actor Prepares* with the performers. These productions were very well received, and Saint-Denis was positioned by some as the 'expert' on directing Chekhov. This reputation was questioned by Deirdre Hurst du Prey in Dartington, where Michael Chekhov, who was both the nephew of Anton and the actor who had trained directly with Stanislavsky, was working in comparative obscurity.

11 The Dartington Hall Trust Archive: Class List and Application Form, 1936, MC/S4/17/A.

12 Interview with Paul Rogers by Martin Sharp, 1 August 2000.
13 Interview with Paul Rogers by Martin Sharp, 1 August 2000.
14 Interview with Paul Rogers by Martin Sharp, 1 August 2000.
15 Interview with Paul Rogers by Martin Sharp, 1 August 2000.
16 The Dartington Hall Trust Archive: *Art Is Higher Activity Than Life*, June–July 1937, DWE 18 B.
17 The Dartington Hall Trust Archive: Dorothy Elmhirst, Lesson Notes, September 1937, MC/S4/15.
18 The Dartington Hall Trust Archive: Deirdre Hurst du Prey, Letter, 3 October 1938, MC/S4/14.
19 Interview with Graham Dixon, 7 July 2010.
20 The Dartington Hall Trust Archive: Deirdre Hurst du Prey, Letter, 3 October 1938, MC/S4/14.
21 Interview with Paul Rogers by Martin Sharp, 1 August 2000.
22 His first wife had also been a student at the Studio in Dartington.
23 Interview with Paul Rogers by Martin Sharp, 1 August 2000.
24 Interview with Paul Rogers by Martin Sharp, 1 August 2000.
25 Interview with Sarah Kane, 7 July 2010
26 Interview with Graham Dixon, 7 July 2010.
27 Having taught at the universities of Birmingham and Exeter, Merlin is currently a professor at the University of California, Davis.
28 See Chamberlain (2003) for further discussion.
29 Response to questionnaire, email to Jerri Daboo, 17 July 2010.
30 Interview with Graham Dixon, 7 July 2010.
31 Response to questionnaire, email to Jerri Daboo, 17 July 2010.
32 Interview with Martin Sharp, 8 July 2010.
33 Interview with Martin Sharp, 8 July 2010
34 Interview with Graham Dixon, 7 July 2010.
35 Interview with Sarah Kane, 7 July 2010.
36 Interview with Graham Dixon, 7 July 2010.
37 Interview with Martin Sharp, 8 July 2010.
38 Response to questionnaire, email to Jerri Daboo, 4 September 2010.
39 Interview with Sarah Kane, 7 July 2010
40 Interview with Graham Dixon, 7 July 2010.
41 Interview with Martin Sharp, 8 July 2010.

Bibliography

Arnot, C. (2002) 'Staging a Survival', *The Guardian*, 13 March, http://www.guardian.co.uk/society/2002/mar/13/guardiansocietysupplement2 (accessed 7 March 2011).

Baldwin, J. (2009) 'Prologue', in Saint-Denis, M., *Theatre: The Rediscovery of Style and Other Writings*, Baldwin, J. (ed.), Abingdon: Routledge, pp. 1–20.

Buckland, T. (2001) 'Dance, Authenticity and Cultural Memory: The Politics of Embodiment', *Yearbook for Traditional Music*, 33: 1–16.

Byckling, L. (2002) 'Michael Chekhov as Actor, Teacher and Director in the West', *Toronto Slavic Quarterly*, 1 (Summer), http://www.utoronto.ca/tsq/01/chekhovwest.shtml (accessed 25 April 2010).

Byckling, L. (2006) 'Michael Chekhov and Anthroposophy: From the History of the Second Moscow Art Theatre', *Nordic Theatre Studies*, 18: 59–72.

Callow, S. (2009) 'Simon Callow on the Changing Styles of Acting', *The Guardian*, 11 May, http://www.guardian.co.uk/stage/2009/may/11/simon-callow-theatre (accessed 28 June 2010).

Chamberlain, F. (2003) 'Michael Chekhov: Pedagogy, Spirituality and the Occult', *Toronto Slavic Quarterly*, 4 (Spring), http://www.utoronto.ca/tsq/04/chamberlain04.shtml (accessed 7 July 2010).

Chamberlain, F. (2004) *Michael Chekhov*, London: Routledge.

Chamberlain, F. (2010) Response to questionnaire, email to Jerri Daboo, 17 July.

Chekhov, M. (1996) *Michael Chekhov on Theatre and the Art of Acting: The Five-Hour Master Class*, Powers, M. (ed.), audiocassettes, New York: Magi.

Chekhov, M. (2002) *To The Actor on the Technique of Acting*, London: Routledge.

Chekhov, M. (2005)*The Path of the Actor*, Kirillov, A. and Merlin, B. (eds), London: Routledge.

Citron, A. (1983) 'The Chekhov Technique Today', *TDR, 27* (3), Special Issue on Michael Chekhov (Autumn): 91–6.

Cohen, E. (1988) 'Authenticity and Commoditization in Tourism', *Annals of Tourism Research*, 15: 371–86.

Dixon, G. (2010) Interview with Jerri Daboo, London, 7 July.

Gordon, M. (1983) 'Michael Chekhov's Life and Work: A Descriptive Chronology', *TDR, 27* (3), Special Issue on Michael Chekhov (Autumn): 3–21.

Hall, P. (2009) 'Foreword', in Saint-Denis, M., *Theatre: The Rediscovery of Style and Other Writings*, Baldwin, J. (ed.), Abingdon: Routledge, pp. vii–ix.

Kane, S. (2010) Interview with Jerri Daboo, London, 7 July.

Keeve, F. (2002) *From Russia to Hollywood: The 100-Year Odyssey of Chekhov and Shdanoff*, Pathfinder, DVD.

Lüdtke, K. (2009) *Dances with Spiders: Crisis, Celebrity and Celebration in Southern Italy*, Oxford: Berghahn Books.

Merlin, B. (2010) Response to questionnaire, email to Jerri Daboo, 4 September.

Morley, S. (1982) 'Interview: Paul Rogers, Greedy for Pinter', *The Times*, 13 October, in *The Times Digital Archive 1785–1985* (accessed 18 October 2010).

Powers, M. (2003) Interview with Jerri Daboo, New York, 17 June.

Rogers, P. (2000) Film interview with Martin Sharp, London, 1 August.

Sharp, M. (dir.) (2002) *Michael Chekhov: The Dartington Years*, Michael Chekhov Centre UK in association with the Dorothy Whitney Elmhirst Trust and Palomino Films.

Sharp, M. (2010) Interview with Jerri Daboo, London, 8 July.

Whyman, R. (2008) *The Stanislavsky System of Acting: Legacy and Influence in Modern Performance*, Cambridge: Cambridge University Press.

4

RIDING THE WAVES

Uncovering biomechanics in Britain

Amy Skinner

> We turn to Meyerhold not for nostalgic conversation about the theatre of the past, nor for grim judgement of the theatre of today, but for inspired guidance to the theatre of the future.
>
> (Chambers 1998: 60)

Identifying the influence of the Russian director Vsevolod Emilevich Meyerhold on British theatre is a problematic process. Productions are called 'Meyerholdian' for any number of reasons, from a revisionist approach to the role of the text to a constructivist-influenced set design. Our instinct is that many of the innovations of contemporary theatre owe no small debt to Meyerhold's aesthetic, but, to quote Robert Leach, that debt appears 'unquantifiable' (Leach 2004: 96).

What follows is an attempt, not to quantify the unquantifiable, but to begin to locate Meyerhold's influence on British theatre through focusing on one specific aspect of his aesthetic: his actor training programme, biomechanics. A systematic approach to training performers, biomechanics is, in effect, Meyerhold writ small, encapsulating the key features and priorities of his theatre in terms of structure, rhythm, line, shape, and narrative.[1] Evident in Britain since the 1930s, biomechanics is central to the story of Meyerhold in the UK, with the history of British applications of the system addressing not only the tricky question of Meyerholdian legacy, but also the wider issue of transmission, particularly as it is related to body-based theatre practice.

Biomechanics is a case-study in the complexities of theatrical transmission: the physicality of the system privileges body-to-body communication, but the political circumstances surrounding Russia's relationship with the West have significantly restricted the opportunities for this sort of training in practice. This tension lies at the centre of British biomechanics and raises questions concerning the system's purity, longevity and utility outside its original context. The relative emphasis which individual practitioners or scholars have placed on these issues determines the form that biomechanics has begun to take.

Bringing biomechanics to the UK is a story of transmission rather than transplantation. The latter implies the lifting of something intact from one context to another; the former is an organic process, taking into account origins, journey, and the intervention of individual human beings. As Richard Schechner observes, 'every acorn is an oak-in-process. But between acorn and oak is sun, rain, wind, lightning and men with axes' (Schechner 1988: 37). The question of how circumstances have shaped individual engagement with biomechanics, and how, in turn, these individual approaches have shaped understanding of the system as a whole, is at the heart of this investigation into Meyerhold's legacy.

Travelling backwards in time through three significant periods in biomechanics' British history, this chapter takes in three 'waves' of the system's transmission: today's practice (based on survey material from 2010); work from the period after the fall of the Iron Curtain (*c*. 1990 leading into the present day); and, finally, practice which preceded the imposition of the Iron Curtain (1930s–1940s).[2] The backwards trajectory from the present day to Meyerhold's lifetime is an intentional choice, aiming to uncover, layer by layer, how the current situation came to exist, ultimately indicating some of the sources of the tensions surrounding biomechanics in Britain today.

For the sake of clarity, attention should be drawn at this point to three significant Russian figures whose influence on British biomechanics is particularly prominent. The first is Meyerhold's collaborator Nikolai Kustov, who outlived the director and was instrumental in establishing biomechanical training in Russia. Amongst Kustov's students are Gennady Bogdanov and Alexei Levinsky, who are responsible for the dissemination of Meyerhold's system outside Russia, and whose influence can be felt throughout British biomechanics. As such, their names occur consistently throughout the story which follows.[3]

Meyerhold's biomechanics: theatrical training for actors

Devised in the 1920s, biomechanics was Meyerhold's contribution to the spectrum of systematic models of actor training emerging in twentieth-century theatre. The director envisaged a system through which the performer would develop a controlled and conscious corporeality, creating actors who relied not on moments of psychological inspiration, but on a clear physical framework for performance. The mastery of physical forms is central to biomechanical training; however, to focus only on the acrobatics of

Meyerhold's system is to miss what makes biomechanics unique: that is, its consciously and resolutely *theatrical* approach to the physical. More than a simple programme for physical fitness or dexterity, biomechanics is theatrical training for actors whose ultimate goal is performance.

This emphasis on theatricality can be seen in biomechanics' key philosophical tenet, the predicament of the actor's duality. Meyerhold writes:

> The actor embodies in himself both the organizer and that which is to be organized (i.e. the artist and his material). The formula for acting may be expressed as follows: $N=A_1+A_2$ (where N=the actor; A_1=the artist who conceives the idea and issues the instructions necessary for its execution; A_2=the executant who executes the conception of A_1).
>
> (Braun 1998: 198)

Through biomechanical training, the actor becomes conscious of this dual status, and learns to master the relationship between A_1 and A_2, as Meyerhold observes:

> The actor must train his material (the body), so that it is capable of executing instantaneously those tasks which are dictated externally (by the actor, the director).
>
> (Braun 1998: 198)

The formal organisation of biomechanics as a system emerges from the director's concern with this ultimate goal. Biomechanics advocates a physical system of training which pushes the body outside its normal comfort zone in terms of intensity, balance, rhythm and shape. The constant re-orientation of the body and the need for consistent physical control teaches the trainee to master the interaction between the thinking self and the moving self, dissolving any distance which might exist between A_1 and A_2. The outcome of biomechanical training for the performer should include increased self-awareness, a heightened ability to locate the body in three-dimensional space and greater skill in responding to external stimuli – what Meyerhold calls 'reflex excitability' (Braun 1998: 201). The ultimate goal, however, is for the actor to use the physical forms as a route to creative and imaginative freedom.

At the centre of the theoretical framework for biomechanics, Meyerhold posits the Acting Cycle, a tripartite rhythmic structure which ensures maximum efficacy of movement, bringing the principles of industrial Taylorism into a theatrical frame. Through the Acting Cycle, each movement is broken down into the three stages: the *otkaz* (intention or refusal), *posil'* (realisation) and *tochka* (reaction). Meyerhold describes the stages of the cycle:

The intention is the intellectual assimilation of a task prescribed externally by the dramatist, the director, or the initiative of the performer.
The realization is the cycle of volitional, mimetic and vocal reflexes.
The reaction is the attenuation of the volitional reflex as it is realized
mimetically and vocally in preparation for the reception of a new intention (the transition to a new acting cycle).

(Braun 1998: 201)

These stages form the basis of every biomechanical movement, resulting
in the distinctive rhythmic pattern of the system. In the training room, the
stages of the cycle are actively acknowledged through a count of *i* – *ras*
– *dva* ('and – one – two'). Jonathan Pitches describes the acting cycle in
action for the relatively simple activity of throwing a stick:

i	*otkaz*	the preparation to throw or a dipping in the legs
ras	*posil'*	the throwing itself
dva	*tochka*	the movement where all the force of the throw is brought back under control and the actor is once again balanced with the stick in hand, ready to throw again.

(Pitches 2003a: 124)

The centrality of the Acting Cycle reflects Meyerhold's belief in the theatrical power of efficiently executed movement, and this analytical approach to
physicality is an aspect of biomechanical practice which has proved most
enduring in contemporary theatre.

In terms of content, biomechanical training is twofold, combining general training exercises with more specific physical studies, the études. The
exercises incorporate a range of activities, including work with balls and
sticks, and the use of tap dance steps; the études are more complex set patterns of movement, each incorporating a basic narrative structure, framed
by Meyerhold as a 'melodrama' (Braun 1998: 176). Some are designed
for individual performers ('Shooting the Bow', 'Throwing the Stone');
others for pairs ('The Slap to the Face', 'The Leap to the Chest') or groups
('Building the Pyramid', 'The Circle') (Figure 4.1).[4] To develop the actor's
understanding of rhythm, the études are frequently performed to, although
not necessarily in time with, music. The daily biomechanics sessions at the
Meyerhold Workshop featured a combination of exercises and études.

The formal construction of the études is distinctive, and, within the context of the tricky question of legacy, biomechanics stands out as a space of
undisputable connection: where the system is practiced, Meyerhold has had

Figure 4.1 The biomechanical étude 'The Leap to the Chest', performed by Stefan
        Kozikov and Zosima Zlobin, 1927.

a direct and tangible influence. It is a natural starting point for considering
his place in British theatre today. However, even within this relatively direct
sphere of influence, that is, practitioners consciously using a practice which
they refer to as 'biomechanics', there is a wide range of applications.

What is most striking in the work of today's biomechanics practitioners is the expression of two consistent concerns. First, there is, as would
be expected, an interest in the utility of biomechanics as a system and its
perceived benefits for performers and directors. There is also, however, a
concern with the accuracy of the practitioners' own use of the system when
compared with Meyerhold's original work. This interest for some in a kind
of biomechanical 'accuracy', constructed as objective through comparison
to Meyerhold's own practice, leads to conflicting interpretations of the
system and a fundamental tension between purity and adaptation in British
biomechanics.

Biomechanics in Britain since the millennium: the 'third wave' of biomechanical transmission

Biomechanics in Britain today falls broadly into two categories: the first concerns professional performance practice through theatre companies; the second, biomechanics and the actor's education in the university sector and in conservatoires.

In the sphere of professional practice, Proper Job Theatre (Manchester/ Huddersfield) is the only British company whose aesthetic fully integrates biomechanics. Directors James Beale and Chloe Whitehead, who together created Proper Job's forerunner Talia Theatre, Britain's first biomechanically trained theatre ensemble, have been instrumental in establishing biomechanics in Britain, and in bringing Bogdanov, who has been their biomechanics master since 1995, to the UK (Figure 4.2). Beale and Whitehead have been training actors personally in biomechanics since 1998, and have, in collaboration with Bogdanov, produced a total of seven biomechanical productions in Britain, including *Dracula*, winner of the 2005 Creativity Works award. Using actors who have undergone extensive biomechanical training (Beale notes that the company knows eight or nine actors trained in this way), Proper Job sees biomechanics as key to its productions, incorporating two weeks training prior to a four-week rehearsal process. The aesthetic of Proper Job's performances reflects the conscious theatricality

Figure 4.2 Biomechanics workshop (led by Gennady Bogdanov) at Proper Job Theatre Company.

of biomechanical training, something Beale notes is particularly appealing to audiences without much theatre experience, who enjoy the physical prowess of biomechanically trained performers. In Beale's words, 'people appreciate physicality' (Figure 4.3).[5]

Proper Job has an ongoing commitment to biomechanics as an aesthetic. In contrast, other companies have made a brief investigation into Meyerhold's system as part of a single rehearsal process. In Red Shift Theatre Company's 2004 revival of *Bartleby*, movement director Katie Normington adopted Meyerhold's system to serve a specific purpose within the production, developing physical competence in actors who had been trained using predominantly psychological techniques (Normington 2005). Normington's work on *Bartleby* indicates an alternative model of biomechanical practice, whereby isolated elements of the system are used as tools to solve specific problems.

Within the university and conservatoire sectors, evidence of interest in Meyerholdian theatre is reasonably pervasive, particularly at undergraduate level.[6] The extent of this interest varies between institutions, and includes analysis of the director as an historical figure, theoretical discussions of his practice, and opportunities for practical biomechanical training. Amongst the universities offering practical training, the BA Acting programme at the University of Central Lancashire (UCLan) is unique in its commitment to Meyerhold's system. Working in collaboration with Bogdanov, UCLan's Head of Acting, Terence Mann, is developing a model for the integration of

Figure 4.3 Proper Job Theatre Company: *Romeo and Juliet.*

biomechanics into British actor training, moving towards the creation of a British MA in Biomechanics with connections to the European centres for biomechanical training that Bogdanov has already established in Germany and Italy.[7] The approach at UCLan is the result of a deliberate choice to invest in Mann's personal specialism in biomechanics: as a former actor and associate director with Talia Theatre, he has now undergone ten years of training with Bogdanov (Figure 4.4).

The intention of biomechanical training at UCLan is the development of the actor's critical and embodied understanding of performance, and the course combines practical study of the études with their critical evaluation and application to a performance process, integrating theory and practice. The course mimics Meyerhold's approach to actor training in establishing what Mann calls the 'disciplines of an ongoing daily practice', that is, a serious and consistent attitude towards training which should inform the actor's professional life, post-university (Figure 4.5).[8]

In the theatre conservatoire sector, the Central School of Speech and Drama (CSSD) also incorporates an element of biomechanical training. The school's undergraduate Acting programme, which includes both 'classical and contemporary actor training', sees first-year students undergo a term of biomechanics taught by the professional theatre maker Sinéad Rushe (Central School of Speech and Drama 2011). In describing these classes,

Figure 4.4 Bogdanov and Mann.

Figure 4.5 Bogdanov teaches biomechanics at UCLan.

Rushe notes the importance of students encountering vigorous physical practice early in their professional training. Her students, she observes, are often shocked by the physical demands which biomechanical training places on them. It is this discomfort which is the crux of the training process, as the students attempt to work through the physical constraints of the system towards embodying the empty form with its theatrical potential. Rushe talks of students developing a 'physical fearlessness' through their training, stepping towards a creative freedom which it takes a lifetime to master.[9] In contrast, Cariad Astles, also teaching at CSSD, uses biomechanics to train students specialising in puppetry. Here, the biomechanical training has the advantage of developing students' understanding of the 'principles and processes of movement', both for themselves and for the puppet, allowing them to master communication as a physical process.[10]

The contrast between practitioners working with an extended approach to biomechanics (Proper Job or the UCLan programme), and those with a more selective approach (Normington or Astles) highlights the issue of adaptation faced by biomechanical practitioners. Although it is clear that any practitioner will shape a system to their own ends to some extent, British biomechanics demonstrates two broad approaches to the system, which might be identified as purist and adaptive. The purist approach is the less common, in which workshop training is provided over an extended period of time. The purity is one of form: pure biomechanics attempts to recreate the formal construction of Meyerhold's system as it was envisaged by Meyerhold. This is generally reflected in a purity of usage as well, whereby all the major elements of biomechanics are incorporated, including the études. This is the practice seen at Proper Job, or in Mann's work at UCLan. In these instances, the priority is to use the system in a way which is as true to Meyerhold's original practice, in terms of form and philosophy, as is possible within the context of today's theatre.

In contrast, practitioners whose work takes an adaptive approach emphasise aspects of Meyerhold's system, resulting in a wide scope of practice, ranging from that which broadly preserves key philosophical or formal elements of Meyerhold's work, to that which makes significant alterations. In some instances, adaptive work is motivated by a respect for Meyerhold and a belief that insufficient training or partial understanding could lead to an inaccurate use of the system, particularly the études. Practitioners who subscribe to these concerns turn instead to the theoretical basis behind Meyerhold's work, incorporating that into their processes through a combination of exercises, some taken directly from Meyerhold, some from other sources. Other adaptive practitioners, whose approach to Meyerhold is less deferential, take a more interpretive approach, actively reworking elements of the system, including the études.

Bryan Brown, an American practitioner of laboratory theatre currently based at the University of Leeds, describes an engagement with biomechanics which typifies the adaptive process. Brown has trained with Bogdanov, but at his own company, the American Russian Theatre Ensemble Laboratory (ARTEL),[11] he notes that he does not use the full system because 'we do not know the études well enough to train in them'.[12] Brown's reluctance to use the biomechanical études results in his emphasis on Meyerhold's principles rather than his literal practice. It seems that Brown's and ARTEL's adaptive approach to biomechanics is in part a response to their (actual or perceived) lack of expertise in the études. Given this, they incorporate Meyerhold's ideas into a wider system of training, interweaving biomechanical techniques with other, body-based training methods to create their 'own training [. . .] revolving around similar principles to Meyerhold's work'. An alternative form of adaptation is seen in Astles's work, in which Meyerhold's three-part Acting Cycle is extended to a five- or seven-part structure which better suits her work with puppeteers.

In some instances, the decision to change aspects of biomechanics results from choice, a desire to incorporate Meyerhold's ideas into a bigger theatrical context: Normington, for example, describes a process in which rehearsals using biomechanical techniques are integrated into a more traditional, text-oriented, rehearsal process. For others, however, adaptation has been a necessity, a result of restrictions which have occurred as Meyerhold's system has made the journey from 1920s Russia to twenty-first-century Britain. Where changes to the system are seen as a necessity, rather than a choice, a hierarchical relationship may be established between practice which is perceived as accurate, that is, closer to Meyerhold's original approach, and practice which has been adapted.

This attitude is in part a result of the intensely physical nature of biomechanics as a system. Body-to-body transmission through training workshops has been vital in the preservation of biomechanical training. The commitment of Bogdanov and Levinsky in communicating the system around the world has resulted in an increasing number of people who have had firsthand training with Russian masters, and the experience of training with Bogdanov runs as a theme through today's British biomechanics practitioners.[13]

Bogdanov is extremely selective about which of his students are released as biomechanics teachers: only a limited number of his British pupils, including Beale, Whitehead and Mann, have officially received his endorsement to teach in the UK. The limited number of students whose practice has been endorsed by Bogdanov emphasises the relative closeness between today's students of biomechanics and the system's creator. Through contact with Bogdanov or Levinsky, British practitioners can experience a living link to Meyerhold which is relatively rare: from Meyerhold, via Kustov, to Bogdanov and Levinsky. This intimate connection with the master is far closer than can be imagined for the majority of actors training in Stanislavsky's System, for example.

Bogdanov's correspondence with Mann makes the value he places on this connection clear:

> In your work I can see the connection with a theatre tradition that started with Vsevolod Meyerhold, continued through my teacher Nikolai Kustov, and which Kustov, in turn, passed onto me [. . .] Having worked with you before, as both your teacher and director, I can clearly see a consistency in your work. Your process of learning and using Meyerhold's Biomechanics is conscious, accurate and correct.[14]

Bogdanov's work endorses the purist approach to biomechanical practice.

From establishing an authorised line of biomechanical practitioners and endorsing Mann's work as 'correct', the implication follows that it is possible, and indeed undesirable, to deviate and therefore practise 'incorrect' biomechanics. There emerges, then, a hierarchical approach to biomechanical training which privileges those uses of the system which might be described as 'pure'. This notion of purity, particularly in Bogdanov's case, is defined by the relative generational closeness of the practitioner to the source, that is, to Meyerhold himself, a closeness which, as Jonathan Pitches notes, is consciously emphasised by choices Bogdanov makes in presenting his practice to the world:

> What is [. . .] evident in Bogdanov's video [of the étude 'Throwing the Stone'] is his choice to echo the garb of his teacher, Kustov. Clearly, this decision is in part to reveal to the uninitiated the musculature of biomechanical action and to celebrate Bogdanov's physique. But it serves equally well to define Bogdanov's place in the Kustov lineage, a theatrical signifier of 'invariance' across 6 decades.
>
> (Pitches n.d.)

Bogdanov's contribution to the establishment of purist biomechanics is considerable, and may also be seen, in turn, to have sown the seeds of an adaptive approach: some practitioners who have studied with Bogdanov have turned to adaptive forms of the system which allow them to continue to engage with Meyerhold's work without claiming to teach biomechanics in its pure form. Bogdanov adds a further caveat to the understanding of purist biomechanics, notably that it is not a question of simply preserving the external forms of Meyerhold's system. Emphatic in his insistence that biomechanics is not a museum piece, Bogdanov's concern is that the transmission of Meyerhold's work to future generations is undertaken by the 'correct' people, those who he judges as best understanding both the form and philosophy of biomechanical training.

The purist and adaptive approaches establish the landscape of British biomechanics today, and give the scholar or practitioner a starting point from which to locate different biomechanical practices. As with any attempt at classification, the issues are more complex than the model suggests. The notion of purity in itself is an unstable one, and although practitioners such as Bogdanov, whose work has a relative generational closeness to Meyerhold, appear to be working in a purist vein, this purity relies on a veneer of objectivity which cannot be verified. The individuality of human beings is such that any engagement with another's work will include an element of interpretation: even the purist biomechanical practice is not pure, and even those endorsed in Bogdanov's authorised line are practising a third-generation version of biomechanics, that is, Meyerhold's biomechanics, as seen by Kustov, as seen by Bogdanov, as seen by today's practitioners. The origins of these categories, as well as their complexity, become readily apparent as the history of biomechanical practice in the UK is explored. The categories of purist and adaptive are not modern constructions or choices. Instead, they are born out of the process of transmission which biomechanical practice has undergone since the 1920s, and they carry within them the concerns of nine decades of people and events which have shaped the British perceptions of Meyerhold, his theatre and Russia itself.

The fall of the Iron Curtain and the birth of practice as research (1989–2000): the 'second wave' of biomechanical transmission

In 1995, the Centre for Performance Research (CPR) dedicated the first in its series of PastMasters conferences to Meyerhold.[15] The conference advertising located the event in terms of the growing presence of Meyerhold in Western academia during the 1990s:

> In the last two decades translations of [Meyerhold's] writings have appeared in the West, along with a growing number of critical studies. More recently, much hitherto unavailable material has surfaced in Russia, allowing for further re-appraisal of his work. It is now time to reassess Meyerhold – as a director, teacher, theorist, polemicist and scholar of theatre.
>
> (Centre for Performance Research 1995)

Implicit in this statement is the change in political circumstances in Russia during the 1990s. The fall of the Iron Curtain had eased cultural exchange between Russia and the West, and the CPR's list of symposium contributors reflected the new level of openness, featuring prominent Russian guests including Meyerhold's granddaughter, Maria Valenta. There is a sense, in the advertising, that a new era was dawning for Meyerhold, a director whose multi-faceted contribution to theatre now merited 'reappraisal'. The reference to Meyerhold as 'teacher' indicates the significant role which biomechanics played at the 1995 conference. With both Bogdanov and Levinsky in attendance, the symposium included demonstrations, films and discussions of Meyerhold's system. A series of biomechanics workshops was also offered by the Russian masters, highlighting the practical applications of the training for actors and directors. Video footage of the sessions led by Levinsky in that year, documented by Arts Archives in Exeter, has become the starting point for many British students of Meyerhold's system.[16]

Alongside the changing political circumstances, PastMasters also reflected developments in the British Higher Education (HE) sector, in which the turn towards Practice as Research (PaR) projects had begun to highlight the utility of Meyerhold's training for contemporary performance. The construction of a tripartite model of practice at the Meyerhold Theatre, combining training with laboratory work and public performances, indicates the director's integrated approach to theory and practice.[17] The emergence of PaR created a niche for Meyerhold in British scholarship, with his critical approach to integrating training within the rehearsal process establishing him as a proto-PaR practitioner. Jonathan Pitches and Anthony Shrubsall's reflections on their 1997 production of *The Government Inspector* at Nene College of Higher Education are an insight into one such project in which the unique environment of HE is used to consciously and critically analyse the contribution of biomechanics to a performance (Pitches and Shrubsall 1997).

The research-oriented environment of the HE sector can allow for a different engagement with biomechanics than normally possible within professional theatre. In its original context, biomechanical training relied on a theatre company with an ongoing relationship, that is, an established ensemble, who used their biomechanical knowledge as a starting point for communication during rehearsals. Pitches and Shrubsall note this advantage of biomechanics in their *The Government Inspector*, in which the étude itself creates a common aesthetic language for director and performer:

> In effect we [the actors and the director] spoke the same language, as I was able to relate the theatrical moment in rehearsal to the physical experience of the étude by saying: 'It's the moment when you see the stone and turn your head' [from the étude 'Throwing the Stone']. This resulted in the effective internalisation and acknowledgment of the direction by the cast and set the tone for the last image [of the production].
>
> (Pitches and Shrubsall 1997: 122)

The complication which emerges in the transference of this process to the British theatre, however, is primarily one of economy: biomechanical training is notoriously time-consuming. Beale notes the need for extensive training to establish a biomechanical ensemble, such as is seen at Proper Job:

> It is extremely difficult with financial constraints but we continue and have now developed an ensemble of actors with over five years experience. It is only when you get to around this level of training that you are able to really develop an ensemble.[18]

Normington echoes the issues of time constraints by concluding her reflections on the four weeks of rehearsals for *Bartleby* with an imagined rehearsal process which would allow for a fuller exploration of biomechanics:

> It would be thrilling one day to have the luxury of time to make a performance piece that created a physical outline for each scene: a system which engaged firstly with corporeal responses to the text, and then elaborated this through the application of words. But it was noticeable within rehearsals that I could only get through a couple of pages of script during an afternoon; about a fifth of the proportion that traditional rehearsing produced.
>
> (Normington 2005: 126)

Both of these concerns – the need for an ensemble of actors trained in biomechanics to make the system viable, and the economic and time constraints placed on professional theatre practice in the UK – are reflected in the shift to HE as a preferred arena for biomechanical experimentation. These concerns filter through to today's work at UCLan, as Mann observes:

> My wife Julia and I formed our own Theatre Company, Motion Loco in 2001 and we talked about staging [Nikolai Erdman's play] *The Suicide* with a cast of Biomechanically trained actors. The problem was, there weren't any, training in Theatrical Biomechanics takes time and where would those actors come from? When I began working at UCLan in 2008 it seemed it may eventually be possible to start the process.

At UCLan, Mann has an opportunity to connect his teaching with practical research into biomechanics by working with a biomechanically trained ensemble of students. He also notes the privileged economic position of the HE system in terms of creating theatre as regards his production of *The Suicide*:

> In 2008 and [Bogdanov's] first visit we began an initial practical exploration of Nikolai Erdman's play. We intend to continue with this work in the coming months and hope to work with [Bogdanov] again in 2011. There is little pressure to stage the production in the near future and it is good to take time with a piece of work, something we can never afford to do in this country. So at present the process is the most important thing and hopefully that may lead to some work in progress next year and a production in 2012.

The HE sector provides time and resources for student actors to engage critically with their biomechanical training, in an environment where the emphasis is on process rather than product. Inevitably, this leads to the question of how these trainee actors can use their biomechanical skills after graduation. Biomechanics is a consciously collective training system. The emphasis is on collective movement and activity, and the individual is always framed within the context of the group. Notes taken by Meyerhold's collaborator Mikhail Korenev make this clear:

> In each collective exercise, every participant must give up forever the constant desire of the actor to be a soloist.
>
> (Law and Gordon 1996: 136)

Outside Higher Education, however, biomechanics in British theatre is experiencing a shift away from this notion of collective commonality. Instead of a professional acting ensemble where a common aesthetic language dominates, the majority of graduates with biomechanical training will enter an individualistic theatre economy. This shift is not reflected in the exercises themselves, or in the content of biomechanics workshops, but in the transition which the actor must make from the training ground into professional performance.

Discussing the utility of biomechanics for students graduating from the course at UCLan in summer 2010, Mann highlights this issue: the whole of the programme, he explains, is tailored towards the development of the individual actor's vocabulary. In answer to the question of how an actor might use biomechanics in his career, Mann outlines an individual working alone, rather than a collective working with a common language:

> I don't believe the emphasis has to be on collective movement and activity [. . .] For me, an actor who truly understands biomechanics, one who has a genuine, embodied knowledge of the system, will always use it, wherever they perform, even in front of the camera.[19]

This post-Soviet phase of transmission to the UK uncovers some of the foundations of the post-millennial perception of biomechanics in Britain. In terms of developing and preserving biomechanics within the UK, the contribution of higher education is fundamental. The rise of Practice as Research and the development of the HE sector as a site for biomechanical experimentation in the 1990s set the scene for the more extensive courses taught at CSSD and UCLan today. Rushe, teaching at CSSD, sees the future of British biomechanics as dependent on the system being extensively integrated into the curricula of universities and drama schools: the more students who have trained in biomechanics, the more chance there is of common ground being found in professional companies.

It is the duality of this period, however, which is most intriguing. Key to *Bartleby* and the Nene *Government Inspector* is the investigation of how Meyerhold's system operates today, within a twentieth-century production process. This emphasis on biomechanics as useful begins to forefront utility over purity in British applications of the system, and the framing of Meyerhold's training as a tool rather than an encompassing system is fundamental in opening it to the notion of adaptation. However, as these projects forefront biomechanics as a tool for today's theatre, the greater freedom in cultural exchange between East and West introduce a new intimacy with Russia, and with Meyerhold himself. As adaptive biomechanical practice takes hold, accuracy is finally offered as a new, tempting, possibility, establishing the groundwork for the duality in biomechanical practice seen in twenty-first-century Britain.

Before the Iron Curtain: the 'first wave' of biomechanical transmission

The imposition of the Iron Curtain, and the circumstances surrounding Meyerhold's death, have significantly complicated international attitudes towards biomechanics. Whilst political circumstances pushed Russia and the West apart, and Stalin's infamous purges began to gain momentum, Meyerhold found himself in an increasingly precarious situation. By the late 1930s, the director had become *persona non grata* in the USSR: the State Meyerhold Theatre was officially closed in January 1938, and Meyerhold was arrested and subsequently executed under falsified charges of spying. The government went onto secure the complete suppression of his work within Russia extending as far as the publication of commemorative books for his productions which do not mention his name, as if, as Laurence Senelick observes, 'the *mise-en-scène* had been generated spontaneously' (Senelick 2003: 157).

For fifteen years, Meyerhold did not exist in the USSR. Limited publications kept him in British consciousness, but the atmosphere of secrecy surrounding Stalin's personality cult meant that foreign reports of the Purge victims' fates were extremely restricted: Joseph Macleod even claims that Meyerhold is 'still alive and active' in his 1943 publication *The New Soviet Theatre* (Macleod 1943: 99). Meyerhold's Russian rehabilitation began in 1955 with the posthumous repeal of his death sentence, and was well under way when Khrushchev's 'Secret Speech' initiated a new period of openness regarding the government's activities during the Stalin years.

Meyerhold's first mention in print, in Victor Komissarzhevsky's (1959) *Moscow Theatres*, is far from thorough or complimentary, but did at least signify his reappearance in theatrical scholarship.

In the West, inaccurate scholarship on Meyerhold (Yury Yelagin's discredited account of Meyerhold's 'last speech,' for example) is a direct consequence of the suppression of information in the USSR under Stalin, which created a difficult situation for those scholars writing in English on Meyerhold during and after the Khrushchev Thaw.[20] The schism in transmission caused by Meyerhold's eradication constructs in effect a hierarchy in biomechanical practice, establishing an information economy: information on Meyerhold is hard to come by, and, as such, imbued with value. An echo of this process is seen in the practitioners today who choose to adapt Meyerhold's system in order to sidestep the problems of not being able to access extensive and ongoing training.

The restrictions surrounding Meyerhold's work following his death interrupted an organic process of transmission which had already begun. Throughout the 1920s and 1930s, the Meyerhold Theatre had received foreign visitors from across the world, including Britain. Their reports formed the beginning of the first wave of interest in biomechanics in the UK, a process of transmission which would, to some extent, sidestep the schism of the Cold War.

By far the most comprehensive early investigation of biomechanics published in Britain is in André van Gyseghem's (1943) *Theatre in Soviet Russia*. Van Gyseghem dedicates two chapters of his book to Meyerhold's theatre, the latter dealing primarily with biomechanics. Alongside a description of a biomechanical training session, and some explanation of the theory behind Meyerhold's system, van Gyseghem also gives a detailed description of the étude 'Throwing the Stone'. It begins:

1. *To concentrate the attention of the pupil* – the hands are clapped twice together in a downward movement, the arms hanging loosely.
2. *Preparing to run* – with a jump, turn and face the right, landing with the left foot in front.
3. *Preparing to run* – knees bent, right hand in front, left hand behind.
4. *Running.*
5. *To arrive where the stone lies* – stop running with a jump, landing on the left foot with the left shoulder in front.
6. *Return to the normal position* [. . .]

(p. 29)

Even in this brief description, contradictions are apparent. Despite the detailed outline of the étude's physical shape (totalling 20 points), van

Gyseghem explicitly states that written descriptions of practical exercises are inadequate:

> It is difficult to give a clear picture of such physical exercises with the written word, and the explanatory sentences are only for the dancer or gymnast who has a technical knowledge which will make it easy for him to visualize each position and movement from the description.
>
> (p. 30)

Here van Gyseghem engages with the same issue which characterises contemporary biomechanics: the complexity of communicating body-based theatre forms without any direct contact. From the purist point of view, written descriptions can only go so far, and are wrought with potential misinterpretation and inaccuracy: it is questionable whether even a 'dancer or gymnast' would be able to interpret such ambiguous descriptions of movement as point 6 ('return to the normal position'), or indeed achieve the level of accuracy with which Meyerhold's biomechanical actor would perform the études. The reference to dance and gymnastics in itself further complicates the recreation of Meyerhold's exercise: these practices have their own rhythmic and formal structures forming the basis of the 'technical knowledge' to which van Gyseghem refers. In practice, it is hard to see how the dancer or gymnast could avoid merging these traditions with biomechanics, and creating a hybrid form which did not reflect the distinctive rhythmic structure of the acting cycle which Meyerhold created. Van Gyseghem concludes that:

> There is little or no written material on the subject, and the only satisfactory way of grasping the essential points is to enter the Meyerhold dramatic school for a term and take practical lessons.
>
> (p. 27)

Implicit in this statement is the establishment of the authorised line of 'correct' or pure biomechanical practice; van Gyseghem privileges body-to-body transmission as more accurate than the model of 'text plus reader interpretation' which he has been forced to use. His conclusion is simple: to establish biomechanics in the UK, practitioners will need to travel to Russia, study with the master, and return to Britain with their new skills. This conclusion, of course, sits under the shadow of hindsight: by the 1940s, travel to Russia from the West would become restricted and dangerous. The Cold War would shape prejudices and attitudes in Western thinking which would make Russia seem an alien and inaccessible place.

It is here, then, that the original problem with the transmission of biomechanics comes to light. The early descriptio⟨...⟩ ⟨...⟩re never intended to facilitate the reproduction of the system. Where ⟨...⟩ have been used as a resource for creating theatre practice, they have resul⟨...⟩d in interpretations which are different from those used by Meyerhold in Russia. Even at this early stage, the attempt to bring biomechanics to the UK has become a process of adaptation: the reader must interpret van Gyseghem's instructions according to their own level of experience. Later developments, particularly the introduction of photographs, film, and the opportunity to study with Bogdanov and Levinsky, create new levels of understanding, allowing the development of the various biomechanics narratives in the UK, falling roughly into the categories of purist and adaptive. The hierarchies associated with the level of interpretation involved in recreating Meyerhold's system exist even at this early stage, only to be magnified by the schism caused by the director's death, the fall of the Iron Curtain, the advent of Practice as Research, and the development of an authorised line of practice through specialists such as Bogdanov. Where biomechanics sits today in the UK is not a corruption of Meyerhold's original system, but a reflection of a complex process of transmission across countries, eras and political circumstances.

Whose biomechanics?

Arguably the greatest difficulty experienced with defining Meyerhold's role in contemporary Britain is establishing what his legacy should entail or achieve. For better or worse, Meyerhold's death remains central in defining his reception worldwide. His unjustified execution, the suppression and near loss of his work altogether, and the notes for projects he never completed (including *Hamlet*) all contribute to a profound sense of loss surrounding the director. The question of legacy becomes clouded by the issue of preservation, the desire to afford Meyerhold's practice the status which, through Stalin, it was denied. Similarly, the relative generational intimacy between today's practitioners and Meyerhold is perceived as a unique advantage. As more people are included in the chain of biomechanics practitioners and more change is potentially made, to quote Rushe, 'something is lost'. Maybe this something is a perceived accuracy; maybe it is intimacy, that privileged place in a chain which, spanning only two generations, stretches from Meyerhold to today. In this desire not to lose Meyerhold, however, we must also guard against his preservation in aspic, a theatrical Lenin lying in state, whose life story overshadows his place as a unique contributor to the evolution of contemporary theatre.

The shock of Meyerhold's death and the schism it creates has an almost formalist effect on the notion of transmission itself. The artificial break in the transmission of Meyerhold's work is a moment of what the Russians call *ostranenie*, or estrangement: through the suspension of the seemingly natural process of transmission, we are made aware of the complexities of theatrical practice crossing countries and eras. The story of Meyerhold's biomechanics is unique in that two processes of transmission work alongside one another. The natural transmission began before the director's death, through the accounts of van Gyseghem and his contemporaries. This process had barely begun when Stalin's intervention attempted to destroy the Meyerhold line. The destruction, however, was only partial, and, like Mayakovsky's Prisypkin, Meyerhold found himself frozen in time. When the director's rehabilitation began, and the Iron Curtain fell, the second line of transmission was unfrozen and joined the first. The result is two parallel processes of transmission operating side by side. One is the initial line begun by van Gyseghem, and now distanced ninety years from the director's own creation of the system. As such, it favours interpretation and the adaption of biomechanics to today's theatre, using the system as a tool to inform contemporary practice. The second is a preserved line, the reanimation of process of transmission which was suspended by political circumstance but brought back to life through Kustov, Bogdanov and their students. This line, in effect, has progressed only two decades from the director's death, and is tied closely to his ideas and memory. In Britain today, biomechanics exists in a range of forms, from the purism of Bogdanov's students at Proper Job or UCLan to the adaptive approaches of Brown and Normington, and the interpretive extension of the system into new fields, such as puppetry, or even dramatherapy.[21]

The existence of two lines of transmission is arguably in itself the greatest definition of the director's legacy. Away from the idea that a lineage must be unified, Meyerhold's legacy might rest in neither model of biomechanical practice alone, but in the tension which exists between the both. The director whose aesthetic privileged juxtaposition, the grotesque and the free adaptation of ideas from international theatre history, popular psychology, industrial theory and fine art – to name but a few – would perhaps revel in the multiple approaches to his system today, and in the tensions which these have created at the heart of British biomechanical practice.

Notes

1 To avoid confusion regarding the word 'system', when capitalised, 'System' should be taken as referring to the specific Stanislavsky System of actor training, and, when not capitalised, as referring to acting training systems in a more general sense.
2 The 2010 survey material comprises a series of case studies carried out by the author. The projects included in this study have a sustained involvement with

biomechanical theory, practice, or both, and are believed to make up the mainstay of theatrical biomechanics in the UK. Details of interviews carried out can be found in endnotes and in the bibliography below.

3 It should be noted that, although they are the best-known in Britain, Bogdanov and Levinsky are not the only Russian practitioners of biomechanics in the West: Elena Kuzina (University of St Petersburg) and Sergei Ostrenko (International University 'Global Theatre Experience'), for example, also offer this sort of training in Europe.

4 Video footage of the étude 'Shooting the Bow' is available on line at the website of the Meyerhold Memorial Museum (http://www.meyerhold.org).

5 All quotations from Beale are in interview with the author (26 January 2011), unless otherwise stated.

6 Research through correspondence with academics at eighteen Drama and Dance departments in the UK conducted by the author has shown that half incorporate some teaching on Meyerhold, with biomechanics making a specific appearance on two thirds of those programmes.

7 Dedicated biomechanics centres can be found in Perugia, Italy, at the Centre for Theatrical Biomechanics (http://www.microteatro.it/public/cisbit/en/content/ChiSiamo.asp) and at the Mime Centrum Berlin (http://www.mimecentrum.de/index_en.htm). It should be noted that, when working in the Higher Education (HE) sector, Mann uses the name Terence Chapman.

8 All quotations from Mann are in correspondence with the author (September 2010), unless otherwise stated.

9 All quotations from Rushe are in interview with the author (13 September 2010).

10 All quotations from Astles are in correspondence with the author (May–September 2010).

11 It should be noted that ARTEL is an American company, whose context and lineage are American. Although its work has been influenced by biomechanics, Brown does not classify the work of ARTEL itself as biomechanical, identifying more with 'a Grotowski-based American tradition filtered through [. . .] Stephen Wangh.' As a practitioner currently based in the UK, and teaching in British HE, Brown notes that he 'more and more utilize[s] Meyerhold's theories in [this] context' (personal correspondence with the author, March 2011).

12 All quotations from Brown are in correspondence with the author (May–September 2010), unless otherwise stated.

13 In 2010 alone, four intensive biomechanics workshops were hosted in the UK, all led by Bogdanov, lasting between two and twelve days each. These workshops were hosted by two different institutions: the University of Central Lancaster hosted two back-to-back workshops in June 2010 (one for beginning students, one for more advanced); Proper Job Theatre Company hosted two workshops (May and June 2010) at the Courtyard Theatre, London. These courses are described as 'an introduction to theatrical biomechanics' and 'basic level training' on the theatre's website (http://www.thecourtyard.org.uk/whatson/112/theatrical-biomechanics-2010-workshops-with-proper-jobs).

14 Personal correspondence between Bogdanov and Mann (2009).

15 http://www.aber.ac.uk/~cprwww/pastmast/index.htm

16 http://www.arts-archives.org/cat15.htm

17 See http://www.bris.ac.uk/parip/pitches.htm for the outline of a paper by Jonathan Pitches which specifically posits biomechanics as a site for PaR investigation.

18 In correspondence with the author (March 2011).
19 In correspondence with the author (March 2011).
20 Yelagin's (1956) book *Dark Genius* gives a distorted account of Meyerhold's speech at the All-Soviet Directors' Conference in 1939, in which he is portrayed as a hero, courageously defending his work in the face of government persecution. As Senelick (2003) highlights, more reliable accounts of the conference portray Meyerhold as broken, uninspiring and backtracking (see, for example, pp. 64–5).
21 Anna Seymour, editor of *Dramatherapy* (Taylor and Francis, publication from 2011), uses the physical containment of biomechanical training to explore the therapeutic notion of paradox, finding that structured physicality of biomechanics provides a framework for providing security and order, as well as, ultimately, emotional release (in interview with the author, 16 September 2010).

Bibliography

Arts Archive (2006) *Catalogue (15)*, http://www.arts-archives.org/cat15.htm (accessed 24 January 2011).

Beale, J. (2011) On Biomechanics at Proper Job Theatre Company (A. Skinner, interviewer, 26 January).

Braun, E. (ed. and trans.) (1998) *Meyerhold on Theatre*, London: Methuen.

Central School of Speech and Drama (2011) *Acting BA (Hons) Acting*, http://cssd.ac.uk/content/acting-ba-hons-acting (accessed 21 January 2011).

Centre for Performance Research (n.d.) *PastMasters*, http://www.aber.ac.uk/~cprwww/pastmast/index.htm (accessed 24 January 2011).

Centre for Performance Research (1995) *Past Masters Conference: Vsevolod Meyerhold*. Advertising Flyer.

Chambers, D. (1998) 'Reconstructing Revizor: An Introduction to "After Penza"', *Theater*, 28 (2): 56–60.

Courtyard Theatre (2010) *Training in Theatrical Biomechanics with Proper Job Theatre*, http://www.thecourtyard.org.uk/whatson/112/theatrical-biomechanics-2010-workshops-with-proper-jobs (accessed 7 January 2011).

Hodge, A. (ed.) (2000) *Twentieth Century Actor Training*, London: Routledge.

Komissarzhevsky, V. (1959) *Moscow Theatres*, Moscow: Foreign Languages Publishing House, Central Books.

Law, A. and Gordon, M. (1996) *Meyerhold, Eisenstein, and Biomechanics: Actor Training in Revolutionary Russia*, Jefferson, NC: MacFarland.

Leach, R. (1989) *Vsevolod Meyerhold*, Cambridge: Cambridge University Press.

Leach, R. (2004) *Makers of Modern Theatre*, London: Routledge.

Macleod, J. (1943) *The New Soviet Theatre*, London: George Allen and Unwin.

Meyerhold Memorial Museum (n.d.) *Biomechanics*, http://www.meyerhold.org (accessed 7 January 2011).

Micro Teatro (2011) *About the International Centre for Theatrical Biomechanics*, http://www.microteatro.it/public/cisbit/en/content/ChiSiamo.asp (accessed 7 January 2011).

Mime Centrum Berlin (n.d.) *Mime Centrum Berlin*, http://www.mimecentrum.de/index_en.htm (accessed 23 March 2011).

Normington, K. (2005) 'Meyerhold and the New Millennium', *New Theatre Quarterly*, 21: 118–26.

Pitches, J. (n.d.) 'The Evolution of an Aesthetic: Tracing the Living Link from Kustov's Biomechanics to Levinsky, Bogdanov and Beyond', unpublished article.

Pitches, J. (2003a) *Vsevolod Meyerhold*, London: Routledge.

Pitches, J. (2003b) *Tracing the Living Link: Documentary Complexity in the Archive of Biomechanics*, http://www.bris.ac.uk/parip/pitches.htm (accessed 7 January 2011).

Pitches, J. and Shrubsall, A. (1997) 'Two Perspectives on the Phenomenon of Biomechanics in Contemporary Performance: An Account of Gogol's *The Government Inspector* in Production', *Studies in Theatre Production*, 16: 93–128.

Rushe, S. (2010) On Biomechanics. Interview with A. Skinner, 13 September.

Schechner, R. (1988) *Performance Theory*, London: Routledge.

Senelick, L. (2003) 'The Making of a Martyr: The Legend of Meyerhold's Last Public Appearance', *Theatre Research International*, 28 (2): 157–68.

Seymour, Anna. (2010). On Biomechanics and Dramatherapy. Interview with A. Skinner, 16 September.

van Gyseghem, A. (1943) *Theatre in Soviet Russia*, London: Faber and Faber.

Yelagin, Y. (1956) *Dark Genius*, New York: Imeni Chekhova.

5

'WHO IS SKIVVY?'

The Russian influence on Theatre Workshop

Robert Leach

Theatre Workshop was probably Britain's only genuinely *avant garde* theatre company. Though it flourished for little more than a decade and a half from the end of the Second World War in 1945, its practice was hugely, even disproportionately, influential, and its methods and ideas informed subsequent work in the British theatre for decades, from the way school plays were approached and performed to the basic proceedings of companies as prestigious as the Royal Shakespeare Company and the National Theatre.

Theatre Workshop's roots may be traced back to the Workers Theatre Movement of the late 1920s and early 1930s. This brief but fascinating flowering of 'proletarian' theatre in its turn owed its existence to the theatre of revolutionary Russia, and in particular to the Blue Blouse groups of that country. After the 1917 Bolshevik revolution, very large numbers of ordinary Russian people set off what became known as the 'theatre epidemic', joining 'proletarian culture' (Proletkult) groups or other 'theatres of revolutionary satire' which created dramatisations of current affairs, 'living newspapers', presenting news items, cartoons, opinion pieces, discussions in a newspaper-like montage which celebrated and propagandised the Revolution across the vast lands of the newly Sovietised country (see Leach 1994: 36–42).

The first Blue Blouse group as such was led by a journalist, Boris Yuzhanin, whose group was able to turn professional when in early 1924 it obtained funding from the Moscow Trades Council. Yuzhanin also published a magazine, *The Blue Blouse*, which not only encouraged theoretical discussion of proletarian theatre, but also contained scripts, photographs and other documentary material. This spawned other, specifically 'Blue

Blouse' groups, the name referring less to their costume than to the type of living newspaper review-style show they created. Rarely lasting for as long as an hour, the presentations included plenty of music (jazz or folk music), dance (folk dance as well as more expressive forms), brief sketches, monologues, clowning and more. The shows were given in village halls, in trade union meeting places, on the backs of lorries, in town squares and on street corners. The performers wore blue shirts, black trousers and red head-scarves, and donned a beard, a hat or other accessory to indicate a particular character's social position. For this was a blatantly tendentious theatre, whose heroes were Red Army men, young Komsomols (Communist youth cadres), coolies and peasants, who bravely faced the array of villains to be found in the world: Mensheviks, capitalists, speculators, foreign imperial-ists and their like. The Blue Blouses were perhaps like highly politicised *commedia dell'arte* troupes (Leach 1994: 168–74).

In October 1927, Yuzhanin's Blue Blouse troupe was invited to tour Germany. Giving their first performance in Breslau on 5 October, they toured strenuously for a month: on 7–9 October they were in Berlin, on 10 October in Dresden, on 11 October in Chemnitz, on 12 October in Leipzig and so on. Ironically, the following year, the Blue Blouses became an early victim of Stalin's increasingly oppressive dictatorship. Their magazine was closed, Yuzhanin was removed from the movement entirely, and the Blue Blouse's efforts were ordered to be redirected to shows which heav-ily endorsed the Five Year Plan and the collectivization of agriculture, and which extolled the personal leadership of Joseph Stalin (Leach 1994: 172).

The irony was that their tour of Germany had sparked huge interest there: almost everywhere they went, they inspired local workers to establish a similar group of their own. They had performed in twenty-five cities before over 200,000 working-class spectators, and the kind of dynamic agit-prop theatre they had stimulated found a new home in Weimar Germany. Among the German 'Blue Blouse' groups was the Berlin-based Red Megaphones, who themselves – also perhaps ironically – toured the Soviet Union to nota-ble acclaim for five weeks in the summer of 1929. They wore blue boiler suits, and performed on temporary platforms, often outdoors, hard-hitting, propagandistic review-style shows to considerable enthusiasm among their Russian audiences. They appear in the 1931 film *Kuhle Wampe*, made by Bertolt Brecht, Hanns Eisler, Ernst Ottwald and Slatan Dudow, and by 1932 they had fifty members who formed four 'brigades', including one perform-ing exclusively for children. However, in January 1933 Adolf Hitler came to power in Germany, and the Berlin Red Megaphones disappeared for ever (see Stourac and McCreery 1986: 153–69).

But they were not forgotten. A British Red Megaphones group, con-sciously taking its name from its German predecessors, made its debut in Platt Field, Manchester, on May Day 1931, presenting mostly satirical propaganda songs from the back of a coal lorry. The members of this group, mostly out-of-work Manchester youths, had come together because they 'were possessed by a terrible sense of urgency, a need to create a political theatre which would help to change the world' (Goorney and MacColl 1986: xxi). This significant Communist imperative would last for more than three decades for some of them. The Red Megaphones were part of the British Workers' Theatre Movement, which had been founded originally by a number of largely middle-class socialists and theatre enthusiasts grouped around the progressive theatre scholar and enthusiast for all things Russian, Huntly Carter, at the time of the 1926 General Strike. Their intention was to encourage agit-prop drama for the working class. However, by late 1928, the movement was virtually moribund. Late that year, though, Tom Thomas's Hackney People's Players took it over, aiming to explore the possibilities of agit-prop theatre themselves. Their initial experiments received an enormous fillip when Thomas returned from the first Congress of the International Workers' Dramatic Union, held in Germany in June 1930, with news of workers' theatre groups flourishing all across the capitalist world: Britain, he urged, should have a similar movement. New companies and red theatre groups sprang up across Britain, largely Communist-owned and all of them deriving inspiration from Russia (though they appear not to have realised that by now Stalin had emasculated the originals of their movement). Thomas coined the slogan 'a propertyless theatre for the propertyless class' (see Samuel, MacColl and Cosgrove 1985: 77–96), and these propertyless groups were usually to be found where political struggles were being waged: housing evictions, strikes and the like. They were utterly unlike any other theatre organisation then known. Jack Loveman, a founder member of the Deptford Red Blouses, explained this:

> The drive [was] to go to the people rather than expect them to come to us. No catering for middle class audiences in well-equipped theatres. We went to the streets, co-op halls, TU premises, pits and labour exchanges . . . We were a Spartan lot. Also unisex. Dungarees for dress. A top hat to indicate bossdom. Outdoors, a cart to spout from if you were lucky.
>
> (Loveman 1982: 44)

By November 1931 the WTM had taken another leaf out of the Russian Blue Blouse book, and begun publishing its own monthly magazine, *Red Stage*, which continued until the end of 1932. Like *The Blue Blouse*, *Red Stage* offered scripts, news from various groups across the country and articles of general interest, such as whether artistic sophistication had a place in working-class agit-prop drama. It also published material about the theatre in the Soviet Union, and the Russian influence remained dominant, though some of it may have been filtered through the German experience.

The Red Megaphones, based in Salford, was a typical Workers Theatre group. Its leader was Jimmie Miller, an energetic teenager, unemployed but gnawed by anger at the world and teeming with ideas of how to change it. He was to change his name to Ewan MacColl later, and become one of the two significant figures in the evolution from this fairly crude agit-prop of the early 1930s to the remarkable fully realised work of Theatre Workshop twenty years later. An active member of the Communist National Unemployed Workers Movement, Miller/MacColl's political commitment was as strong as his artistic yearnings, and the Russian influence on him was suddenly unexpectedly personal. Sometime very early in the 1930s, he met 'a Russian girl', whom he only ever knew as 'Comrade Ludmilla'. She told him about the European agit-prop troupes she had encountered, especially in Germany and Czechoslovakia (Samuel, MacColl and Cosgrove 1985: 228). She was, apparently, some sort of spy, and in Britain illegally, having been sent from the Soviet Union to learn about the peasant movement in Manchester! However, she knew about the Blue Blouses, and, however much truth there was in her explanation of her presence in Britain, the fact was that she gave young Jimmie Miller hope, an example and a focus for some of his ardour.

The Red Megaphones toured their shows for a little over two years throughout Lancashire, and occasionally further afield. They performed from the stages of Labour or Co-operative Party meetings, from the backs of lorries at factory gates, where Communist candidates were standing for election or where workers were in dispute. For example, during the cotton trades' harsh 'eight-looms' strike, when weavers were asked to work twice as many looms for no increase in pay, and violence broke out across much of industrial Lancashire, the Red Megaphones were frequently to be seen – in Wigan, Blackburn, Burnley, Nelson etc. – performing their propaganda pieces, partly to encourage and support the strikers, partly to raise funds for them, and food and clothing for their children. Theirs was a theatre which consciously made itself *useful* in the class struggle. They wore bib-and-braces overalls, and developed an acting style which was crude but energetic. Miller tried to 'train' his company, although, as he admitted, he was 'the same age as everyone else in the group and I really knew no more than they did' (Samuel, MacColl and Cosgrove 1985: 231). The worst feature of the experience was that too often, even sometimes at factory gates, people were utterly indifferent to their efforts:

Often they would pass by with heads averted so as not to be involved, occasionally one or two would stop to jeer, others met us with blank apathy and this was harder to take than the abuse.

(Goorney and MacColl 1986: xxiii)

Miller tried to console himself with the thought that 'audiences would improve when we ourselves improved with hard work and rehearsal' (Goorney and MacColl 1986: xxiii), but it was becoming clear that agit-prop drama on its own was not enough to 'change the world'. More would be needed.

This feeling of inadequacy was not confined to Jimmie Miller in the Workers Theatre Movement. Philip Poole of the Hackney Red Radio group felt something of the same, as he recalled:

About this time we had an invitation to send a group of the Workers' Theatre Movement players to Moscow. I wasn't able to go, but about fifteen to twenty members went on this organised trip to Moscow to see the theatre . . . they landed at Leningrad. The first night they went to see a classical ballet . . . Then they went on to Moscow and they saw classical operas as well as some of the modern theatrical experiments that were going on at that time in Russia. One name I remember is Meyerhold. He was doing some startling things like producing plays without curtains . . . when they came back of course there was a furious discussion. And I thought, this is ridiculous, this 'propertyless class must have a propertyless theatre' . . . I said, 'How can we maintain this? This group's been to Russia and they've seen all sorts of things, classical things. Surely the thing is to take the best out of the old style and marry it with what we're trying to do'.

(Poole n.d.)

The Russians had moved on from agit-prop, and British progressive and workers' theatre groups felt they must do the same. However, it should be noted that Jimmie Miller/Ewan MacColl retained something from the Red Megaphone phase: the fragmented structure of a show, the review-like putting together of different kinds of scene to create a jagged, unsettling whole, the deployment of what is called in film criticism 'collision montage'. It can be seen in MacColl's later plays, such as *Uranium 235*, Theatre Workshop's biggest success in the immediate postwar period, in *The Hostage* by Brendan Behan (a good deal of the structuring of which was actually done by Theatre Workshop's other pillar, Joan Littlewood) and notably in *Oh What a Lovely War*, probably the high point of Theatre Workshop's achievement. 'Collision montage' derived directly from the Russian revolutionary 'theatre epidemic'.

In 1934, Ewan MacColl obtained from the New York Laboratory Theatre a copy of the script of the American living newspaper, *Newsboy*. Renaming themselves 'Theatre of Action', he and the other remaining members of the Red Megaphones put it into immediate rehearsal for performance indoors. It was while these rehearsals were proceeding that he met Joan Littlewood, a disaffected actress who had left RADA and tramped on foot to Manchester hoping to obtain work at the BBC. MacColl and Littlewood found an immediate *rapport*, and Littlewood's help in the realisation of *Newsboy* was the beginning of an artistic partnership which lasted for two decades. At first, however, *Newsboy* simply demonstrated the problems which the ambitions of the group raised: they needed actors who could dance, sing, perform acrobatics, speak verse and more; and they needed stage lighting and an understanding of stage space and stage settings, to say nothing of sound effects. It was a formidable list, but one which MacColl and Littlewood determined to tackle with relentless thoroughness.

Initially they went for answers to the Manchester Central Library, where MacColl had spent time already desperately trying to educate himself. They discovered here Léon Moussinac's *The New Movement in the Theatre* (1931), which directed them towards the theatre of revolutionary Russia, but now less to its original agit-prop manifestations than to some of the 'startling things' being created by Meyerhold and his professional peers in the mainstream. Moussinac, a French critic and political activist, had fought in the First World War, and had adopted Communism in response to political developments since that conflagration. In 1932 he had been elected to the Moscow-based Central Committee of the International Association of Workers' Theatres, and in the same year had founded in Paris his own Theatre of Action – perhaps the inspiration behind the name of MacColl and Littlewood's company in Manchester. He was a poet, novelist and playwright, as well as an eminent film critic, and had made a short film, as it were 'for fun', with Sergei Eisenstein in 1929.

The New Movement in the Theatre is a monumental tome, with large photographic plates of scenes from many of the most exciting productions of the 1920s from virtually every developed country in the world. Significantly, there are thirty plates showing performances from the USSR, more than from any other country, followed by twenty-seven from France, twenty-three from Germany and fifteen from the USA. Then there are seven from Austria, six from Czechoslovakia, five from Belgium, followed by a paltry three each from Yugoslavia and Britain, and two from Poland. It demonstrated with alarming clarity how far Britain was behind in theatrical modernity. It should be added in passing that MacColl and Littlewood drew inspiration not only from the USSR sections of the book. Pictures of German productions by Jessner, Martin, Brecht and Piscator were also exhilarating, and depictions of the latter's *The Adventures of Gallant Private Schwejk* were probably the first MacColl or Littlewood had seen of this work as a stage drama: it was to prompt one of their own most inventive works.

The most exciting photographs in Moussinac's collection, however, were almost certainly those of the Russian theatre. They included Tairov's *Salomé*, *Phèdre* and *Giroflé-Girofla*, *Don Carlos* directed by Sakhnovsky, Vakhtangov's best-known productions, *Turandot* and *The Dybbuk*, and Nemirovich-Danchenko's *Lysistrata* (Figure 5.1). The photograph of this last production, showing the setting of ramps, pillars, stairways and platforms, probably inspired MacColl's version of the same play, which was reworked several times and, as *Operation Olive Branch* (MacColl 2008), proved one of Joan Littlewood's most telling directorial successes (Figure 5.2). Photographs of her production demonstrate the link extremely clearly. Even more significantly, Moussinac reproduced photographs of a series of Meyerhold's productions, including *The Magnificent Cuckold*, *The Forest*, *The Warrant* and *The Government Inspector*. No wonder MacColl later wrote of this book as 'a veritable treasure-trove of concepts and ideas' (Goorney and MacColl 1986: xxxiv).

The Introduction by R. H. Packman elucidated some of the import of the pictures. Of the productions of Ostrovsky's *The Forest* and *The Warrant* by Nikolai Erdman (now usually known as *The Mandate*), he writes of 'the imaginative use of empty space punctuated with significant accessories' (Moussinac 1931: 14) whose power comes from their 'relying on the

Figure 5.1 Lysistrata, in the production by Vladimir Nemirovich-Danchenko at Moscow Art Theatre Musical Studio in 1923, from Leon Moussinac's (1931) *The New Movement in the Theatre*.

Figure 5.2 Operation Olive Branch, Ewan MacColl's adaptation of *Lysistrata,* directed by Joan Littlewood, 1947.

imaginative collaboration of the spectator' (p. 15). Of Meyerhold's productions in general Packman notes that:

> The material accessories are usually of extreme simplicity. 'I construct the idea: a scaffold is enough for me,' is Meyerhold's boast. His production (1926) of *Revizor* (*The Government Inspector*) is one of his most complete successes. Here he permits himself the uniforms and dresses, and an occasional table and chair, of the 1830s; but their function is purely symbolic, like the column or the tree in a Greek vase painting which imply a façade or a landscape. There is no naturalism. The acting, too, is stylised to a degree which would be impossible in the so-called realistic theatre of Western Europe, because the actor has to bear the responsibility of creating his environment. There is no scenery to help him. On the other hand, there is no scenery to hamper him.
>
> (Moussinac 1931: 13)

Such comments directly opened new perspectives. Meyerhold's abolition of the proscenium arch, his abandonment of the conventional back cloth, and his designs which used varying levels for the actors to climb up to or descend upon, were a clear challenge to the audience's preconceptions. He used scaffolding, platforms, playground furniture like seesaws and swings, industrial erections and even, in *The Government Inspector*, moving scenery (Figure 5.3).

All this made for a new (to them) Russian aesthetic, austere and aesthetically provocative, and MacColl and Littlewood began to try to incorporate something of it into their own work. For *Newsboy*, they rejected a front curtain and used a deliberately open stage, without proscenium arch. A note appended to the text of *John Bullion* states:

> The set is constructivist, being designed to facilitate the movement of the actors rather than to represent anything. Curtains are dispensed with and the transitions from one movement to another are achieved by using documented sound sequences. The stage is divided in to three levels or planes these being 1. A five-foot level which runs from left to right upstage, which is used for purposes of dramatic generalisation. 2. A level consisting of two sections, the meeting point of the sections being up centre just below the first level; they are placed at an angle of 90 degrees from each other (i.e. each section at an angle of 45 degrees from the first level). The height of the planes at this point is two feet. From here they slope down to stage level. These planes are used for stylised dance movements. The ordinary stage level completes the list.
>
> (Goorney and MacColl 1986: 2)

Figure 5.3 Revizor (*The Government Inspector*), Meyerhold's 1926 production, from Moussinac (1931).

More subtle was the use of lighting on the bare stage for Clifford Odets's *Waiting for Lefty*, produced in 1934. A semi-circle of taxi drivers is seated facing the audience:

> *The lights fade out and a white spot picks out the playing space within the space of the seated men. The seated men are very dimly visible in the outer dark, but more prominent is Fatt smoking his cigar and often blowing the smoke in the lighted circle.*
>
> (Mann and Roessel 2002: 353)

Other works which MacColl and Littlewood almost certainly consulted included periodicals such as the Moscow-based *International Literature*, which published a significant article by Yuri Olesha on Meyerhold's sixtieth birthday, and – probably – *The New Spirit in the Russian Theatre* by Huntly Carter, an earnest English journalist, a Theosophist and something of a polymath. He had studied medicine, tried his hand at playwrighting and before the First World War had written in support of women's suffrage as well as about state socialism and syndicalism. He was also the art critic of *The New Age* and had hailed 'Picassoism' (Cubism) when few in Britain had heard of it. In the 1920s he had become extremely excited by the post-revolutionary Russian theatre and cinema, its vitality and – as he saw it – its potential for good, and had founded the Workers Theatre Movement in Britain to try to emulate something of this here. He visited Russia, and wrote more than one book about its theatre. His description of Meyerhold must have appealed to the romantic in Ewan MacColl:

> I can remember Meierhold [*sic*] looking . . . like a typical workman in blouse, top boots and cap, dining on black bread and hard-boiled eggs, living in a bare, cold and cheerless flat, and yet doing work that might reasonably cause English theatre managers to give up their jobs and take to road-sweeping.
>
> (Carter 1929: 203)

Carter reported on how in Russia there was developing a new and stimulating view of the theatre worker: Smyschlaiev, for example, a comparatively undistinguished Russian theatre director, 'wanted the actor to be a citizen, a bolshevist and a social politician' (Carter 1929: 36) and systematically trained his actors accordingly. Meyerhold ('the greatest living creative and interpretative producer') similarly 'reshaped the actors by a system of training, scientific, biological, and psychological' (Carter 1929: 51). It was not clear precisely what this entailed, but at one point Carter noted that Meyerhold 'sought to make the actor's movements resemble those of a dance' (Carter 1929: 56), and MacColl and Littlewood leaped on this. As one of their first acts when working on *Newsboy*, they inveigled a young woman who had trained with Margaret Morris to work with their group, because *Newsboy* is suffused with dance. Scene 3, for example, is a 'ballet scene':

> *As the blind woman comes across the stage and turns to go back, all the figures who have thus far passed in the street scene come on stage and, working on three parallel planes with the same dance movement, go through movements which bring out their individual characteristic movements. All face the audience. They combine voices with characteristic gesture, i.e. the young lady keeps repeating* 'Why don't you go away! I'll call a policeman! I'll call a policeman!' *The blind woman repeats her singsong. The 2nd Newsboy shouts* 'News Chronicle Empire. CUP FINAL DRAW. PLANS FOR ROYAL JUBILEE.'
>
> (Goorney and MacColl 1986: 14)

Newsboy was often coupled with *John Bullion* in Theatre of Action's programmes. The latter was described by its authors, James H. Miller and Joan Littlewood, as 'a ballet with words'. Their commitment to theatre which included dance can be seen from another angle in their last work as members of Theatre of Action. For this, they were drafted in to help at Rusholme Repertory Theatre in February 1935 with the staging of Ernst Toller's *Draw the Fires* under the direction of the author. The opening of the play, performed by MacColl and other men from Theatre of Action, depicted sailors, shovelling coal into the ship's engine's fire, a scene which became in this production, according to one reviewer, 'a sort of ballet' (Davies 1996: 381).

From the books they devoured, they learned, too, about Meyerhold's insistence on training, and this chimed with MacColl's own feelings even during his Red Megaphone days. Starting with the engagement of the young lady dancer, MacColl and Littlewood from the beginning worked hard to train themselves and their colleagues, and this survived virtually to the end of Theatre Workshop itself in the late 1950s.

Some notes for training evenings from the 1930s survive. One, headed 'Training class – Tuesday. Eurhythmics and the beginnings of Biomechanics', lists the exercises the group would undertake:

1. Walking – running – to various rhythms
2. Two people running round room – one pulling forward – the other backwards
3. *Last Edition* unemployed man[1]

4. Wrestling, finishing up with leaping on partner's back
5. Leap frog to different rhythms
6. Tug of war to different rhythms
7. Scrubbing the floor
8. Shovelling
9. Throwing heavy weights
10. Throwing a ball
11. Pick axe[2]

Some of these exercises are unexpectedly like Meyerhold's actual biome-chanics exercises – especially the wrestling which 'finishes up with leaping on the partner's back', though it almost certainly lacked the nuances of Meyerhold's now-famous étude.

Littlewood's surviving notes from the 1940s and 1950s similarly con-tain plenty of pieces of paper with headings such as 'Class for Tuesday' or 'Exercises for Thursday', followed by lists of activities for the training session.[3] Even though Theatre Workshop at that time was a touring com-pany, with no base of its own, they always found a place and a time for training. When they were in Felixstowe in June 1947, for example, we find the company's programme for their third week of evening performances included also:

Wednesday	10.30–11.0	Movement (Rosalie)
	11.15–	Voice (in pairs)
	11.45	Stanislavsky (Ewan)[4]
Thursday	9.30–11.30	rehearse scene (*Blood Wedding*)
	10.0–11.0	Movement (Rosalie)
	11.45–1.0	Singing
Friday	9.30–11.30	rehearse scene
	10.0–11.0	Movement (Rosalie)
	11.45–12.15	rehearse scene
	11.15–12.15	Voice (in pairs)[5]

Such timetables could also be multiplied many times over, and indicate the thoroughness and dedication to systematic training which was to char-acterise especially Joan Littlewood's career. When in the later 1950s her productions began to transfer to the West End, and her company was no longer available to her, she more or less retired. She was offered produc-tions by the most mighty of British theatre impresarios, but felt unable to accept because whatever actors she would work with would lack what she felt was the requisite training.

Simply knowing the Russian (and other European) theatre through pictures and somewhat unclear descriptions was, however, not enough for MacColl and Littlewood. They determined to visit and study in the country of their dreams. In the autumn of 1935 they were accepted by the Soviet Theatre and Cinema Academy in Moscow as students. They applied for visas, and set off to London to collect them. However, there was a hitch. The visas were delayed. For nearly half a year they stayed in London, hoping with increasing despair that the visas would be granted. During this period, however, they were able to formulate and put in order their own ideas: they set up a sort of theatre school, with a few working-class students, based on what they supposed were Soviet lines, and formed a theatre company (which did no productions) called the Miller Theatre. (They were married by now, so the name covered both 'regisseurs', as they styled themselves.) However, they had no money, and finally had to return to Manchester utterly poverty-stricken, though with a considerably clearer idea of the theatre they were trying to create.

They were hired by the Peace Pledge Union to create a production of Hans Chlumberg's *Miracle at Verdun*, the success of which led to the foundation of yet another theatre company, this time called Theatre Union. MacColl wrote a manifesto which thinly disguised their political agenda, and the new group began a thorough study of theatre history as well as initiating a training programme of up to four hours per evening after members had finished work. They were still amateur, though the members were not shy of affirming that theatre was their 'real work' (Leach 2006: 34).

It was just at this time (1937) that Stanislavsky's *An Actor Prepares* appeared in English translation. MacColl and Littlewood seized on it, read it with minute care and brought its insights and ideas into everything they did. For several years, Stanislavsky's techniques – as far as they understood them – were the bulk and mainstay of all their practical work with actors (Figure 5.4).

Joan Littlewood's surviving notes from this period show just how slavishly they attempted to work through Stanislavsky's book. This, presumably, is from a talk she gave to her actors:

> In the art of acting the finest moments are the moments of inspiration. At such moments it is impossible for the actor to understand how certain hidden feelings in him found expression. If you ask an actor how he feels at such moments, he perhaps cannot tell you – and yet at these moments he is in fact *living the part*.[6]

Compare this with Elizabeth Hapgood's version of Stanislavsky:

> The very best that can happen is to have the actor completely carried

Figure 5.4 Theatre Workshop actor training session, c.1947.

away by the play. Then regardless of his own will he lives the part, not noticing *how* he feels, not thinking about *what* he does, and it all moves of its own accord, subconsciously and intuitively.

(Stanislavsky 1937: 13)

Littlewood asserts:

First our art will teach us how to create *consciously* and *rightly* – that is the mastery of our technique – *conscious* and *right* creative moments in our role will in turn open the gates of inspiration. To play *rightly*, that is *truly*, our acting must be logical, it must be coherent, we must think, strive, feel and act in unison with our role.[7]

And here is Stanislavsky:

Our art teaches us first of all to create consciously and rightly, because that will best prepare the way for the blossoming of the subconscious, which is inspiration. The more you have of conscious creative moments in your role the more chance you will have of a flow of inspiration . . . To play truly means to be right, logical, coherent, feel and act in unison with your role.

(Stanislavsky 1937: 14)

More interesting, perhaps, are the exercises she developed to explore his concepts. For instance, Stanislavsky discusses his idea of the power of 'if' by getting his imaginary professor, Tortsov, to describe different ways of opening a door in different situations, and similarly lighting a fire under different circumstances (Stanislavsky 1937: 42–3). Joan Littlewood's first notes for 'Exercises on "if"' are:

1. Close door . . . imagine cops come to arrest us and beat us up, how would you do it?
2. Light a fire . . . as if Okhlopkov and one of Stanislavsky's actors were coming.[8]

Further exercises on 'if' are still very close to Stanislavsky:

Training class for Tues 18 Sept
Notes on the imagination from Stanislavsky.
Play a series of if and giv[en] circ[umstance]s thought up by the author:
Actor's *imagination* turns author's imaginings into theatrical reality

. . .

Exercises
1. Imagine that this class is being held not in 42 Deansgate but in a Lakeland Youth Hostel at 11.0am on a sunny summer morning. After the class is over, what are you going to do?
2. that the class is being held on a spring early evening on the banks of the Seine in Paris.
3. in a London night school on a November evening. It is thick yellow fog outside –

. . .

What are you doing?
Sitting on a chair.

(a) imagine you are sitting in a stall on the first night of a Theatre of Socialist realism in Moscow. Describe it.
(b) on an electric chair condemned to death
(c) in an opium den
(d) waiting for the result of your child's serious operation
(e) waiting for an audition for the best acting academy in the world
(f) waiting to murder someone.[9]

Examples of Joan Littlewood's exercises in her exploration of Stanislavsky's ideas could be greatly prolonged.

It is worth adding here, however, that the discovery of Stanislavsky was as liberating for Ewan MacColl as it was for Joan Littlewood. For instance, here are some exercises devised by MacColl around Stanislavsky's ideas about observation:

> Take that chair. It exists outside me. I look at it and I have a sensation of putting out visual feelers. Now I close my eyes and see that chair on my inner vision. Examine an object. Notice its form, lines, colour, detail and characteristics. Time 30 secs. In the dark you will tell me all that your visual memory has retained. This time should be finally shortened to 2 secs.
>
> A Lappish hunting knife. Describe it. Do you like it? What do you like or dislike in it? What could you use it for? What has it been used for? Imagine some circumstances which will transform that object in your eyes, make it part of some real or imaginary event.[10]

Finally, one example from many of an exercise devised by MacColl or Littlewood (or both perhaps) on 'objectives and units':

> You have just got home, you are shortly going to bed. Will you go and close the curtains, change your shoes, examine the gramophone records, put one on, listen, rest in a chair, take the record off, look at a book, and then go to bed. *Count the units.* Main objective – to go to bed. Going to bed is the channel you are following. Cut out the detail. Find out the units which keep you in the creative line, which point towards the objective.[11]

Later in these notes, MacColl uses a vivid image which shows how deeply he understands Stanislavsky's concept of what Hapgood translates as 'units and objectives': the creative objective, he notes, is 'like an egg in a shell – an organic part of the unit – and *more important* it creates the unit which surrounds it'.[12]

From even such a brief examination of the work of Ewan MacColl and Joan Littlewood in these last years of the 1930s, it is clear how deeply imbued they became with the work of Stanislavsky, as they received it from *An Actor Prepares*. No other British actors were anywhere nearly as conscientious in their application of Stanislavsky as these two and their Theatre Union colleagues.

In light of this deliberate immersion in Stanislavsky, the choice of what plays the Theatre Union should stage is especially interesting, for at first sight they seem a far cry from the expected naturalism. Theatre Union's main productions from the period at the end of the 1930s were almost all comparative classics: Lope da Vega's *Fuente Ovejuna*, with songs from the Spanish Civil War, then raging, by Ewan MacColl, and MacColl's adaptations of *Lysistrata* by Aristophanes and the novel *The Good Soldier Schweyk* by Jaroslav Hasek. In these presentations, the use of Russian-style constructivist scenery was continued: the ramps, pillars and platforms of *Lysistrata* have already been mentioned. *The Good Soldier Schweyk* adapted certain motifs from Piscator's Berlin production of 1928 (from the photograph in Moussinac's book), but where Piscator had used cartoons by George Grosz, for instance, Littlewood and MacColl employed line drawings by the Manchester artist Ernest Brooks, and projected these onto the backcloth. As for *Fuente Ovejuna*, here the stage was dominated by a large, stylised sheep (the play's alternative title is *The Sheep Well*), and the backdrop used abstract, almost Futurist designs (Melvin 2006: 21, 24, 26, 28, 29).

What is instructive, though, is that MacColl's adaptations of these plays, though they employ the montage structure which originated in the Red Megaphone days, are actually composed of short, *highly naturalistic* scenes, which provide almost perfect grist for a Stanislavskian mill. A sort of synthesis between Stanislavsky and something more Meyerholdian was being created. Here is a small excerpt from the opening of *Lysistrata*. It is important to visualise the scene set on the conventionalised steps and rostra of Joan Littlewood's design:

A public square in Athens, it is the moment before dawn. Lysistrata, cloaked and hooded, stands against a pillar; a bell with a silvery chime strikes the hour of six.

LYSISTRATA:	Not a soul in sight! Wonderful. I call the women together to save Greece and nobody turns up! Greece bleeds and Athens snores. If peace was the reward for sleep, we'd have peace in perpetuity. Oh, what fools we are! Had I called them for a feast of Pan or Aphrodite this place wouldn't have been big enough to hold the eager crowds. But peace! I must be mad to think I could rouse them from their beds.
CALONICE (*off stage*):	Lysistrata! Lysistrata! Darling, where are you?

LYSISTRATA: I'm here.
CALONICE (*entering*):   I'm so sorry for being late. I had an awful
                         time getting away. But where are all the
                         others? I expected to find everybody here.
                                              (MacColl 2008: 10–11)

This is a far cry from Aristophanes as we are usually presented with him.
Here, for purposes of comparison, is Jack Lindsay's more traditional
version:

Lysistrata stands alone with the Propylaea at her back.

LYSISTRATA: If they were trysting for a Bacchanal,
                         A feast of Pan or Colias or Genetyllis,
                         The tambourines would block the rowdy
                         streets.
                         But now there's not a woman to be seen
                         Except – ah, yes – this neighbour of mine
                         yonder.
(Enter Calonice.)
                         Good day, Calonice.
CALONICE: Good day, Lysistrata.
                         But what has vexed you so? Tell me, child.
                         What are these black looks for? It doesn't suit
                         you
                         To knit your eyebrows up glumly like that.
                                               (Hadas 1962: 289)

This is a perfectly respectable translation, but offers the actor nothing like
MacColl's subtle 'I'm here', for instance. This is an excellent example of
the challenge MacColl's (much underestimated) scripts offer to the actor:
what is Lysistrata's objective when she says: 'I'm here'?

The Good Soldier Schweyk, by contrast, employs an almost Pinteresque
naturalism. Brettschneider, the police informer, enters Palivek's bar:

BRETTSCHNEIDER: Fine summer we're having.
PALIVEK: Think so?
(Pause.)
BRETTSCHNEIDER: Things are very quiet tonight.
PALIVEK: Oh, yes.
(Pause.)

BRETTSCHNEIDER:	That's a fine thing they've done for us at Sarajevo. (*No answer.*) I said, that's a fine mess they've made of things at Sarajevo.
PALIVEK:	Oh.
BRETTSCHNEIDER:	What do you think of it?
PALIVEK:	I don't think.
BRETTSCHNEIDER:	Oh? Why not?
PALIVEK:	It gets you into trouble.
BRETTSCHNEIDER:	I see.
(*Pause.*)[13]	

This is one of a series of small vignettes of which MacColl's *Good Soldier Schweyk* is composed. The script is a montage of small scenes, each of which, independently, provides excellent material for a Stanislavskian approach. When the whole is put into the highly stylised stage setting, it suggests the possibility of something genuinely original.

However, the progress of Joan Littlewood and Ewan MacColl was horribly interrupted by the advent of the Second World War, and the inevitable demise of Theatre Union. At the war's end, in 1945, MacColl, Littlewood, and three or four others from their pre-war troupe, together with half a dozen new members, formed themselves into a new Theatre Workshop, based in the north of England, and with the self-imposed task of taking theatre to the working class. The new company, which was to be full time and professional, consciously (almost self-consciously) took as its model what its members believed was Russian practice, most particularly the practice of the Moscow Art Theatre. Stanislavsky himself had described formulating the Art Theatre's founding principles:

> We also spoke of artistic ethics and entered our decisions into the minutes, at times even using aphorisms.
> 'There are no small parts, there are only small actors.'
> 'One must love art, and not one's self in art.'
> 'Today Hamlet, tomorrow a supernumerary.'
> (Stanislavski 1962: 298)

In Theatre Workshop, consequently, there were to be no stars; and no star salaries – all would receive precisely the same pay. Equal pay meant equal esteem between all members of the company. It was somewhat disillusioning a decade or so later when Theatre Workshop finally got to visit the real Art Theatre in Moscow:

Each dressing room had a brass plaque on the door bearing the name of some famous Moscow Art performer.

'Which is your leading lady?' he (the *regisseur*) asked.

'We don't have one – Lady Macbeth may be playing the skivvy tomorrow.'

'Who is Skivvy?'

(Littlewood 1994: 482–3)

However, by adhering to the principles of equality, Theatre Workshop was, in its best years, a genuine co-operative. In 1970, *The Times'* theatre critic, Irving Wardle, called Theatre Workshop 'an egalitarian ensemble, for whom the creation of fine work on stage is inseparable from the creation of a freely co-operating collective' (*The Times*, 3 December 1970). The spirit of the collective clearly fed into the work. This is suggested by the *Glasgow Herald*'s highly enthusiastic review of Theatre Workshop's 1952 production of *The Imaginary Invalid*:

> The salient quality of the acting was teamwork. Even the most subsidiary character had something to contribute and was encouraged to do so. The leading parts were woven into the play's texture with easy authority without monopolising the limelight. The highly satisfactory result was the impression of a fellowship of players sharing an enjoyable experience with the audience.
>
> (Littlewood 1994: 433)

This is a clear advance on the achievements of the 1930s, and such reports could be multiplied many times over.

Perhaps the most notable development of this post-war period artistically stemmed from Littlewood's dissatisfaction in 1945 with the quality of movement in her actors. The dance they had experimented with in the 1930s was always fairly crude and inconsistent. A reliable member of the group, Rosalie Williams, had tried to teach some elementary dance, which was charming but seemed to lack a true dynamic. So, in 1946, Littlewood contacted the German master of movement, Rudolf Laban, now based in England since his flight from Nazism. Laban was impressed with the company, and 'lent' them his star dancer, Jean Newlove, to direct their endeavours. In a short time, Newlove had joined the company as actor, dancer and choreographer, and she it was who turned the group into one of which no less a luminary than Sigurd Leeder was able to remark that they moved 'as some of the best dancers I've ever seen' (Goorney 1981: 160). Ewan MacColl concurred: 'It was because of her efforts that Theatre

Workshop achieved a standard of movement which would not have disgraced a company of dancers' (MacColl 1990: 389).

The basic characteristic of Laban's system is that movement is not something that somehow simply happens; it is always undertaken for a purpose. In other words, all movement must have an objective. In this sense, it dovetails perfectly with Stanislavsky's insistence that in each unit of a scene the actor must have an objective. Newlove began with the bases of Laban's understanding of movement, how the limbs may move up and down, back and forward, and from side to side. Once she had freed the actor of inhibitions, she added work on Laban's concept of the eight basic efforts which produce movement. Her work – constant, thorough, insistent – enormously increased the actors' range and technical armoury (see Laban 1980; Newlove and Dalby 2004). Over and over again, in production after production, Jean Newlove's work bore fruit. Howard Goorney quotes her description of the work on *Uranium 235*:

> In *Uranium 235* we had to split the atom, and because our actors were trained as modern dancers, it wasn't much trouble to get them to understand that they had to actually present the atom in a ballet. The bodies were intertwined and twisted, leaning over in the most difficult, extraordinary positions, legs up in the air. An actor from the ordinary theatre, asked to do this, would probably walk out, saying it was ridiculous, but of course it wasn't. We wanted to show the splitting of an atom, not simply describe it in words.
>
> (Goorney 1981: 160)

However, Newlove's training in the techniques of Laban movement did not simply pay dividends in dance sequences. There were other scenes, such as those in the anonymous Elizabethan melodrama *Arden of Faversham* when the villains, Shakebag and Black Will, are stalking their victims, when they have to traverse rough meadowlands and bog, through a dense fog which hides their prey from them. They stop and listen. They hold onto one another. They move with twitchy timorousness. Newlove was in her element with these scenes.

By 1950, Theatre Workshop as a touring theatre without a base of its own was becoming an untenable proposition. For many of the actors, as well as for Joan Littlewood herself, a permanent base was a necessity, and, after some bitter arguments, the company settled in early 1953 into a dilapidated theatre in the east end of London, at Stratford-atte-Bowe. However, the quality of the work did not diminish. Some members, including Ewan MacColl, drifted away, considering the stabilisation in London to be a betrayal of the original Communistic ideals of taking theatre to working-class communities. Yet Littlewood herself knew in her heart of hearts that if her work was to reach its true potential, and for the collective to flourish, this stopping place was necessary. It was at Stratford East that Littlewood's art probably reached its finest level.

This did not originate wholly from the Russian theatre. Laban was German, and Jean Newlove's Laban work provided the final piece of the jigsaw which enabled Joan Littlewood's achieved directing style to find itself. Nevertheless, and perhaps paradoxically, her style was clearly of Russian type: it was extraordinarily close to the 'Method of Physical Actions' of Stanislavsky's last phase, and equally surprisingly it was also close to Meyerhold's mature employment of biomechanics. Her own intuitive brilliance as a theatre practitioner seems to have led her onto the same path these Russian masters had trodden two decades earlier, for she knew nothing of the last creative flowerings of either of them. Yet, in the end, it is at least arguable that her work was as notable as theirs.

Stanislavsky's Method of Physical Actions was an attempt by him to supersede the too-cerebral nature of his system as it is embodied in *An Actor Prepares*, and which his own practice for some years after 1910 had largely followed. This entailed the company sitting round the table and discussing, arguing, deducing the play's overall meanings and intentions, characters' actions, motivations, desires, the given circumstances surrounding the action, and more. The aim was to inspire the actors with an ever more urgent desire to give physical expression to their discoveries, to unravel the inner truth of the play, and thereby to be able to authenticate whatever they actually came to perform on stage. Thus, it was only after a tortuous and extremely lengthy series of sessions that they were permitted to stand up and begin to try to embody what their discussions had uncovered. However, by 1930, Stanislavsky himself had acknowledged the weaknesses and problems inherent in this method. He now set out to short-circuit these problems by relying increasingly on the power of movement itself to fire the actors' imaginations and to reveal the truths his round-the-table analyses had previously worked at. It is highly ironic, of course, that, by the time *An Actor Prepares* was published in Britain, many of its ideas had long passed out of Stanislavsky's own practice.

Around 1930, he changed tack, and explored this new approach. The basic premise behind the Method of Physical Actions was, according to Bella Merlin:

> quite simply that actors could generate many of the creative discoveries in a rehearsal room through their *bodies*, rather than their *brains*. By

getting up on their feet and inhabiting the rehearsal space, the actors' bodies could feed their imaginations and prompt them into all sorts of emotional discoveries.

(Merlin 2007: 187)

The method now was to discover the sequence of *actions* which would allow the actor to access the inner truth of the script. In practice, this led to something remarkably like Littlewood's or MacColl's exercise above, when the character enters the room and listens to a gramophone record before going to bed. That list of actions was remarkably similar to what Stanislavsky called a 'score of physical actions'. The difference is that MacColl/Littlewood's was merely an abstract acting exercise, whereas Stanislavsky's 'score of physical actions' relates to a text being rehearsed. In his new system, the improvisations which produce the physical score are alternated with something like the round-the-table discussion of the text. After each improvisation, the actors return to the script and assess their work in its light; after each discussion round the table, they return to improvising the scene, recreating and refining the physical score. The advantage of the method is that the actors come to inhabit the action before they 'learn the lines': their 'truth' (Stanislavsky's word) is thus embodied physically in their own limbs, muscles and so forth, and works personally for each actor, whose improvisations lead towards the script – a reversal of the usual process.

It is important to note, however, that Stanislavsky learned a good deal of this from his younger colleague, Vsevolod Meyerhold, who as early as 1905 was developing what he called then 'the theatre of the straight line' (Braun 1991: 50). This involved the director saturating himself in the playwright's work, and sharing that knowledge with his cast. They too might then be expected to research the author, and there were sessions when they read excerpts or poems from the author's work aloud to each other. This work aimed to uncover the themes and forms of the writer's work as a whole. Then the specific play to be produced was read aloud together by the cast; there was a minimum of discussion before they stood up and began to improvise. Here Meyerhold was trying to uncover the inner truth of the play, as well as the superobjectives driving the characters, and he did this *through improvisation* (see Leach 2003: 52–7). Throughout the rehearsal period Meyerhold encouraged improvisation, including the use of 'parallel scenes' to investigate relationships, social tone and so on. The extent and direction of the improvisations were controlled not so much by the script as by the director's understanding of the script, and as the production took shape the director inserted breaks into the action, moments not unlike the Victorian 'tableau', to summarise the moment in a picture or formal 'silhouette'. Thus, improvising did not in Meyerhold's theatre imply simply doing as one pleased, any more than it did for Stanislavsky. Rather the creation of the production was a matter of collaboration, with both actor and director contributing and compromising. According to Meyerhold:

> Self restriction and improvisation – these are the two main working requirements for the actor on the stage . . . By self-restriction within the given spatial and temporal composition, or within the ensemble of partners, the actor makes a sacrifice to the whole of the production. The director makes a similar sacrifice in allowing improvisation. But these sacrifices are fruitful if they are mutual.
>
> (Gladkov 1997: 160)

This was the 'theatre of the straight line' from author through the director, on to the actor and so to the spectator.

The key difference between Meyerhold and Stanislavsky entailed training. Meyerhold insisted that all his actors be trained thoroughly in his system, Biomechanics, before he could work fruitfully with them, whereas for Stanislavsky the rehearsal itself was often the training. Whereas Stanislavsky's 'studios' in the 1910s, for instance, were in the hands of Leopold Sulerzhitsky, Evgeny Vakhtangov and others, Meyerhold's studios were firmly in the hands of Dr Dapertutto – that is, Meyerhold himself. Meyerhold continued to insist throughout his career that his actors must continue training whatever the difficulties. By the mid 1930s, when Stalin's butchers were closing in on him and he no longer had a theatre of his own, André van Gyseghem attended a biomechanics class in the theatre in which his company was temporarily housed:

> The long foyer around which the audience patrol in the evening before the play begins, is turned into a gymnasium. Chairs are cleared to the walls, and down the centre are a series of mattresses such as are used in any school gymnasium.
>
> (van Gyseghem 1943: 27)

All this is unexpectedly consonant with Joan Littlewood's theatre practice, especially as it found its maturity at the Theatre Royal, Stratford East. Like the Russian masters, her early rehearsals were devoted to exploring the play's 'final objective', the characters' relationships, the play's structures and rhythms, and so on. Her actors, like Meyerhold's, were frequently asked to research particular topics of relevance and report back to the company. She still believed in Stanislavsky's 'round the table' method of play analysis in the early stages of rehearsal, but, interestingly, this often took the form of a *physical* exploration. Using Laban's system of movement, her actors would get up from the table to explore the character's 'weight' (heavy/light, fast/slow etc.). Alternatively, they would improvise instead of dissecting a scene at the table, and, as they improvised, each physical action had to be justified. Like Meyerhold, she continued to employ improvisation, including the use of 'parallel scenes', and her special variant on improvisation, games, throughout the whole rehearsal period. She noted: 'When artists or scientists set out, they don't know what the end product will be. It changes. It changes in collaboration, each man trusting and mistrusting the people he works with' (Tynan 1967: 316).

What this method achieved for Littlewood (and the Method of Physical Actions or biomechanics achieved for Stanislavsky and for Meyerhold) was an *organic* production, one in which movement, speech and the responses and reactions from one actor/character to another were deeply honest and truthful. It led to performances which were absolutely fitting: the production *became* the play. On the one hand, we have a comment such as that by the poet Hugh McDiarmid, who, having seen Joan Littlewood's production of *Uranium 235*, wondered whether stage groupings had ever been more naturally achieved. On the other hand, we can look at photographs of the productions and see the stylized or formalised groupings which Littlewood often achieved (like Meyerhold's 'silhouettes'). The photograph of the 1954 *Richard II*, for instance, shows the king and queen on a balcony (like that of the Elizabethan theatre), with courtiers on ramps on either side, maintaining a visual symmetry, and soldiers in the well below (Figure 5.5). It provides a perfect emblem for the hierarchical society depicted in this reading of the play. A photograph of *The Prince and the Pauper* by Mark Twain, adapted by Ewan MacColl, also from 1954, shows three gentlemen in smart top hats and flowery neckties on steps, each one a step higher than the last, confronting a shabby figure standing on the ground in a battered topper with a grimy scarf round his neck. The meaning is immediate, though the photograph certainly does not seem posed, for the 'picture' is truly dynamic (Melvin 2006: 53, 66).

In case this should create an impression of something pre-conceived or static, the final point to note about Joan Littlewood's productions is that, unlike almost any other productions, certainly from that period in the British theatre, they were never 'fixed'. Two visits to the same production were unlikely to yield up precisely the same response. The second would be subtly, sometimes indeed radically, different from the first. 'As soon as a production is fixed, it is dead', she insisted (Tynan 1964: 90). Every production continued to change and evolve over its series of performances. She took copious notes during performances, and kept the actors after the curtain was down to give them her thoughts. Alexander Fraser recorded

Figure 5.5 Shakespeare's *Richard II* at Theatre Royal, Stratford East, with Harry H. Corbett in the title role, 1954.

'her view [that] no two nights of a play should be the same. Lines should be given new emphases, calling for a new emphasis in the response' (*Daily Telegraph*, 1 February 1973). This was 'improvisation in performance', and echoes precisely the ultimate aims of both Stanislavsky and Meyerhold, who said that:

> the good actor is distinguished from the bad by the fact that on Thursday he doesn't play the same way he did on Tuesday. An actor's joy isn't in repeating what was successful, but in variations and improvisations within the limits of the composition as a whole.
>
> (Gladkov 1997: 108)

He also said: 'The actor must not rivet his role tightly, like a bridge builder with his metal construction. He must leave some slots open for improvising' (Schmidt 1980: 207). Improvising during performance, 'playing in the present moment', rather than just regurgitating remembered rehearsal, is extremely difficult for actors to achieve and few actors or directors even attempt it. Yet it is what transforms the interesting performance into the exciting. Richard Harris recalled Joan Littlewood saying 'Don't practice how to say a line – it's whatever comes out tonight' and, on another occasion, 'You're getting used to that, change it' (*Omnibus*, BBC television, 19 April 1994). Clive Barker recalled Harry H. Corbett, 'who could stand for the epitome of the Theatre Workshop actor', saying that:

> his ambition was to give one performance in which he had only one motivation, the one which took him out of the wings and onto the stage. From that point, he wanted to play only off his reaction to the other actors.
>
> (Hodge 2010: 139).

Corbett had understood what Littlewood dedicated a lifetime to realising. It was what the great Russian masters had also realised, and she achieved it through thirty years and more of unremitting work. Of course, there were other influences which helped to make Theatre Workshop unique, especially German influences – the Berlin Red Megaphones, the dramaturgy of Ernst Toller, the mastery of movement of Rudolf Laban and so on. However, from the earliest days of the Red Megaphones' agit-prop experiments in Salford and Manchester, through the later 1930s, as Ewan MacColl and Joan Littlewood struggled to understand the dynamics behind photographs of Meyerhold's most brilliant productions, and on to the discovery of Stanislavsky through *An Actor Prepares*, from the unrelenting insistence on actor training, to the foundation of Theatre Workshop on Russian lines, and the final synthesis of all these endeavours in the brilliant productions by Joan Littlewood in the later 1940s and 1950s, it is the Russian light which shines most brightly, illuminating a path which few if any other British theatre practitioners were able to follow.

Notes

1 *Last Edition* was a living newspaper produced in 1939.
2 Joan Littlewood and the Theatre Workshop Collection, Harry Ransom Humanities Research Center, University of Texas at Austin, Box 1 folder 5. For other examples, see Leach (2006: 81–4).
3 See Joan Littlewood and the Theatre Workshop Collection in Harry Ransom Humanities Research Center, University of Texas at Austin.
4 For Theatre Workshop's Stanislavsky work, see below.
5 Joan Littlewood and the Theatre Workshop Collection, Harry Ransom Humanities Research Center, University of Texas at Austin, Box 1 folder 6.
6 Joan Littlewood and the Theatre Workshop Collection, Harry Ransom Humanities Research Center, University of Texas at Austin, Box 1 folder 5.
7 Joan Littlewood and the Theatre Workshop Collection, Harry Ransom Humanities Research Center, University of Texas at Austin, Box 1 folder 5.
8 Joan Littlewood and the Theatre Workshop Collection, Harry Ransom Humanities Research Center, University of Texas at Austin, Box 1 folder 5.

9 Joan Littlewood and the Theatre Workshop Collection, Harry Ransom Humanities Research Center, University of Texas at Austin, Box 1 folder 6.
10 Joan Littlewood and the Theatre Workshop Collection, Harry Ransom Humanities Research Center, University of Texas at Austin, Box 1 folder 6.
11 Joan Littlewood and the Theatre Workshop Collection, Harry Ransom Humanities Research Center, University of Texas at Austin, Box 1 folder 6.
12 Joan Littlewood and the Theatre Workshop Collection, Harry Ransom Humanities Research Center, University of Texas at Austin, Box 1 folder 6.
13 Unpublished script in MacColl and Seeger Archive, Ruskin College Library, Oxford.

Bibliography

Braun, E. (ed.) (1991) *Meyerhold on Theatre*, London: Methuen.
Carter, H. (1929) *The New Spirit in the Russian Theatre, 1917–28*, London: Brentano's.
Davies, C. (1996) *The Plays of Ernst Toller*, Amsterdam: Harwood Academic.
Gladkov, A. (1997) *Meyerhold Speaks, Meyerhold Rehearses*, Amsterdam: Harwood Academic.
Goorney, H. (1981) *The Theatre Workshop Story*, London: Eyre Methuen.
Goorney, H. and MacColl, E. (eds) (1986) *Agit-Prop to Theatre Workshop*, Manchester: Manchester University Press.
Hadas, M. (1962) *The Complete Plays of Aristophanes*, New York: Bantam Books.
Hodge, A. (ed.) (2010) *Actor Training*, 2nd edn, Oxon: Routledge.
Laban, R. (1980) *The Mastery of Movement*, 4th edn, revised by Lisa Ullman, London: Macdonald and Evans.
Leach, R. (1994) *Revolutionary Theatre*, London, Routledge.
Leach, R. (2003) *Stanislavsky and Meyerhold*, Bern: Peter Lang AG.
Leach, R. (2006) *Theatre Workshop: Joan Littlewood and the Making of Modern British Theatre*, Exeter: University of Exeter Press.
Littlewood, J. (1994) *Joan's Book: Joan Littlewood's Peculiar History as She Tells It*, London: Methuen.
Loveman, J. (1982) 'Workers Theatre', *Red Letters*, 13 (Spring): 44.
MacColl, E. (1990) *Journeyman*, London: Sidgwick & Jackson.
MacColl, E. (2008) *Plays 1*, London: Methuen.
Mann, E. and Roessel, D. (eds) (2002) *Political Stages*, New York: Applause.
Melvin, M. (2006) *The Art of the Theatre Workshop*, London: Oberon.
Merlin, B. (2007) *The Complete Stanislavsky Toolkit*, London: Nick Hern Books.
Moussinac, L. (1931) *The New Movement in the Theatre*, London: B. T. Batsford.
Newlove, J. and Dalby, J. (2004) *Laban for All*, London: NHB.
Poole, P. (n.d.) 'The Workers' Theatre Movement: A Propertyless Theatre for the Propertyless Class', *Red Letters*, 10: 10.
Samuel, R., MacColl, E. and Cosgrove, S. (1985) *Theatres of the Left, 1880–1935*, London: Routledge and Kegan Paul.
Schmidt, P. (ed.) (1980) *Meyerhold at Work*, Austin: University of Texas Press.
Stanislavski, C. (1962) *My Life in Art*, London: Geoffrey Bles.

Stanislavsky, C. (1937) *An Actor Prepares*, London: Bles.

Stourac, R. and McCreery, K. (1986) *Theatre as a Weapon*, London: Routledge and Kegan Paul.

Tynan, K. (1964) *Tynan on Theatre*, Harmondsworth: Penguin.

Tynan, K. (1967) *Tynan Right and Left*, London: Longmans.

van Gyseghem, A. (1943) *Theatre in Soviet Russia*, London: Faber and Faber.

6

SHARED UTOPIAS?

Alan Lyddiard, Lev Dodin and the Northern Stage Ensemble

Duška Radosavljević

The end

It was a January morning in 2005. I do not remember the details of how the meeting was called, but there was urgency about it, and it was to be a – rarely convened – full company meeting. Amid the refurbishment project of the Newcastle Playhouse, which was to reopen in 2006, Northern Stage was temporarily residing in a warehouse in Ouseburn, overlooking the Tyne. As the company Dramaturg, I was based at the University of Newcastle. By the time I arrived for the meeting, the company, which at this stage consisted of some 30–40 people including the actors and stage management, sat around in a big circle. There was a sense of anticipation – maybe even of bad news. We had just finished working on the new company mission statement, and so much was being lined up: two imminent premieres, the capital project, a new epic production of *The Odyssey* for the opening of the new theatre, the tenth anniversary of the ensemble in 2008, a full repertoire for at least another five years involving various international partners. Alan Lyddiard's announcement, that he was going to resign from his position of Chief Executive and Artistic Director of the company after thirteen years of service, was the last thing anyone expected to hear. The situation seemed absurd, inexplicable, and yet there was absolutely no hope of any compensation for the ideals and hopes invested in a project that had come to such an abrupt end. As a person from the former Yugoslavia, I had been in this situation once before. In both cases I witnessed just the end of the dream.

In reflecting on Alan Lyddiard's ensemble project, which was inspired by Lev Dodin's Maly Theatre from St Petersburg, I inevitably wish to understand what it was that made this highly idealistic project happen in the first place, what kept it going and – crucially – what caused its demise. Having joined the company in 2002, I witnessed the denouement of a story which had begun with Lyddiard's arrival in Newcastle in 1992 and peaked in 1998 with the formation of the ensemble. Inside the organisation, at that fateful time in 2005 an explanatory (perhaps somewhat dystopian) narrative had emerged about political machinations which led to this unfortunate finale. From this temporal distance and through a more objective academic approach, a more illuminating perspective seems possible.

This contextualisation of Lyddiard's ensemble model, by reference to the British and Russian theatre traditions, will also refer to interviews and correspondence with Lyddiard himself, his Executive Director Mandy Stewart, and a number of actors, cultural figures, policy makers and theatre critics familiar with Lyddiard's work. The chapter will therefore piece together an outline of the ensemble's history, its relationship to the legacy of Dodin, its potential impact on its larger context, and its aftermath, using Jill Dolan's concept of 'utopian performatives' as a framework.

Utopias

Writing in the aftermath of September 11, Jill Dolan seeks to define her concept of 'utopian performatives' in relation to Victor Turner's 'communitas' and J. L. Austin's 'performatives' which, she argues, 'make palpable an affective vision of how the world might be better' (Dolan 2005: 5). In their potential to provoke rehearsals for revolution the 'utopian performatives' are also seen as 'cousins to the ideas' of Boal and Brecht (p. 7). Revisiting the etymological origin of the term as first used by Thomas More in 1516, Dolan appears to interpret the notion of 'no place' as an indication of a lack of fixity which allows for a sense of 'hope, possibility and desire' (p. 8). She proposes:

> At the base of the utopian performative's constitution is the inevitability of its disappearance; its efficacy is premised on its evanescence. [. . .] The utopian performative's fleetingness leaves us melancholy yet cheered, because for however brief a moment, we felt something of what redemption might be like, of what humanism could really mean, of how powerful might be a world in which our commonalities would hail us over our differences.
>
> (p. 8)

Dolan is fully aware of the potentially coercive nature of the term and that '[f]ascism and utopia skirt dangerously close to each other' (Dolan 2001: 457), but ultimately she places her faith in the affective power of the theatre to activate civic engagement, and in the 'alchemy' which takes place when a consensus is reached that something 'works'.

Despite an initially problematic reception of Dolan's project,[1] Virginie Magnat (2005) has adopted Dolan's 'utopian performatives' in terms of the 'transformation that [utopia] makes possible' (p. 74). Magnat applies Dolan's notion to collective creativities in theatre as 'the art of losing our moorings in the familiar', which 'yield[s] a kinesthetic and associative form of awareness' (p. 74). It is precisely this kind of application of the positive content of Dolan's 'utopia' that creates a useful context for the forthcoming investigation of Lyddiard and Dodin's respective methodologies. For me, as Lyddiard's former dramaturg and an academic providing a historical narrative and analysis of Dodin's influence on Lyddiard's utopia, there are several ways in which the application of the term 'utopian performatives' will be relevant. For a start 'the inevitability of [utopia's] disappearance' seems immediately pertinent to the abrupt ending of the Northern Stage Ensemble. Secondly, Dolan's academic rehabilitation of such terms as 'idealism', 'alchemy', 'commonality', 'desire', 'love' and 'humanism' creates a useful space for the ideas, rhetoric and ways of working openly advocated by both Lyddiard and Dodin, but otherwise often subjected to scepticism and scrutiny.

Finally, on a historical-political level, it seems significant that both Lev Dodin's and Alan Lyddiard's pursuits of their own artistic ideals are in some way results of the political changes surrounding the end of the communist utopia. Peter Lichtenfels states that 'the Maly Drama Theatre could be considered the first new theatre of post-Soviet Russia' (in Delgado and Rebellato 2010: 59). Meanwhile Lyddiard's most memorable productions with Northern Stage are reinvestigations of Orwell and, one might argue, Orwell's inherent socialist ideals. Nevertheless, Lyddiard's work was always engaged with its current context – his production of *Animal Farm* in 1993 (Figure 6.1) was explicitly prompted by the wars in the former Yugoslavia.[2] It was repeatedly revived and toured internationally for ten years, becoming known within the company as the '*Annual Farm*'.

This essay will therefore investigate the 'utopian performatives' manifested not only in the individual works of those artists but in their chosen work ethos and respective creative methodologies at a particular moment in time.

Lev Dodin and the Maly Drama Theatre: collective spiritual pursuits as a way of life

In outlining the early years of Dodin's career, Maria Shevtsova places a particular emphasis on his 'homeless' years throughout the 1970s. Atypically

Figure 6.1 Animal Farm. Copyright: Keith Pattison.

for any theatre artist in the Soviet Union, Dodin did not have a 'theatre-home' (Shevtsova 2004: 5). So deeply entrenched was this necessity for a theatre artist to belong to an organisation in Russia and in the Soviet Union that Anatoly Smeliansky explains it using the term 'feudal ownership', whereby the artist is owned 'not only by the state but by their own theatrical "family"'. He adds that 'in such conditions the threat of losing one's theatre was tantamount to a death threat' (quoted in Shevtsova 2004: 6). The ensemble way of working has therefore been a default position in Russian theatre and very often, as in the case of the Moscow Arts Theatre and the Maly, there were clear links between training and ensemble membership. In fact, Shevtsova mentions that, despite being 'homeless' until he was invited to take over the Maly in 1983, Dodin was 'not without a roof' (p. 6) as he retained a permanent teaching position at his own *alma mater*, the Theatre

Institute in St Petersburg. He even declined a position at the Moscow Arts Theatre in order to keep his teaching post as he believed 'that he would be able to realise his artistic vision only with actors with whom he shared a whole way of seeing and being, which was more likely if he formed them himself' (p. 6).

It is worth noting that, despite all the political and economic changes that ensued after the end of the Cold War, the pluralist consciousness which goes with postmodernism and poststructuralism has hardly been able to touch this part of the world in any significant way. Of course, they are by no means unknown terms, but they have rarely found any manifestation in practice. Ruth Wyneken charts the way in which the Soviet years vanquished those of Stanislavsky's disciples belonging to the early avant-garde movement such as Meyerhold, Vakhtangov, Tairov and Michael Chekhov in favour of an ' "arithmetic" version of the System' (Wyneken 2006: 3), thus creating a monolithic way of working closed off to any Western modernist influences and purged of any Russian alternatives. This situation remained until the late 1970s and early 1980s when the likes of Lyubimov began to harness theatre's own power of disguised resistance. However, ironically, the eagerly anticipated end of the Cold War ushered in an unexpected anti-climax. Wyneken quotes one of Dodin's star actors Igor Ivanov remembering the company's first trips abroad in 1989: 'There were shiny shop windows, an affluent life. We were simply shocked. For some it was a tragedy. [. . .] There was no dialogue' (p. 5). Meanwhile, at home, the end of censorship meant that 'nobody need[ed] artists anymore'; some attempts at diversifying actor training were made, although the economic situation drove a lot of actors away from the theatre, and crucially:

> Theatre's enthusiastically welcomed liberation from the state revealed problems of a new kind. One of them was internal censorship. The old dogma of conservative, orthodox theatre was still strong among educators, scholars, critics. [. . .] It was very difficult to have contemporary plays included in repertoires, especially outside Moscow and St Petersburg; they were considered trash theatre, an absolute taboo.
>
> (p. 5).

Wyneken adds that Russia's oldest theatre academy GITIS – which 'has no experience with contemporary Western plays' – is still a stronghold of traditionalism and holds the credo that psychological realism is 'the only acceptable method of dramatic art' (p. 6).

Even though Dodin is seen as maintaining 'fidelity to a venerable Russian tradition' (Tarshis 2006: 16), his company's notable successes for over twenty years all around the world point to the kind of work which is certainly engaging and relevant. Lichtenfels notes that:

> In review after review, from all corners of the world, theatre critics invariably comment on the freshness and the memorable qualities of all the acting, whether in a new or early production from their repertoire.
>
> (Lichtenfels 2010: 71)

He adds that the work facilitates an impression among the audiences 'that the portrayed characters' lives are as complex and difficult as their own' (p. 71). Often reported features of the work include the longevity of the ensemble, the length and intensity of the rehearsal period – 'Dodin works on productions until he thinks they are ready' (p. 71) – great attention to detail and the epic proportions of each show. In a 1994 interview, Dodin recalled the ensemble-building process surrounding his first significant production with his students, incidentally for the Maly in 1977 – *Brothers and Sisters* – which involved an expedition to 'the north of the country' and living in a monastery 'with no electricity and no heating' (Dodin in Delgado and Heritage 1996: 73). The renowned Italian director Giorgio Strehler is reported to have said of this particular adaptation of Fyodor Abramov's novel:

> This play is a penetrating message about the fact that all men are brothers, about the value of human life and the need for human solidarity in the face of ever-new political catastrophes.
>
> (Strehler quoted in Tarshis 2006: 16)

Interestingly the Maly actors themselves are extremely loyal and 'they all profess the same artistic faith – they all have the same dramatic blood group' (Tarshis 2006: 17). Dodin has called this feature of his ensemble 'like-mindedness', claiming that this term 'in Russian culture has always meant sharing the same faith, sharing a belief in the existence of some spiritual truth' (Dodin 2005: 47).

In the interviews he has given, Dodin has repeatedly spoken about his work in precisely those terms that arouse scepticism and caution among contemporary academics in the West – 'spirituality', 'humanism', 'universal' and the 'collective'. Clearly, then, he is on a similar ground with Dolan and Turner when he celebrates the 'communitas' of a theatre experience. He distinguishes between 'the official religion' in pre-Soviet Union era, which was 'too close to the government, to the ruling classes and it was bound by dogmas', on the one hand, and 'the arts as a religious cult' (in Delgado and Heritage 1996: 72) on the other. Finding himself in the direct lineage of training coming from Stanislavsky and Meyerhold via his own teachers

Boris Zon and Matvey Dubrovin respectively, Dodin attributes this conception of a 'religious cult' to Meyerhold, who had written in a programme note
that theatre is a 'kind of community' and the 'actor is a dissident':

> The word Meyerhold used denotes the notion of a community that
> does not live according to the official religion of the state. They live
> as hermits in a sort of cave or a catacomb where they don't see others
> and are opposed.
>
> (in Delgado and Heritage 1996: 72)

Meanwhile Dodin's idea of theatre not being only a part of life but 'life
itself' (p. 72) comes from Stanislavsky, whose 'main book was called *My
Life in Art*, exactly because art cannot exist without the "life in it"' (Dodin
2005: 48).

In his more recent interview with Lichtenfels, Dodin has reiterated his
conviction that 'development in culture means carrying on something that
was always there' (Lichtenfels 2010: 75), that 'the issue of the ensemble
being formed is the issue of the [collective] soul' (p. 76) and that 'telling the
difference between what is sacred and what is art is very hard; they usually
go together' (p. 80).

It is possible then to view Dodin's approach to theatre in terms of utopian performatives not only on the level of the work itself featuring utopian
alchemical moments that 'work' for disparate audiences around the world
but also on the level of personal dedication and investment of his whole life
to a collective spiritual pursuit with his theatre company. At first glance,
taking into consideration the often futuristic aspect of utopian ideas, it
would seem illogical that the notion of utopia could be applied to a theatre
collective that is at the same time completely dedicated to 'carrying on a
tradition'. However, Dodin's utopian performatives – like Dolan's – seem to
be aimed at preserving those ways of thinking about theatre that are at risk
of extinction. This is by no means a merely nostalgic exercise concerned
with a conservative and 'obsessive valorization of the past' which Susan
Bennett (1996: 65) has attributed to the nostalgia surrounding productions
of Shakespeare, but an attempt to carry over from the personal past and to
keep that which has 'worked' despite the challenges and demands of changing trends, external pressures and paradigm shifts.

Alan Lyddiard and Northern Stage: building a home for international theatre

In 2001, the *Guardian* reviewer Alfred Hickling famously referred to
Northern Stage as the 'total theatre machine' specialising in 'techno-drama
for the digital age' (Hickling 2001). This was the zenith of Alan Lyddiard's

project, an internationally facing, local ensemble theatre from Newcastle-upon-Tyne which he had formed three years previously. Lyddiard came to Newcastle in 1992 to take over the artistic directorship of the struggling homeless company, which had been given two years by the Arts Council to live or die. Within two years he moved it into the Newcastle Playhouse, on the campus of Newcastle University, giving it an overhaul, a capable administrative and artistic leadership, and a rich and varied repertoire.

Born in London in 1949, and educated at public school, Lyddiard started his career as an actor at Harrogate Repertory Company and later worked at the Blue Box Theatre in Keswick. He received an Arts Council bursary in 1976 to work as a director with EMMA theatre company, and later became the Artistic Director of the Second City Theatre Company in Birmingham. Lyddiard moved to Scotland in 1984 as an Associate Director to Robert Robertson at Dundee Rep, and then became the Artistic Director of TAG theatre company in Glasgow from 1988 to 1992. Several aspects of Lyddiard's Scottish experience seem to have shaped and influenced him in crucial ways as an artist and cultural producer. In an interview he gave me, he recalls a moment upon his arrival at Dundee when the Timex workers were on strike, local unemployment was at 25 per cent 'and the local theatre was doing boulevard comedies from the West End'.[3] He felt that his key job as Associate Director in this situation was to 'change the emphasis of the work and make it much more local'. This meant engaging with local writers and with the community. Many Scottish audiences still fondly remember Lyddiard's community productions of *They Fairly Mak Ye Work* by Billy Kay in 1986 and John Harvey's adaptation of William Blain's novel *Witch's Blood* in 1987 – the latter involving audiences being bussed around Dundee.[4] Another important formative moment for Lyddiard was Glasgow's time as City of Culture in 1990, which facilitated his encounters and the beginnings of his working relationships with Lev Dodin, Peter Brook, Robert Lepage and Yukio Ninagawa.

> So when I came to Newcastle, I wanted to do the opposite of what I had done in Dundee. This is not a local theatre for local people. It's a local theatre but it has an international vision and a desire to create work that is of an international status.[5]

When he arrived in Newcastle, Lyddiard found that the director Max Roberts at Live Theatre was already doing the kind of work with local writers which showed 'a strong working-class commitment to creating work for, by and with [local] people' that Lyddiard had pioneered at Dundee. Instead, Lyddiard concentrated first on finding a home for his theatre, which was at the time based in offices, as well as building a creative team and an audience for his work. He was fortunate to be asked by Brian McMaster to participate in the Edinburgh International Festival's 1992 retrospective of the work of C. P. Taylor with a Geordie production of *And a Nightingale Sang*. The cast featured Robson Green, Denise Welch, Angela Lonsdale and David Whittaker and it was a major success, which caused some local tensions. The path from then on was by no means smooth, but by 1994 Lyddiard brought to Newcastle two of his key former collaborators: his long-term friend and Head of Design from the Dundee Rep, Neil Murray, whom he made Resident Designer and Associate Director, and his general manager from TAG, Mandy Stewart – the daughter of the actor-producer Michael Reddington – who became the Executive Director of Northern Stage and occupied half of the post of Chief Executive with Lyddiard as the Artistic Director.

Stewart recalls that she first walked into Northern Stage's new home, the Newcastle Playhouse, in March 1994. On the same day Peter Brook's company were presenting *The Man Who*,[6] and the next week Lev Dodin's company arrived, as part of an international season – which meant that 'we spent all our money for the whole year in two weeks'.[7] Several of my sources concur that, within these first stages of his leadership of Northern Stage, Lyddiard made a huge impact on the local artistic scene, partly through inspired and adventurous programming and partly through his continued commitment to creating 'a local theatre of international standing'. The core principle of his vision was that bringing 'the best in the world into Newcastle' would make it possible to also 'create a company of local people that would aspire to become as great as the people that have visited the organisation'.[8] Lyddiard traces the origins of this vision to Glasgow City of Culture in 1990 and to his encounter with Dodin, which actually initially took place in Moscow in 1986 as part of a Scottish delegation led by John McGrath of 7:84. This was the early phase of Soviet Union's own internationalisation under Gorbachev through *glasnost* and *perestroika*, and the visit was prompted by an invitation from the Actors' Union of Russia. In St Petersburg Lyddiard saw Dodin's production of William Golding's *Lord of the Flies* – a memory which may have led to his interest in the similarly dystopian works of Orwell.

Before proceeding with an analysis of the influence that Dodin had on Lyddiard's project, it is important to consider here for a moment the confluence of several strands of British theatre tradition that manifested itself in Lyddiard's Northern Stage. For a start, Lyddiard's early roots in the British repertory theatre as an actor suggest a particular approach to theatre making which, according to Rowell and Jackson's history of British regional theatre, had 'run its course' by the early 1980s (Rowell and Jackson 1984: 173). Rowell and Jackson trace the beginning of the 'movement' to the efforts of Harley Granville-Barker, William Archer, George Bernard Shaw and Basil Dean to direct British theatre away from the Victorian business model and more in line with the enlightened 'Continental' practices of significant state subsidy of the arts. Even though the arts subsidy in Britain did not occur until the Second World War and the creation of the Arts Council's predecessor – the Council for the Encouragement of Music and the Arts – Granville-Barker did manage to create a form of 'short run' repertory (p. 175) during his management of the Royal Court in the first decade of the twentieth century. Rowell and Jackson note that, despite several examples of reps in London in the pre-Second World War era, the model took off only with the advent of the Arts Council, resulting in the creation of the Old Vic, National Theatre and Royal Shakespeare Company (RSC) ensembles in the 1960s. They find that the model does carry certain strengths such as frequent changes of repertoire, lengthening rehearsal time, low ticket prices, promotion of new writing, rise of touring theatre, youth theatre and community workshops, risky revivals of lesser-known classics and increased degree of security and continuity (p. 183). However, by the early 1980s it becomes evident that dependence on a single funding body makes 'theatre's future vulnerable to changes in political control', large subsidy can 'buy its way out of trouble rather than [solving problems] by critical ingenuity', and the model ultimately results in increased levels of bureaucracy and administration (p. 184). This leads them to proclaim:

> Does Continental theatre practice in this respect offer a goal to be aimed at? It would seem not. While the actor on the European stage may enjoy the security and other benefits of a long term contract with his company, the British actor, by and large, especially in repertory, prefers to be mobile.
>
> (p. 180)

Another important factor they propose here is the influence of television-style naturalism on directors who aim 'for the most suitable casting character by character rather than at the development of ensemble playing' (p. 180).

Whereas Lyddiard's first apprenticeship at Harrogate in the late 1960s to early 1970s would have been closer to the model of repertory theatre catering for a more middle-class audience, it is interesting that his second significant theatre home, the Blue Box Theatre at Keswick (at a site which is nowadays known as Theatre by the Lake), is remembered as a touring theatre with a particularly strong impact on the community. Indeed, Theatre by the Lake's website states that:

> The refurbished Blue Box is now at Snibston Discovery Park in Leicestershire where it serves as a community theatre and as a tribute to

an extraordinary touring theatre enterprise which inspired many towns and cities around the country to create permanent theatres during nearly 25 years on the road.[9]

Lyddiard's later engagement as director with EMMA theatre company – highlighted by Baz Kershaw (1993) as an example of 'radical community theatre' – would also perhaps suggest a potential genealogical link to the strand of British theatre which has come to be known as 'alternative' (Craig 1980) to the Oxbridge-influenced mainstream. The values Craig highlighted around his definition of 'alternative theatre' of the late 1960s in Britain – the emphases on performance rather than text as well as the political, community and theatre-in-education – certainly manifested themselves in the structure of Northern Stage as an ensemble and the inherent non-literariness of its repertoire.

The ultimate home of Northern Stage, the Newcastle Playhouse, was a university theatre, built in 1970 as part of the trend of post-war new theatre buildings characterised by 'more egalitarian auditoria and more flexible staging' (Craig 1980: 12). The main auditorium had a capacity of 550 and the Gulbenkian studio 200.[10] It is interesting that by the time of Lyddiard's departure in 2005, and during the new wave of building regeneration in Britain under New Labour, the Newcastle Playhouse was being refurbished to create a bigger flexible stage by fusing the two pre-existing spaces. The intention was to rebrand the building using the name of the ensemble – Northern Stage – and to eventually turn it into the 'Centre for European Performing Arts' or the 'Home for International Theatre' in the region. Even though Lyddiard's vision for Northern Stage would have evolved and modified itself over the years, the most prominent principles – in addition to 'internationalism' – that were upheld until the end of his artistic director-ship were the notions of 'projects rather than plays', 'performers rather than actors' and a 'produced, presented and participatory' approach to program-ming. An example of Lyddiard's articulation of his vision was recorded in an article in *The Independent*:

> The theatre's got to become an event. [. . .] We've got to get away from the sense that each production is just another one off the conveyor belt. We want it to be dangerous and exciting.
>
> (Bayley 1995)

The 'project-model' approach meant that each new Northern Stage production would be accompanied by a number of satellite events ranging from conferences to workshops in schools, exhibitions or, during my time, writer's events. An interesting example was a conference to accompany the production of *1984* in 2002, whereby a group of local eighteen-year-olds, born in 1984, were brought together with local decision makers to voice their opinions about politics. The 'project-model' approach required joined-up thinking across the organisation and was fully complementary with the Northern Stage idea of 'produced, presented and participatory' programming. These principles were also core to the 'New Ways of Working' bid which Lyddiard and Stewart submitted to the Arts Council in 1997 as part of the Arts for Everyone scheme.[11] The main argument of this bid was that, in order for Lyddiard's vision to be delivered fully and functionally, the mechanism of ensemble was required – the ensemble of performers would carry out projects rather than just performances, facilitate participatory work, and in this way promote the work of the company locally, nationally and internationally.

Stewart recalls an interesting anecdote concerning the bidding process to the Arts Council for £500,000, when an assessor questioned Stewart and Lyddiard on what their exit strategy was – what would happen when the pilot period of two years was over, and how they would fund the continuation of the project?

> Alan and I hadn't thought about it at all. But we both looked at each other and we looked at this person and we said: 'The work will fund it! Because we will have created this national and international demand for the work and producers will call us from all over the world and take the work and that will provide the funds to keep paying the company.' And it's pretty much what happened. Because of the repertoire of work that was created during the pilot stage, like *Animal Farm*, *Clockwork Orange* – there was continual demand for touring, which really helped sustain the economy. The piece that we were making as I left was *1984*, and that piece was commissioned by four or five different theatres or arts centres that really wanted the Northern Stage Ensemble brand, and they were prepared to put in £5–£10,000 apiece to co-commission the work. So what we rather cheekily but defiantly said without any rehearsal – we just looked at each other and went 'this is how it is' – it actually was the truth.[12]

The bid was successful and the Northern Stage Ensemble was formed on 13 July 1998.[13]

Dining with Dodin

Prior to the Maly Theatre season in 1994 with *Brothers and Sisters*, *House* and *Gaudeamus*, Dodin had already visited Newcastle to mentor Lyddiard during his production of Alexander Galin's *Stars in the Morning Sky* in

Figure 6.2 Lev Dodin and Alan Lyddiard in Allenheads, Northumberland. Copyright: Keith Pattison.

1993. This play about the treatment of the Moscow dispossessed during the Olympic Games in 1980 had been staged by the Maly in 1987, and Lyddiard, who had seen and admired Dodin's production in Glasgow in 1988, was keen to have his blessing.[14]

It may be useful to elaborate on the nature of the relationship which evolved between Dodin and Lyddiard (Figure 6.2) over the years between their meeting in Glasgow in 1990 and the early 2000s. Referring to him as a 'mentor' and a 'guru' and to their relationship as a 'master–student' relationship, Lyddiard describes how he travelled around Europe to see Dodin's work and regularly dined with him on these occasions. Dodin's dramaturg Michael Stronin was often present as an interpreter, and Dodin talked about his work and his artistic beliefs and shared his views on theatre with Lyddiard. In a moment of a personal confession, Lyddiard intimates:

> I was quiet. I never said anything really. I just listened to him! Because he is amazing. I have a book called *Journey without End*. It is written by Lev Dodin. He has written in my version a message to me in Russian which, of course, I can't understand. But it says something very beautiful. The other thing about Lev, and I warmed to this so much, is this kind of ability to be in love with you. I think it was a love affair. I think it was. In some strange way.[15]

Clearly this statement also evokes Dolan's 'performative utopias', in as much as it is hard to protect from academic cynicism, and yet it is so essential in understanding the artistic make-up of Lyddiard's project. In anticipation of the reopening of the theatre in 2005, Graeme Rigby, a former board member of the theatre, writer and film maker, wrote a paper entitled 'Love and Roots'. He borrowed this phrase from a speech that the Maly Theatre's Michael Stronin had made at an international gathering of theatre directors in Newcastle in 2002. On that occasion, Stronin had used the phrase 'love and roots' to encapsulate what Lyddiard's Northern Stage stood for. In his paper, Rigby also remembers how those ensemble values of 'love and roots' were instilled by Dodin and how, during his visit in 1993, Dodin emphasised that 'Theatre is not the name of the building; theatre is a spiritual substance' (Dodin quoted in Rigby 2003). Even though Shevtsova too worries that some of Dodin's 'fluid conceptions' might have 'a hint of New Age go-with-the-flow' about them (Shevtsova 2004: 38), she finds the key in the fact that Dodin defines his approach to actor training, for example, not in terms of tangible results, but as a 'training of the heart and the nervous system' (p. 39) – an idea that she further explores in relation to non-canonical Stanislavsky but also to Grotowski and with regard to Dodin's notion of 'aliveness', which concerns the exchange of energy between the actor and the audience.

How did this translate into the Newcastle rehearsal room?

Work on *Stars in the Morning Sky* began early in 1993. Lev Dodin, his wife Tatiana Shestakova (a Maly actress)[16] and Michael Stronin spent two out of four weeks of rehearsal working with the company. My recent correspondence with two of the actors from this production – Deka Walmsley and Val McLane – suggests that the process had its difficulties. This is confirmed by Rigby, who in 'talking to the actors at the bar' found that the work had taken them 'a long way out of the comfort zone' (Rigby 2003). McLane recalls that the cast members had to do homework 'as per Stanislavsky i.e. writing biogs of our characters and accounts of the character's previous 24 hours', but some cast members were so terrified by the intensity of the process that they 'ran away and had to be persuaded to return'.[17]

Deka Walmsley observes that 'all the frustrations felt by the actors on the project stemmed from the same source – namely the clash of cultural working methods'.[18] Whereas Dodin had had the luxury of time to work with his company for eighteen months on their production of the play, the rehearsal period in this instance was very limited. This led to the feeling that working with Dodin under such conditions was not a true collaborative process 'but one in which we somehow felt obliged to embrace a working method which was rooted in a completely "alien" theatrical culture'. Although he provides an account of a rather uncomfortable exercise he underwent with another actor he had never worked with before, similarly to McLane, Walmsley finishes on a positive note, stating that this was an experience he 'would not have missed for the world':

> I was genuinely fascinated by [Dodin's] approach, and could fully understand Alan's desire to bring about some kind of co-production.

And out of that clash of approaches we moved forward and developed ways of working on future productions that were shaped by the experience.[19]

Interestingly, Walmsley notes that the production in which the ensemble values Lyddiard was pursuing actually did emerge was *Animal Farm*. Walmsley recalls that this production was initially made before Dodin's visit, with another touring version emerging later in 1993. According to Lyddiard, the production was made on a shoestring budget at the end of a financial year and was intended as a schools project. Nevertheless this was 'the first piece of work that I had done that came out of a desire to create a company of Geordie actors'.[20] He used Ian Wooldridge's adaptation, which had previously been done in schools in Strathclyde. Even though this project took place five years before the Northern Stage Ensemble was created, Walmsley observes that 'all the elements blended' to create an ensemble-like environment:

> Strong script that very much suited Alan's visual strength, strongly bonded actors and a choreographer [Frank McConnell] who both understood that we were not dancers and whose sense of theatricality was sublime. And all in 3 weeks!![21]

The production had only six cast members, including Lyddiard as Farmer Jones, as he could not afford another actor. According to Lyddiard, the key aesthetic influences on this production included Pina Bausch's *Rite of Spring*, and a photographic exhibition of Duane Michael which yielded the idea for its most memorable stage image – boots being worn on hands to indicate legs and the concept of 'Two legs good, four legs better'. In addition, Lyddiard cites Brith Gof's piece *Gododdin* as influential too, partly because of its use of music and physicality, and partly because it deals with a heroic and tragic uprising of a group of Welsh mercenaries against the British Army. This seems to have resonated with Lyddiard's pre-existing and ongoing concern with marginalised people, and of course his production of *Animal Farm* too – in which the protagonists are refugees from a war-torn land taking a rest in their journey – was a take on the war in Bosnia. This show was an immediate success. Peter Mortimer (1993) wrote in his *Guardian* review '[D]are I say it? – as good as the book!', and the popular demand for this production was so high that it was repeatedly revived for ten years and toured nationally and internationally.

What is particularly striking about this example is that it features none of the psychological realism that is the hallmark of Dodin's way of working. This suggests a key distinction between Lyddiard's work ethos, which is modelled on Dodin's, and his aesthetic approach, which is more easily traceable within his own development as an artist in the UK. By further extension, one might consider Dodin's influence on Lyddiard to have been methodological rather than necessarily artistic, and based on shared values rather than a dogmatic following. Even with *Stars in the Morning Sky*, Lyddiard seems to maintain an unquestioning commitment to Dodin's way of working and is grateful for the fact that, at the end of the fortnight, he had 'a company of performers who were entrenched in the world of the play, given to them by the original director'.[22] However, he is particularly excited when he recalls the opening to his show, which had 40 extras on stage, and the walls of the set, which spectacularly closed in on the protagonists.

Lyddiard's ability to maintain his creative integrity and individuality of vision while following the leadership of his 'guru' is perhaps the most interesting feature of this particular chapter. Even though he finds himself amid 'the clash of cultural working methods' – and distinct artistic sensibilities – he is able to transcend the perceived binary and engage with the core values of these different approaches. What he takes from Dodin therefore is not a methodology which has to be followed dogmatically, but a reinforcement of shared ideals – or even reinforcement of shared 'utopian performatives'.

Shevtsova notes that the phrase 'common language' is used frequently by Dodin 'to identify what is specific to the company' (Shevtsova 2004: 36). Dodin and Lyddiard appeared to find enough 'common language' between them to sustain their intense relationship for over ten years, even though they almost always communicated via an interpreter. Then again, the notion of 'common language' in Dodin's terms has as much to do with feelings, and 'is used intuitively rather than strategically, as dancers use their idiom [. . .] or jazz musicians when they improvise' (Shevtsova 2004: 47).

In this respect it is also valuable to consider Dodin's conception of adaptation itself, or his 'theatre of prose'. In the British theatre system we have grown accustomed to the idea that the best-qualified person for any adaptation or translation job is another playwright. Whereas a British playwright will then set about restructuring and rewriting their text to fit a dramatic concept of their choice, Dodin will instead go through the novel with his actors reading it aloud line by line, occasionally acting out certain segments or improvising around others. Contrasting Dodin's adaptation practice with that of Lyubimov, Shevtsova highlights that Lyubimov 'essentially adapted novels within literary parameters – that is by establishing texts – rather than striking out to create new, performance-led texts' (p. 46). This turns Dodin's rehearsal process into a kind of 'research' giving the actors a lot of responsibility for both immersing themselves in the context and for the 'writing with their bodies'. The actors are elevated from the position of 'interpreter' to 'co-author' of the production, which is always considered a 'living organism' (p. 51). The work exists for a long time memorised in actors' bodies instead of in the form of a script. Shevtsova likens this process to a choreographic practice and to the practice of an oral culture in which narratives are 'remembered and transmitted orally, long before they are written down' (p. 52). It is worth remembering that a Maly rehearsal process could easily take years. Eventually, Dodin makes decisions about how to layer and arrange the material and it is not unusual for him to make radical decisions at the last moment before the opening.

What is illuminating about the process described above is the way in which the language of performance is given its own autonomy and, by being open to judgement on its own terms, the work is potentially liberated from any sense of comparison or indebtedness to the 'original' – a practice which also brings to mind the work of Kneehigh, for example.[23] In other words, the respect towards the prose text on which the performance is based is bestowed on it not by a celebration of its literariness but by a deep investigation of its inner meanings, which – as in any process of translation, whether between art forms or between cultures – can only ever find an approximate semantic equivalent in another idiom. Thus, the only fidelity that is possible in the process of adaptation is the fidelity to one's own understanding of the text's meaning and the deployment of one's own expertise and language to enable it to effectively communicate the meanings of what has been understood and is being translated. Interestingly, this notion of translation between cultures points to another possible interpretation of the term 'utopian', meaning literally 'no place': that in order for something to be translated it has to be uprooted from the specificities of a particular place or culture – or 'unmoored from the familiar'. Translation (and by extension adaptation) itself is a 'utopian' endeavour.

The significance of this is twofold in relation to Lyddiard. As explained above, his relationship to Dodin involved a certain element of loyalty and ethical equivalence without dogmatic imitation. In addition, Lyddiard's own work – which was often based on adaptation of prose – similarly privileged the performance idiom over any attempted 'fidelity to the original text', although Lyddiard's performance idiom (which will be discussed further) was distinct from Dodin's.

Evidently then, Dodin's arrival in a Newcastle rehearsal room in a somewhat utopian manner in 1993 – to work with a number of actors, some of whom had never met each other before – led perhaps to a situation of cultural misunderstanding. However, by 1999, when he was invited again to lead a three-day workshop with the newly formed Northern Stage Ensemble on Chekhov's *Uncle Vanya*, the parameters were very differently set.[24]

It is worth noting that at this point the Northern Stage Ensemble was coming to the end of an extremely successful first season of work. Its first production, *A Clockwork Orange* (Figure 6.3) was touring around the

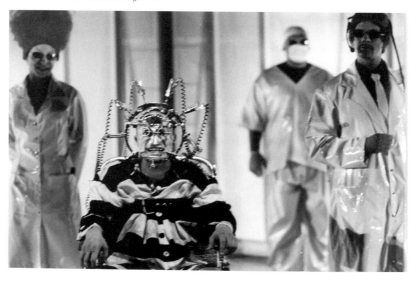

Figure 6.3 A Clockwork Orange. Copyright: Keith Pattison.

country and had only just missed going into the West End because Lyddiard was not prepared to recast it for ten instead of the fourteen people that were in it.

Following Dodin's request for a place in the country where the company would live together for the duration of the workshop, an old school was hired in the village of Allenheads in Northumberland and transformed by Neil Murray into 'something between a stage set and an installation' (Fisher 1999). Describing in detail the lit candles, vases, drapes, a log fire and a stack of newspapers tied with red ribbon, Fisher considers this to have been a space created not just to facilitate the right ambiance for the play but also to signal 'a place for serious artistic study'. During the three days, Dodin read the text aloud in Russian and spoke in an 'erudite' way about various aspects of the text and its analysis. In dealing with actors' insecurities and vulnerabilities on this occasion, Dodin came across as sympathetic and capable of 'perfect advice': 'You explored your knowledge of what was missing. [. . .] You will remember how uncomfortable it feels when you miss something' (quoted in Fisher 1999).[25]

Even though Lyddiard never persuaded Dodin to direct *Uncle Vanya* in Newcastle, the Ensemble went from strength to strength, both making projects in the region and in collaboration with European partners. Aside from Dodin and Brook, Alain Platel, Calixto Bieto, Gabor Tompa and Robert Lepage were all household names in Northern Stage and have all either produced and co-produced or presented work in the theatre. Of British companies, Complicité, Cheek by Jowl and DV8 were regular visitors, and Northern Stage co-created *Pandora's Box* with Kneehigh in 2002.

What was distinctive about Lyddiard's ensemble and his way of working?

Despite sharing with Dodin the interest in longevity and the ensemble way of working, Lyddiard understood that it would be pointless to try and adopt the Stanislavskian approach to acting with his ensemble, which consisted of individuals trained in very disparate traditions, if they had been trained at all.

Even though some of Lyddiard's actors did go to drama schools before embarking on their careers, the majority had emerged from university drama degrees (which by their nature tend to foster collaborative ways of working), or came into the theatre without any prior training in theatre at all (Darren Palmer had been a footballer, and Stephen Lamb came in through Northern Stage's work in schools). Lyddiard explains:

> I started from the premise of not necessarily wanting to work with actors, but with people who were from a particular place and a particular background and a particular ideology. And that was mainly working-class male actors . . . My principle idea about performance is that what I'm interested in is: who you are and what you do . . . And when I say 'express who you are' that's not an intellectual approach, it's a kind of emotional statement of being: 'I am here, this is me and I am fine'. That's what I wanted to get from the actors, or rather the performers – I always called them the performers, because I felt that they weren't necessarily in the traditional mode of training as an actor. You were a performer, and your self was the tool which you used to perform. So 'I am here, this is me and I am fine, and now what I'm doing is I'm approaching Shakespeare, or I'm approaching Chekhov, or I'm approaching *Clockwork Orange*, or I'm approaching George Orwell'. So my next step was to try to get who you are to confront what we were doing.[26]

In reviewing Lyddiard's production of *The Ballroom of Romance* in 2000, Lyn Gardner noted that the defining characteristic of Lyddiard's work was that 'it takes the lives of ordinary people surviving on the margins and makes them seem special, almost blessed' (Gardner quoted in Radosavljević 2009: 47). In a recent interview she gave me, she also recalled *The Factory Romeo and Juliet*, which was made in the first Ensemble season in 1998. Gardner admired this highly controversial adaptation which portrayed the main protagonists as people with special needs,[27] seeing it as 'absolutely subversive':

> [Whereas] so much British theatre is really about actors sitting there or standing somewhere and hurling situational chat at each other, none of Lyddiard's work was like that. The work owed as much to movies, to dance – it bled, it always bled.[28]

To illustrate the individuality of Lyddiard's style further, it is worth noting an observation made by the former Chief Executive of Northern Arts (and current CEO of Creative Scotland), Andrew Dixon, that Lyddiard was ahead of his time in his use of technology and live audio-visuals in performance:

> He was almost thinking digitally and thinking like a website before thinking digitally emerged.[29]

Most significantly however, the *Guardian*'s northern correspondent Alfred Hickling recalls that what struck him the most when he first went to Northern Stage was that upon opening the programme he found that everyone in the company was listed alphabetically starting with a cleaner, 'and then somewhere you got to L and it said Alan Lyddiard, Artistic Director'. He offers a further sobering comment that:

> The idea of everyone egalitarian and equal, I mean – you already sound like you are describing a communist utopia. I'm not making a value judgement whether it's right or wrong, all I'm saying is that there's an aspect of social utopia which is going to make some people suspicious and it's going to make other people feel energised and empowered. I think you don't make it any easier for yourself to find funding and support for all these things to survive.[30]

After the utopia

Hickling suggests that there is something 'almost intrinsically militant' and 'quite confrontational' about the championing of a model of working such as was Lyddiard's ensemble. As it turns out, Lyddiard admits that his project did make a lot of people angry in Newcastle; they were people in power and they were very passionately opposed to the kind of work that Lyddiard did.[31]

In my quest to discover what indeed led to the demise of the Northern Stage Ensemble I found that the explanation was a lot less dramatic than it seemed to be at the time. In January 2005, unexpectedly and despite the fact that he had lined up a whole series of projects for the near future, Lyddiard decided to resign and take a two-year Arts Council bursary to develop his international work. The situation in the organisation at the senior management level had not been healthy for a while. Things took a downward turn in 2002 when Mandy Stewart made the difficult decision to leave Northern Stage to run Leicester Haymarket and head up the refurbishment campaign of the Curve. This left Lyddiard in a vulnerable position as he was not fully supported by the then Chair of the Board, Fiona Ellis. A new Executive Director was selected and appointed by the Board without Lyddiard's approval. As a result, Lyddiard did not see eye to eye with the new Executive Director nor the newly appointed Marketing Director and this led to tension, ineffectiveness and a period of reduced productivity, especially after the closure of the theatre for refurbishment in the summer of 2004. Even though Lyddiard's resignation seemed like an outcome of a cloak and dagger scenario, he is very gracious when he recalls the circumstances of this event:

> That battle raged and it raged for months, maybe even as long as a year. And it destroyed me as an artist. I wasn't able to work well, I wasn't able to function well and I made some very bad mistakes. I made mistakes, I didn't do things right and I started losing my grip on the whole situation.[32]

A criticism often levelled at Lyddiard was a sense of patriarchalism which was inherent to his ensemble project and even confessed to by Lyddiard himself. A former ensemble member, Jim Kitson, observes that the main way Dodin influenced Lyddiard was 'by holding over the head of Alan Lyddiard the idea of a god-like director at the creative heart of a theatre company, a father figure and presiding artistic genius'.[33] This is indirectly confirmed by Lyddiard's admission:

> I lived the whole thing every day of my life, and I continued to live my life as my work. So I was living this ensemble, they were my family. I was like a father in a family and sometimes I was very, very bad tempered and pissed off with people but I loved them dearly and I tried to work with that love and I tried to work with that despair that they didn't do what they were told, and like a father, I tried to let them flourish but always held them back a little bit.[34]

Joanna Holden, a founder member who then went on to work with VTOL, Cirque du Soleil and Kneehigh, recalls a sense of 'great freedom' during her time with Northern Stage – everyone was free to voice their opinions, make requests related to their personal training needs and invited to participate in regular meetings where the 'way of working' would be discussed by ensemble members.[35] Similarly Kitson observes that 'Alan was extremely tolerant of mistakes, personal obsessions, arguments and hostility'.[36] As well as Dodin's belief that theatre is 'life itself', the notion of artistic director as 'father of the family' is compatible with the rhetoric shared by both directors concerning the ensemble as a 'family' and the theatre building as 'home'.[37] Interestingly, many of the outside observers I interviewed proffered this view of Lyddiard and Stewart as the parents of the company who held it together, and tended to see Stewart's departure in 2002 as the beginning of the end of the ensemble.

The second issue was financial. As noted above, although he was very much interested in engaging the community, Lyddiard was not interested in pandering to popular taste or to the commercial factor. Stewart testifies that Lyddiard was not averse to financial risk and they both saw more value in individual members of the public phoning in to say 'that performance last night changed my life' than a hundred people saying 'I quite liked that'.[38]

Mike Worthington, a supporter of Lyddiard, who succeeded Fiona Ellis as Chair of the Board in 2002, explains that for him the default position always was that 'ideally theatre in this country should be 50 per cent subsidised and 50 per cent generating its own income'. However, he points out that, when he took over as Chair, he found that the ratio at Northern Stage was 75:25 in favour of subsidy, which led him to believe that the ensemble model was not financially sustainable. He also expressed his belief that 'when the theatre closed for the best part of two years, there was an inevitable end to the ensemble'.[39]

Similarly, Andrew Dixon confesses that Lyddiard's project presented a dilemma for funders as on the one hand they wanted the public to see 'a whole range of work' rather than just one company of actors, but on the other hand they could also see the benefits of longevity and the success that it yields.[39] Dixon claims that, by creating opportunities for his ensemble members to perform both in village halls and internationally, Lyddiard gave them confidence and key experiences they would not have had otherwise. Although he does not consider the ensemble to be 'the most efficient use of the salary bill' he believes that Lyddiard took individual actors and turned them into 'theatre professionals', some of whom are now producing, directing and project managing very successful projects in the region.

Ruth Levitas claims that the recent resurgence of investment in utopias owes much to Ernest Bloch, a German theorist who during his exile in the United States in the 1930s wrote a major work *The Principle of Hope*, published upon his return to the German Democratic Republic in the 1950s. Levitas explains that the key principle of Bloch's thesis is that the human experience is marked by a sense of lack or longing which can be articulated only through imagining 'the means of its fulfilment' – a mechanism which gives rise to various kinds of fantasising, including utopian thinking itself. This brings to mind a particular lesson that Dodin bestowed on his Newcastle disciples: 'You explored your knowledge of what was missing' (Fisher 1999).

Shevtsova too finds that the existentialist distinction between 'being' and 'becoming' is particularly useful in relation to Dodin's creative process and that in such a context his work 'looks very much like research into potentiality, into what might become' (Shevtsova 2004: 55). This process of imagining a 'potentiality' certainly extends to the audience too, in the form in which Dolan explores 'utopian performatives' through the majority of her volume. In this sense, another insight of Levitas proffered in the domain of scientific enquiry is crucial – and applicable to both theatre experience and to Virginie Magnat's idea of utopia-inspired creative process as 'the art of losing our moorings in the familiar':

> Utopia creates a space in which the reader is addressed not just cognitively, but experientially, and enjoined to consider and feel what it would be like not just to live differently, but to want differently – so that the taken-for-granted nature of the present is disrupted. This is what sociologists call defamiliarising the familiar.
>
> (Levitas 2005)

Perhaps the point of Lyddiard's project was just to offer a possibility, or a potentiality, of a different way of working which would unmoor us from the familiar. It seems interesting that similarly to a typical dystopian narrative – such as Lyddiard's signature piece *Animal Farm* – the story of this particular utopia seems to have met its end as a result of the crisis of leadership. However, unlike Orwell's suggestion that a crisis of leadership, and therefore of utopia itself, is linked to moral corruptibility of the leaders, this particular situation seems to point to a more pragmatic conflict between irreconcilable ideological positions.

Acknowledgements

I would like to thank everyone whose testimonies are quoted in this text for giving their time so generously to this research project. Thank you also to Alex Elliott and Tracey Wilkinson for their testimonies, which have sadly not survived to the final draft, and to Annie Rigby for sending me the only surviving copy of a video made during the Dodin and Northern Stage residency in Allenheads. Special thanks are due to Neil Murray and Saša

Savić for helping to digitise Keith Pattison's photographs for use in this publication. Finally, many thanks to Paul Allain and Jonathan Pitches for comments on earlier drafts of the paper.

Notes

1 Most critics of Dolan's book were sceptical of her endeavour, cautioning against her 'rehabilitation of humanism' and 'a modified version of universalism' (Reinelt 2007: 215). It might be speculated that, since the end of communism, any kind of utopianism, alongside other varieties of idealism, became unfashionable or just synonymous with implicit forms of oppression. In a 2005 lecture, the sociologist Ruth Levitas recognised that the term had started to regain currency in scientific research, with writers such as Susan McManus proposing that 'the "fictive" is an inescapable ground of political theory' (McManus 2005: 1) and that indeed the very process of political theorisation should involve an element of utopian imagination. Meanwhile, a fellow-survivor of the Yugoslav utopia, Slavoj Žižek, has also noted that in the post-Socialist age, we should make space for the kind of utopia that is not just based on 'free imagination', but 'is a matter of innermost urgency' (Žižek in Taylor 2007). Interestingly most of these cases for the rehabilitation of the term coming from political philosophers seem to be focusing on the creative and empowering potential of the utopian mode of thinking.

2 Underscored with a recorded version of *Jerusalem*, the piece opened with a group of refugees who pause in their migrations to tell each other the story and ended with a choral rendition of a folk song from the Balkans.

3 Interview with Alan Lyddiard, Canterbury, 3 December 2009.

4 See Dawson-Scott (2009) and Facebook discussion thread on 'Witch's Blood – the Play', http://www.facebook.com/topic.php?uid=2217782995&topic=3790 (accessed 10 July 2010).

5 Interview with Alan Lyddiard, Canterbury, 3 December 2009.

6 *The Man Who* was inspired by Oliver Sacks' neurological study *The Man Who Mistook His Wife for a Hat*; it was originally made by Brook in French in 1993 and presented in English in 1994.

7 Interview with Mandy Stewart, Queen Elizabeth Hall, London, 23 April 2010.

8 Interview with Alan Lyddiard, Canterbury, 3 December 2009.

9 Theatre by the Lake website, http://www.theatrebythelake.co.uk/about_us.asp?page=22 (accessed 14 July 2010).

10 To give an idea of scale, it may be worth noting that, during the annual RSC residence in Newcastle, work from the Royal Shakespeare Theatre would usually be presented at the Theatre Royal, and work from the Swan would go onto the Playhouse main stage.

11 Lyddiard claims that his and Stewart's project bid also inspired the formation of the Dundee Rep Ensemble under Hamish Glen – an ensemble that is still going strong under a new leadership.

12 Interview with Mandy Stewart, Queen Elizabeth Hall, London, 23 April 2010.

13 It had thirteen performers in it: Francisco Alfonsin, Mark Calvert, Alex Elliott, Rebecca Hollingsworth, Mark Lloyd, Anthony Neilson, Peter Peverly, Janine Birkett, Maggie Carr, Craig Conway, Joanna Holden, Stephen Lamb and Darren

Palmer. The first seven of these performers stayed until 2005, although others came back occasionally. Two new permanent members, Jim Kitson and Jane Arnfield, joined the ensemble in later stages and stayed until the end. The Northern Stage Ensemble also had Company Manager Amanda Purvis, Stage Manager Niall Black, Deputy Stage Manager Colin Holman, Assistant Stage Manager Nicola Irvine. The information here has been verified with both Irvine (who later became the Deputy Stage Manager) and Purvis.

14 Glenny's (1989) introduction to his translation of the play states that the Maly's Russian-language production was shown as part of the Glasgow Mayfest on 9 May 1988 and at the Riverside Studios in London on 18 May 1988.

15 Interview with Alan Lyddiard, Canterbury, 3 December 2009. For the purposes of this research I also attempted to arrange an interview with Dodin through his assistant Dina Dodina. Although in her last piece of correspondence Dodina intimated that she knew 'Lev would enjoy speaking about Alan' (email correspondence, 5 May 2010), this interview was sadly never completed because of Dodin's travelling commitments.

16 Shestakova is credited in Glenny's translation of the play as a co-director of the original production as well as the actress playing Anna (Glenny 1989: 64).

17 Correspondence with Val McLane, 7 June 2010.

18 Correspondence with Deka Walmsley, 7 May 2010.

19 Correspondence with Deka Walmsley, 7 May 2010.

20 Interview with Alan Lyddiard, Canterbury, 3 December 2009.

21 Correspondence with Deka Walmsley, 7 May 2010.

22 Interview with Alan Lyddiard, Canterbury, 3 December 2009.

23 In a recent interview Emma Rice explained how her six months of working with Gardzienice in Poland in 1990 was extremely influential on her as an actress and artist, and it affected her own relationship to her work profoundly. However, her work is ultimately based on her own British identity and heritage (Radosavljević 2010: 95). Similarly, her adaptation methodology is based not on the principle of 'fidelity' to the original work but on her own 'emotional memory' of it (p. 97).

24 Initially Lyddiard wanted Dodin to direct the play with the Northern Stage Ensemble, but Dodin was adamant that he only worked with his own actors. He did agree to a workshop instead and, replicating one of his own rehearsal techniques, asked for a place in the country where the company could live together in isolation for the duration of the workshop – and where they could sing together, sleep together and eat together.

25 The actor and musician Jim Kitson, who was a newcomer to the process, recalls that working with Dodin was 'essentially a cerebral experience'. Even though, in his recollection, Dodin never talked about what the play was about thematically, he gave a very detailed account of why every character did and said everything that they did and why they remained silent. Kitson observes that, as someone who came to this experience from physical theatre and the school of thought that was 'ossifying around the rejection of the psychological as a reason to do anything', he found 'the novelty of being told what to do [. . .] very liberating' as an actor, and the improvisations 'easy and enjoyable' (correspondence with Jim Kitson, 14 July 2010).

26 Interview with Alan Lyddiard, Newcastle, 12 April 2010.

27 In addition, the most unlikely ensemble members, Joanna Holden and Mark Calvert, played the leads. Holden, who is often cast in comic roles, remembers

that she was in her thirties, a bit plump, and that she was very shocked when the casting was announced: 'even from the age of 12, I was nurse material as opposed to Juliet' (interview with Holden, London, 2 May 2010).

28 Interview with Lyn Gardner, Wimbledon, 27 May 2010.
29 Interview with Andrew Dixon, Baltic Place, Gateshead, 13 April 2010.
30 Interview with Alfred Hickling, Arts Café, Leeds, 14 April 2010.
31 This perspective is legitimised as being more than just mere parochialism when we consider the cry of Slavoj Žižek that 'the mother of all crimes' in the context of radical liberalism amounts to the 'brutal imposition of one's own view onto others' (Žižek 2007: para. 3). In capitalism and the free market economy, which according to Žižek exemplifies the principle that 'human nature is egotistic' (ibid.), a vision of egalitarianism – even if only in the context of a 'utopian perfomative' – is clearly untenable.
32 Interview with Alan Lyddiard, Newcastle, 12 April 2010.
33 Correspondence with Jim Kitson, 14 July 2010.
34 Interview with Alan Lyddiard, Newcastle, 12 April 2010.
35 Interview with Joanna Holden, London, 2 May 2010.
36 Correspondence with Jim Kitson, 14 July 2010.
37 Interestingly, as pointed out by Shevtsova, Dodin struggled with professional homelessness at the start of his career. Meanwhile Lyddiard's current theatre project involves collaboration with the homelessness charity Crisis, which is intended to culminate in an international adaptation of Orwell's *Down and Out in Paris and London.*
38 Interview with Mandy Stewart, Queen Elizabeth Hall, London, 23 April 2010.
39 Interview with Mike Worthington, Northern Stage, Newcastle, 13 April 2010.
40 Interview with Andrew Dixon, Baltic Place, Gateshead 13 April 2010.

Bibliography

Bayley, C. (1995) 'No More Fog on the Tyne', *The Independent*, 17 May, http://www.independent.co.uk/arts-entertainment/no-more-fog-on-the-tyne-1619884.html (accessed 14 July 2010).

Bennett, S. (1996) *Performing Nostalgia: Shifting Shakespeare and the Contemporary Past*, London: Routledge.

Bennett, S. (2006) 'Review of Jill Dolan: *Utopia in Performance*', *Theatre Journal*, 58, 4 (December), 728–30.

Craig, S. (ed.) (1980) *Dreams and Deconstructions: Alternative Theatre in Britain*, Ambergate: Amber Lane Press.

Dawson-Scott, R. (2009) 'Billy Mackenzie and the Associates Show Is a Winner in Dundee', *STV Entertainment*, http://entertainment.stv.tv/onstage/102822-billy-mackenzie-and-the-associates-show-is-a-winner-in-dundee/ (accessed 10 July 2010).

Delgado, M. and Heritage, P. (1996) *In Contact with the Gods?: Directors Talk Theatre*, Manchester: Manchester University Press.

Delgado, M. and Rebellato, D. (eds) (2010) *Contemporary European Theatre Directors*, Oxon: Routledge.

Dodin, L. (2005) *Journey without End: Reflections and Memoirs*, London: Tantalus Books.

Dolan, J. (2001) 'Performance, Utopia and the "Utopian Performative"', *Theatre Journal*, 53, 3 (October), 455–79.

Dolan, J. (2005) *Utopia in Performance: Finding Hope at the Theater*, Ann Arbor: University of Michigan Press.

Fisher, M. (1999) Original draft of an article about the Lev Dodin and Northern Stage residency in Allenheads, published in the *Glasgow Herald*, provided by Fisher by email.

Fuchs, E. (2007) 'Review of Jill Dolan: *Utopia in Performance*', *Theatre Research International*, 32: 198–99.

Glenny, M. (introduction and trans.) (1989) *Stars in the Morning Sky: Five New Plays from the Soviet Union*, London: Nick Hern Books.

Gardner, L. (2000) 'Distilled Emotions', http://www.guardian.co.uk/culture/2000/sep/23/artsfeatures1 (accessed 15 July 2010).

Hickling, A. (2001) 'Northern Stage's Staggering 1984', 23 March, http://www.guardian.co.uk/culture/2001/mar/23/artsfeatures (accessed 4 May 2010).

Kershaw, B. (1993) 'Poaching in Thatcherland: A Case of Radical Community Theatre', *New Theatre Quarterly*, 9:34, 121–33.

Levitas, R. (2005) 'The Imaginary Reconstitution of Society, or Why Sociologists and Others Should Take Utopia More Seriously', Inaugural Lecture, University of Bristol, 24 October, http://www.bristol.ac.uk/sociology/staff/inaugural.doc (accessed 10 July 2010).

Lichtenfels, P. (2010) 'Lev Dodin: The Director and Cultural Memory', in Delgado, M. and Rebellato, D. (eds), *Contemporary European Theatre Directors*, Oxon: Routledge, pp. 69–86.

Magnat, V. (2005) 'Devising Utopia, or Asking for the Moon', *Theatre Topics*, 15, 1, 73–86.

McManus, S. (2005) *Fictive Theories: Towards a Deconstructive and Utopian Political Imagination*, Basingstoke: Palgrave.

Mortimer, P. (1993) '*Animal Farm*', *The Guardian*, 10 February 1993 (no page, cutting supplied by author).

Radosavljević, D. (2009) 'The Need to Keep Moving: Remarks on the place of a Dramaturg in Twenty-First Century England', *Performance Research: 'On Dramaturgy'*, 14 (3), 45–51.

Radosavljević, D. (2010) 'Emma Rice in Interview with Duška Radosavljević', *Journal of Adaptation in Film and Performance*, 3, 1, 89–97.

Rebellato, D. (1999) *1956 and All That: The Making of Modern British Drama*, London: Routledge.

Reinelt, J. (2007) 'Review of Jill Dolan: Utopia in Performance', *Theatre Survey*, 48: 215–217.

Rigby, G. (2003) 'Love and Roots: Towards a Centre for European Performing Arts', manuscript from the Board papers of Northern Stage.

Rowell G. and Jackson A. (1984) *The Repertory Movement: A History of Regional Theatre in Britain*, Cambridge: Cambridge University Press.

Shevtsova, M. (2004) *Dodin and the Maly Drama Theatre: Process to Performance*, London: Routledge.

Smeliansky, A. (1999) *The Russian Theatre after Stalin*, Cambridge: Cambridge University Press.

Tarshis, N. (2006) 'Director Lev Dodin and his Maly Drama Theatre (MDT) in Saint Petersburg', in Wyneken, R. (ed.), 'Russian Theatre between Tradition and Revival', special issue of *Kultura*, 11 (November), 16–18.

Taylor, A. (dir.) (2007) *Žižek!*, Hidden Driver Productions, USA.

Wyneken, R. (2006) 'Russia's Opening to the West and Russian Holy Theatre', in Wyneken, R. (ed.), 'Russian Theatre between Tradition and Revival', special issue of *Kultura*, 11 (November), 3–7.

Žižek, S. (2007) 'The Liberal Utopia: The Market Mechanism for the Race of Devils', http://www.lacan.com/zizliberal2.htm (accessed 17 July 2010).

7

RE-VISIONED DIRECTIONS
Stanislavsky in the twenty-first century[1]

Bella Merlin and Katya Kamotskaia

Introduction

Stanislavsky was adamant that his 'system' should not be seen as dogma. Indeed, how could it be, when an overview of his writings reveals the way in which his theories changed throughout his life in response to his discoveries as a practitioner? It may be fair to assume, therefore, that implicit in his legacy is the tacit permission granted to his successors to continue evolving and re-visioning those acting practices prompted by his teachings.

This chapter charts a contribution to such re-visions by two contemporary practitioners – Kamotskaia and Merlin – both of whom are actors *and* teachers; hence, their experiential knowledge is garnered from both sides of the fourth wall.

In the first section, Kamotskaia explores the concept of 'systematic' training (the basis of her doctoral thesis) from her perspective of teaching at the Royal Scottish Academy of Music and Drama (RSAMD) since 1999. Using re-visioned implementations of Stanislavsky's principles, she addresses the nature of 'inner process' (her interpretation of Stanislavsky's 'unbroken line') and how it can be trained, in order to diminish the 'gaps' in onstage logic out of which an actor's fear and self-judgement may spring.

The second section comprises a case-study of *The Seagull*, directed by Kamotskaia with Merlin as Arkadina (Figure 7.1). The ensemble for the production at the University of California (UC) Davis included professional actors and undergraduate students with a diversity of trainings, backgrounds and experience. Merlin records the rehearsal process adopted by Kamotskaia, as influenced by the practices of the Russian director Anatoli Vassiliev (and Kamotskaia's individual interpretation of his *nagavor* or 'talking through'), and informed by Kamotskaia's own training as an

Figure 7.1 Act 1, *The Seagull,* set designed by Jamie Kumf, lighting designed by Jacob W. Nelson, costumes designed by Sarah Kendrick. Photograph: Kristine Slipson © University of California, Davis.

actor at Vakhtangov's Shchukin Institute (Moscow) and Grotowski's Teatr Laboratorium (Poland).

1: Katya Kamotskaia and training 'inner process'

Background

As a student-actor in 1970s Moscow, my experience of Soviet Russian actor training was extremely hard, for three fundamental reasons.

First of all, I personally found Stanislavsky's writings were rather generalised. His ideas are absolutely ingenious and he covers everything we need as actors, and yet he is often unclear in articulating how each component integrates deeply into a whole, implementable 'system'. This generality is understandable: in his desire to turn the art of acting into a valued profession, Stanislavsky sought to commit to paper everything about acting that he possibly could, which in itself was simply too big a process. Added to which, psychology was still very young as a science, leaving certain principles inevitably generalised.

Second, I was scared and demoralised by self-judgement – but that was how we were trained in the Soviet Union because that was how our teachers were trained. When all one ever hears is criticism, the whole process of acting becomes very difficult, as inner – and outer – judgement blocks any creative spontaneity.

Third, I did not always understand how the components of our Soviet actor training fitted together coherently to make us better actors. The early stages involved a very particular sequence of exercises. The first step in this sequence began with very simple, solo, mimed études, to encourage us as actors just to exist on stage without any disruptions to our inner state. The second step introduced into the given circumstances a 'problem'; for example, you are sitting alone and you read a letter, the contents of which provoke a change in you to which you must immediately respond, truthfully and spontaneously. The third step featured études with a partner; the exercises were still silent at first, involving given circumstances which legitimised the silence; for example, you are both in a library together and the only way you can communicate is without words. While these exercises made sense in themselves, their relevance to rehearsals, or to acting practice as a whole, was never overly explained. I now understand that there was no explanation because our tutors did not necessarily have one. They were taking their exercises directly from Stanislavsky's books with (as yet) very little direct questioning or interpreting of his 'system'. They did not necessarily know how to fit all the components together, because Stanislavsky does not specifically explain – probably because he did not yet know. Therefore, the generalisations inherent in Stanislavsky's writings led to generalisations in the classroom – both in our tutors' teaching and our learning.

When I myself started to teach acting in the 1980s, I took these three problems – (1) the obscurity of some of Stanislavsky's works, (2) the actor's need to overcome self-judgement, and (3) the clear purpose of an exercise – as key strategies in developing my own actor training. In some ways, it is hard to tell which aspects of my teaching method are absolutely my own, because of course I am integrating the knowledge that I was given. That knowledge came from my teachers (including Vladimir Poglasov, Professor at the Shchukin Institute; Alla Kazanskaia, who was a direct student of Vakhtangov; Antonina Kutznesova, Professor at GITIS (the Russian University of Theatre Arts); and Albert Filozov, Professor at VGIK, the All Russian State Institute of Cinematography), from my directors and from Stanislavsky, not to mention the books that I have read. Certainly, working on Benedetti's translations clarified some of Stanislavsky's ideas (as I outline below). One of the biggest influences on my professional practice has been the director Anatoli Vassiliev, whom I have known for nearly thirty years, including attendance at many of his rehearsals for Slavkin's *Cerceau* and Gorky's *Vassa* at the Taganka Theatre, Moscow, as well as workshops, conversations, and a one-week international laboratory at the School for the Dramatic Arts (2005).

However, the one area in which I know my method is purely mine is that it comes from my personal actor's pain: my own terrible mistakes and my own horrible feeling on stage. Chekhov knew exactly what he was talking about when he has Nina say in *The Seagull*, 'I didn't know what to do with my hands, I didn't know how to stand, I couldn't control my voice. You don't understand what it's like when you feel you're acting badly' (Chekhov 1993: 122). I know what it feels like when you have no idea what is coming next and your sole preoccupation is how to stop yourself from trembling. When I started to teach, I saw students acting and feeling as horrible as I do when I am acting badly, and it prompted the thought: 'How is it possible to put a system in place to enable them to feel more in balance?' And – more importantly – to provide them with a sense of professionalism: to know *what* they are doing, *why* they are doing it, and *how* to achieve whatever is required of them by the script and the director.

With regard to the third problem – the purpose of an exercise – I knew my task was to make my exercises more and more precise. In my early teaching years, my explanations were too vague: this in turn revealed that my understanding of the *purpose* behind the exercises was too vague – just as it had been with my own teachers. I could see it in the work of my students. When an actor becomes general in his or her onstage actions – usually because they do not know the specific purpose or task – they can become distracted by the *wrong* task: for example, they start to try to impress their audience. This can lead to irrelevant or even uncomfortable sensations on stage. I could see my students were more preoccupied with impressing me than with building their inner state. As an actor trainer, I knew that – if I was to help them – I had to search for clarity in my own understanding of Stanislavsky's exercises. In fact, it was in the process of teaching some of the exercises which I myself had undertaken as a student that I began to uncover many of the hidden truths in my own – albeit painful – training. Not least was to ensure that the actors' onstage tasks were more interesting to them than the desire to be good for the teacher, director or audience.

Creating a methodology: inner process

'Methodology', as I understand it, involves having a very clear picture of what one is aiming for – and that can be curiously elusive in actor training. My primary goal is to guide actors who, most of the time, are going to be working with directors who will not be able to help them in the ways in which they need. One of the striking differences between artistic education in Britain and Russia is the absence of structured director training. Whereas it is rare in Russia to serve even as an Assistant Director without having undergone the requisite five-year training at an established conservatory (during which time, many classes are fundamental actor training, and the same Stanislavsky-based terminology with its general meaning is used right across schools, theatres and studios), in Britain a director's avenue into the industry is predominantly through university experience or comparatively short, postgraduate courses at drama schools. Such education can be haphazard and dependent on opportunity, rather than rigour. As I perceive it, if there is no systematic director training, there will inevitably be no universal system in the rehearsal room, and this in turn can leave actors adrift. In developing my actor training, I have focused on preparing actors to develop their inner creative state[2] and to incarnate truthful characters, regardless of the director or the medium.

At RSAMD, my main responsibility is to teach the first-year 'Foundations of Acting' course. At the end of their first year, these students will have to face performing in a production. Therefore, my 'supertask' is to teach them over the course of that year how to inhabit all the details of a production, how to find what I call a clear 'inner process' and – having found it – how to use and to develop it constantly.

For me, 'inner process' is different from 'subtext', because it is not just about words: it is about the 'understream' or 'undercurrent' running beneath (and maybe contrapuntally to) those words. In *An Actor's Work*, Stanislavsky states that actors should have an 'unbroken line' (Stanislavsky 2008: 286),[3] but he is not absolutely clear what that unbroken line is. I have known this phrase all my working life, but it is only in the last few years – since combining my consultancy work on *An Actor's Work* with my lifetime of teaching and directing experience – that I have really understood what he means. As I interpret it, that unbroken line *is* the actor's 'inner process'.

This inner process is constant: as human beings, we always have plans in our head, inner monologues. Sometimes we have immediate questions to which we have immediate responses. Sometimes, however, those responses are not immediate: they might occur in ten minutes, or an hour, or a month. As my co-director Mark Stevenson (of *The Seagull* and of my company, StanStudio) expresses it, inner process is a constant questioning going on in our heads: we ask ourselves questions, and we get an emotional response, which will lead to an action, which will lead to a thought, and so it goes on.

As human beings, our inner life is very complex. And it is made more complex for an actor playing a character, as some of that inner process is connected with the *fictional* given circumstances of the character and some of it is concerned with the *actual* given circumstances of being an actor on stage or in front of a camera. Inner process is, therefore, a mixture of character and acting task. Nor is it restricted to realism or any other genre: it exists every second in every kind of theatre, just as it exists every second in life. Depending on the style, we apply it differently, we dress it differently, we play it differently – not least because it exists at different speeds. In Chekhov, we can take a pause; in Shakespeare, we do not have time: we have to think a little ahead of the line or the thought is destroyed. Inner process is a fundamental, human activity. My work as a teacher and director is to assist young actors to access for themselves and utilise constructively this natural activity within the artificial structures of theatre and film.

Training 'inner process'

I know from my own experience, that actors feels secure and happy when they achieve a 'level of existence' on stage, when they forget about themselves. By that I do not mean that they forget who they are, as I do not believe in 'losing oneself in the character'. A 'level of existence' on stage means thinking in the logic of the character, and as a result the actor cares about what the character cares about; they care about the other characters on the stage; they forget (in a healthy sense) that they are being watched, and therefore they stop judging themselves.

Finding the unbroken line is about eliminating the gaps in one's onstage existence. Gaps occur when an actor's thoughts become fractured by concerns unrelated to the life of the play, such as 'What am I doing with my hands? Do I have my props? Why are the audience so noisy? Why is that actor not looking at me?' In those moments when the line is broken, fear and panic start, and out of those gaps leap all the falsehoods which have nothing to do with the character's narrative and consequently result in self-judgement and fragmented creativity.

My contemporary application of Stanislavsky to acting processes is consciously geared towards the erasure of those gaps and to the training of the unbroken line. This training has two particular tasks on which I constantly focus my students. The first is to observe their own inner lives: this research on themselves involves observing how their anger 'works', how their happiness 'works', how they respond when they are facing problems, how they talk, how they face difficulties with another person. In many ways, it is primitive psychology. I am inviting them to learn about themselves and their own personal, psychological processes, so that every time they look at a scene they are asking themselves Stanislavsky's fundamental question: 'How would I behave in these given circumstances?' The question 'how' is just the beginning of the enquiry. The more significant question is *why* they behave in a particular way. When can they afford to reveal their emotions? When do they need to hide their emotions? The students' fundamental research on themselves – through which they become increasingly acquainted with their uniquely personal, inner processes – is one very general kind of task, which actually goes all the way from the beginning of their actor training to the end of their professional careers.

The second task is to decode the character. This involves asking questions such as: '*What* are they saying?' And then: '*Why* are they saying it in with these particular words and not others?' I am not concerned with any specific way of saying the words, but rather *why* they are saying these words in the first place. Much of this is to do with 'textual analysis' (see below).

Although these two tasks – observing their own inner lives and decoding the character – inform all their acting work, my training with the first-years at RSAMD is divided into three very clear-cut terms, each of which has a slightly different goal, orientated towards creating and feeling the 'logic and sequence'[4] of inner process.

Term 1: Simplicity, openness, vulnerability

The first term focuses on very simple exercises, often starting with the quality of touch and how we make physical contact (hands, faces etc.). These are deliberately simple games in order to keep the actors focused on themselves, on their task and on their partners. This quality of simplicity ensures that the first stages in building inner process are sure and secure. All we are doing is awakening basic sensory experiences. Despite this simplicity, I pay close attention to the nature of the group, sometimes changing the tasks according to their makeup, as some exercises are too adventurous for certain groups and my primary goal is not to scare them. This fundamental principle of my teaching – not to scare my actors – again arises out of the experience of my own Soviet teaching, which was extremely strict. I regularly heard my teachers shouting, 'No, wrong! False! Do it again!' This teaching tactic was possibly due in part to their own uncertainty about the specifics of Stanislavsky's 'system'. Although they could see that our acting was 'false', they were not necessarily equipped to help us in a very precise way to improve our acting and – as many teachers acknowledge – it is always hard to admit to students that you do not know the answers. They may also have felt vindicated in their approach, given Stanislavsky's own notoriety for stopping actors when they had barely walked on stage with the cry, 'No, I don't believe you!' We know as actors that to be false on stage is extremely dangerous, because we *feel* it. And if we feel it, we judge ourselves, and if we judge ourselves it is very difficult to hear the truth and almost impossible to move forward. So, if we cannot feel the truth, we have to start again from the very beginning. So: simplicity, safety, belief in our own actions – these are crucial steps in laying down the unbroken line of inner process.

Term 2: Textual analysis

The second term focuses on text. Although we may only work on one scene towards a very tiny, in-class presentation, we must understand that, in order to do just one scene, we have to go through the whole play – or at least until the point at which the scene happens, and sometimes further. This is what I call 'textual analysis'. However, I know that even this phrase can be misunderstood or misrepresented, and I am aware that what *I* consider textual analysis can be very different from the norm, as I discovered when one of my colleagues said, 'Oh, textual analysis – you do it at university and it's so boring!' I have no interest in anything too dry or too historically orientated. Textual analysis for me involves treating the characters like human beings and finding out (a) *what* is going on in their minds and (b) *how* their minds operate. This kind of analysis is absolutely necessary, and I personally do not understand how to work on a scene without it.

In my re-visioning of textual analysis, I rarely break a text down formally into bits of action as many directors do – unless it seems to be essential and the actors feel the need for it. That said, I *am* looking for what I call the 'changes'. Changes are absolutely necessary. An actress playing Masha in *Three Sisters* has to know when she changes her inner logic in Act 1 from 'I'm in a bad mood and I want to go home' to 'I'm staying for breakfast'. Of course it is not at the moment when she says, 'I'm staying for breakfast': she changed earlier, and the actress has to know why. How did the thought appear in her head? When did it start? How did it grow? And what prompted her to say it out loud? At the heart of these questions lie her relationship with Vershinin and the effect that he has on her during the first act. Understanding of relationships is the most important research to come from textual analysis. That then gives a very clear task to the actors: 'What am I doing in relation to my partner?'

Most of the textual analysis that I encourage actually happens on the actors' feet. My practice is not dissimilar to Stanislavsky's and Maria Knebel's Active Analysis, though my own 'transmission' of these practices has been filtered through a very brief, but intense, period spent in *The Tree of People* workshop at Grotowski's Teatr Laboratorium in Poland. Based on the work I experienced there led by (amongst others) Ryszard Cieslak, Rena Mirecka and Zygmunt Molik, I have evolved a series of extended improvisations. These are essentially exercises in which – without words – the actors explore their relationships, their conflicts, their connections with characters with whom they do not necessarily have any scenes in the play but still (when they look at this person on stage) they have to know what they feel about them – after all, it is a human being. (See section 2 for further details.)

The result of these extended improvisations is a very deep understanding on the part of the actors of the whole play. Without this deep understanding, they will have to believe *me* as the director and accept *my* understanding of the play, which ultimately will not be enough for them.

Furthermore, the improvisations can be used to create backstory and biography, as well as build up emotional experience. To quote Stevenson again (who was originally one of my students when I first experimented with these extended improvisations at RSAMD):

> If in the play, you don't know how the characters met, then you can use the silent improvisations to explore the first stages of flirting, etc. Although that information might never be cited directly in the script, it's there as a real memory for you as an actor in the play and it feeds your emotional life. It's real. It's something you actually experienced with the other actors, rather than imaginatively having to separate yourself from what's going on in performance to access an analogous [autobiographical] feeling.[5]

The nature of these extended improvisations changes according to the actors with whom I am working, as I watch where they naturally go with a script and what is comfortable for them as a group. Always my task is to encourage them to be open. When they are open, they give me raw material and, as I observe the dynamic of the group, I understand the kind of questions I can provoke and the direction in which the improvisations can go, as well as the help that I can offer them individually. The more mature the actors, the more adventurous the discussions and the improvisations can be. The more research they draw from the physicalised textual analysis, the more it provokes their thoughts and playful imaginations.

Certainly, the second term of my first-years' training is really about 'the playfulness of thought'. I do not want the students' understanding of textual analysis to be heavy and dead. I want them to understand that they are *thinking* and *playing* at the same time. The more playful they can be, the more they will unlock the thought processes of the lines: they will discover when the lines express significant information, and when sometimes the lines express nothing, when sometimes the lines are just noise and mask while something far deeper is going on beneath the words.

Term 3: A proposed ethos for directing; aesthetics, ethics, technique

The third term of the first year focuses on production. Much of the work stems from the discoveries of the textual analysis explored during Term 2, though now we are dealing with the problems of how to keep a whole play in your head, and not just a scene. How can you make the whole story clear? How do you deal with space? How do you deal with props?

Many so-called directors in our current industry are in fact producers. They are very skilful in their ability to produce, and productions remain technically proficient. However, a good director also has to be teacher to the acting company and a creator with an artistic vision. Artistic vision has nothing necessarily to do with concepts, lighting, sounds, *mise-en-scène* and so on. It is a vision of the world: it is the director's personal humanity. A very good director would ideally have an understanding of what Stanislavsky termed Aesthetics, Ethics and Technique.

The Russian actor Petr Ershov (1910–94) trained under Stanislavsky in the 1930s. His book, *Teknologia Iskustvo Aktiorskovo* (*Technology of the Actor*, Ershov 1992) details Stanislavsky's definition of his 'system' (as Ershov was taught it) as a science that could be realised from three sides, like a kind of pyramid. If you develop each of the three sides, working from the surface towards the deepest part, a shared core can be found. This shared, middle core is the whole – the heart – of acting process, and the three sides are Aesthetics, Ethics and Technique. Many confusions concerning Stanislavsky's 'system' stem from one person assessing it from one side of the pyramid, another from the second side and another from the third side. Subsequently, each person claims their one side as *the* interpretation of Stanislavsky's 'system'. And yet, each will only give one perspective of a far more complex and holistic entity.

The first side – Aesthetics – essentially concerns the science of what theatre is and why we need it in human society. Stanislavsky's speech during the first lesson for students and actors at the Moscow Art Theatre in 1911 highlights this:

> The harm caused by a bad book cannot be compared with that caused by a bad theatre, either in the extent of the infection or the ease with which it spreads. And yet, the theatre as an institution . . . [is] an instrument of education . . . primarily, of course, of the aesthetic education of the masses. Thus you see what a powerful force we are preparing ourselves to wield. You see how responsible we are to [ensure] that this force is used as it should be.
>
> (Stanislavsky 1953: 27)

Although many young actors today will go on to film and television rather than theatre, the power they hold as actors and storytellers remains no less relevant, regardless of medium.

The second side – Ethics – is directly connected to the first, and concerns the qualities that an actor needs in order to serve this kind of theatre or acting. Stanislavsky's own writings on ethics arise from a time of serious challenge to the state of theatre – drunkenness, actors not knowing their lines, little experience or understanding of the power of the ensemble. Although the crises in the arts may have changed in our own, economically challenged time, Stanislavsky's words still have resonance:

> Ethics is the science of morals. This science elaborates the correct moral standards, which help to keep the human soul safe from corruption and which regulate the mutual relations between people and whole countries. Like every other citizen the actor has got to know the laws of social ethics and abide by them . . . The first condition is teamwork.
> (Stanislavsky 1984: 107)

The third side of the pyramid connects the first and second, and this is Technique – in essence, the science of the most rational and effective way possible for actors to realise their potential. What are those skills? How do you shape a goal that you can practically achieve using these skills? What activities do you have to undertake in everyday life to build and strengthen these skills so that you can create the art that you wish to create according to the goals you have set yourself?

In brief, Aesthetics is the goal towards which a theatre is striving; Ethics are the meanings that an actor brings to their work;[6] and Technique comprises the practical skills that they employ to bring that ethical meaning to their work. All three are focused on one subject: the real art of acting.

In practice, most people focus on Stanislavsky's Technique, with little reference to – or awareness of – Ethics and Aesthetics. The reason for this in Soviet Russia was that aesthetics and ethics were based on moral, individual choices, and these subjects were too dangerous and too personal to discuss. During Brezhnev's leadership – when I was a student – there was only one aesthetic: Socialist Realism. That said, there were open discussions about our responsibility as creative artists, although the subject was not written about academically. The result of these discussions is that artists such as Vassiliev have succeeded in establishing strong, individual Aesthetics and Ethics, in spite of their restrictive backgrounds. In the West, the reason for the emphasis on Stanislavsky's Technique is different, and probably due to the predominant use in drama training of *An Actor Prepares*, which details the technical aspects of Stanislavsky's 'system' with very little reference to the other two terms. Certainly, Technique is the most accessible and implementable of the three; the notions of Ethics and Aesthetics are more subjective and, therefore, harder both to define and to teach. I myself use these terms cautiously with my own students, and I am aware that many of them will find employment in film and television, with scripts (vampire movies, action series etc.) in which Aesthetics and Ethics may seem irrel-evant.[7] Yet all three terms remain vital components of Stanislavsky's 'system', and continue to reflect the power which actors may hold in social and artistic realms.

Taking Kamotskaia's theories and practices of actor training, we now exam-ine as a case-study her production of *The Seagull* at UC Davis, California, in March 2010, drawing on the rehearsal journals of Bella Merlin, as Arkadina.

2: Bella Merlin and 'inner process' in production

The first tentative steps towards inner process

As Kamotskaia states in the previous section, the guiding principles for establishing a coherent 'inner process' are simplicity, safety and belief in your actions. As you start to build a character, you have to begin with your own self and your own truth to prepare the appropriate terrain. Indeed, this was Kamotskaia's opening gambit at *The Seagull* rehearsals: 'You have to go very easily at first – lightly – because at the beginning, the creative urge is very vulnerable and very delicate. Every false note or false movement will be felt by your spirit and it'll shatter your inner process. So go slowly and catch each moment'.[8] And yet, this degree of simplicity, safety and belief in my actions proved to be particularly tricky, even from the first read-through, as I approached the role of Arkadina.

Reading aloud with my fellow cast members, I found myself uninten-tionally adopting a voice and intonations which were theatrical in a way that was not necessarily my own self, my own truth. I could scarcely help it. It was if there was a hooligan actress inside me, saying, 'Let me at her! Let me give Arkadina a life!' Despite my attempts to bear in mind Kamotskaia's words to keep it light and easy, there was a curious energy inside that was bursting to come out. By the end of Act 1, I felt giggly – lightheaded – like a bubble pushed to its limitations, as if some nascent Arkadina were strug-gling to be freed. It was fun. Yet, at the same time, a part of me was saying, 'Those notes are ringing false at the moment. They might be where I end up, but if I go there now, they'll be "sound and fury signifying nothing".' So what should I do? The horse wanted to gallop, but my inner trainer was rein-ing it in. Already my 'inner process' was in danger of being compromised as I raced towards 'truth'.

The core of the problem, I soon realised, had nothing to do with 'inner process' per se, but lay in the nature of Arkadina, as the issue of truth (or lack of it) lies at the heart of her character. She is an actress – so, to what extent is she playing? How many of her speeches are imitations of those she has performed in a lifetime of repertoire? Although I knew it was too early for definite answers, I could feel – even in this first read-through – that *giving too much* obviously felt false, but (paradoxically) going *too lightly* did, too. Neither course led to belief in my actions.

To overcome this temporary dilemma, I turned to one of my favourite Stanislavsky tools: 'here-today-now'. Whatever you feel 'here, today, now', use it. If *I* feel false, constrained, unconvincing, then let that be how *Arkadina* feels too: moment by moment she is sussing out whether or not her actions are convincing Trigorin of her love.

Although the problem might be solved for the time being, this was just the beginning of unlocking Arkadina's inner process and allying it with my own.

Week 1: Early stages of textual analysis

Following the read-through, Kamotskaia began the various stages of her intricate 'textual analysis'. For the first stage, the entire cast was assembled for a close reading of the play and collectively invited to contribute to the ensuing discussions. The intention was that, through this collaborative sharing of knowledge, we would all 'own' the entire production and be able to make creatively informed choices towards each and every other character, whether we had any scripted dialogue with them or not. This stage correlated to Stanislavsky's 'round the table analysis' (also known as 'cognitive analysis' or 'affective cognition') (Carnicke in Hodge 2010: 13).

The second stage of Kamotskaia's textual analysis involved the cast working in groups of two or three to create backstories and contexts for the events in the play. This work was highly imaginative, while always (and necessarily) feeding off clues in the text. The results of these discussions were fed back to the group through the hot-seating of each duo or trio. However, unlike my previous experiences of hot-seating, the actors were to answer as themselves and not 'in character'. This relieved us from making hasty assumptions about how our characters might talk, sit or interact. Any false assumptions at this stage could disrupt the delicate structuring of an 'unbroken line' in our characters' logic.

Sharing these imaginative backgrounds provided unexpected opportunities to widen our knowledge of the play's undercurrents in a non-intellectual, intuitive way. On hearing the actors playing Nina (Cody Messick) and Trigorin (Michael Davison) discuss their love affair – a discussion I found unexpectedly and genuinely upsetting as if loyalties really *had* been betrayed – I began to understand how much Arkadina likes control. I sensed how she adapts her tactics to do whatever is necessary to bring about the appropriate outcome for her, and she flounders when circumstances are beyond her control.

Thus it was that, by hearing other actors talk imaginatively about their relationships, the rest of the cast could effortlessly build layers of logic and sequence to our own characters, even in these early days. After just one week of rehearsals, the matrix of relationships was unquestionably deepening in a very time-efficient way.

Week 2: Extended improvisations

It was at this point that Kamotskaia's implementation of textual analysis really came into its own as she introduced extended improvisations, informed by her work at Grotowski's Teatr Laboratorium and clearly influenced by Stanislavsky's Active Analysis. The set-up for these improvisations was as follows: all the actors (usually about ten or twelve) were dotted around the stage on chairs. Little by little, just by making eye contact and sensing the dynamics between the various 'char-actors' scattered around the space, we could begin to move wherever we wished and engage in some kind of silent interaction with each another – maybe in close proximity, maybe at a distance. I coin the term 'char-actors' because, as an actor in these exercises, you begin from yourself, how you are feeling today, and what it may be that you want to research right now in terms of the relationships within the play. (It may be research of the characters' first meeting, or some aspect of the characters' histories not explicitly provided in the script that you want to experience and flesh out.) Then, through a curiously effortless process of osmosis, you find that you have 'evolved' into the character in the course of the exercise without any conscious imperatives. Essentially, you are researching the character *through your negotiation with other 'char-actors'*, rather than from preconceived expectations. In this respect, the premise is incredibly simple: everything is born 'here, today, now'.

Because the extended improvisations were silent, there was no concern to find the character's voice or words. It was simply a question of reading the different signals emitted by each char-actor – through Stanislavsky's 'communion' and 'grasp'[9] – and beginning to forge an imaginative relationship, testing it very delicately through the whole body, intellect, emotions and space.

This stage of the textual analysis proved to be extremely fruitful in its experiences and discoveries. On the first occasion that Kamotskaia introduced the extended improvisations, neither Ben Morowski (Konstantin) nor I was present. Cody Messick (Nina) describes what happened for her:

> Since Bella (Arkadina) and Ben (Konstantin) weren't there, Michael (Trigorin) and I were able to develop our entire love story without any complications. It was totally pleasant and lovely![10]

However, at the following rehearsal, Morowski and I *were* present. This time, Messick describes the experience quite differently:

> Everything became so complicated . . . Previously I'd had a wonderful time with Trigorin, and now Arkadina was there and she's frightening . . . At one point, Trigorin, Arkadina and Konstantin were all in my line of vision, and I didn't know what to do, I was paralysed – with guilt, the fear of Arkadina, issues I couldn't escape. And I felt these emotions *for real* – in that improvisation. The experience added more to my understanding of Nina than I could have ever imagined.[11]

The key word in this stage of Kamotskaia's textual analysis is *experience*. We were finding – and experiencing – true connections with each other, thereby establishing emotion memories that could nourish us creatively and inform our interactions in all future rehearsals and performances.

Week 3: Developing 'levels of existence'

As our collective knowledge of the play grew, Kamotskaia used the extended improvisations to research relationships that still needed attention, and thus develop 'levels of existence' on the stage. One way in which this was achieved was by giving each actor two points of focus – two secret objectives – both of which were to be played throughout the course of the silent improvisation. The two objectives given to me for one such improvisation were aimed at sharpening my relationships with Shamrayev (Brett Duggan) and Dorn (Barry Hubbard). The first objective was 'to seduce Shamrayev', as he seems to be the only person on the estate whom I cannot manipulate. The other objective was 'to keep an eye on Dorn to see why he's paying Masha so much attention'.

Again, this extended improvisation proved to be incredibly lucrative in its experiences and discoveries. Since Dorn/Hubbard did not seem overly preoccupied with Masha during this improvisation, I found myself focusing on my first objective, concerning Shamrayev. For much of the early part of the improvisation, I/Arkadina avoided giving Shamrayev/Duggan too much overt attention; instead, I tried to *feel* where he was in the room. The situation gradually became more and more exciting, as he seemed to be ignoring me. This provoked me to use any strategy I could find to be close to him – moreover I would use any *person* I could use in order to get his attention: befriending Polina, reclining on Sorin, flirting with Dorn, teasing Masha.

When 'using other people' did not seem to work, I turned to 'activities'. I tried to lure Shamrayev's attention by carrying out farm-type activities with the paraphernalia lying about the stage (clanking chains, rolling a rope etc.). The less attention Shamrayev/Duggan gave me, the more frustrated I became. In the end I threw the rope on the floor at his feet. Shamrayev/Duggan picked it up and threw it back at me. So I threw it back at him. So he threw it back at me. When other char-actors intervened, I realised how much I was enjoying the dynamic. This in turn unlocked an inner logic for the argument that Arkadina has with Shamrayev in Act 2 concerning taking the horses to town: she enjoys the spat; it relieves the 'sweet country boredom'. As Arkadina, I wanted to wind up Shamrayev – it was chemical, it was exciting to see a man grow so passionate. After all, Shamrayev is unlike the rather more phlegmatic characters of Dorn and Trigorin, and it was all rather fun.

Much of the reason that this particular extended improvisation proved to be so chemical was that, unbeknownst to me, Kamotskaia had told Shamrayev/Duggan that he was secretly in love with Arkadina, but could not show it. These playful objectives, which stimulated the imagination, yielded great rewards. We uncovered a very exciting dynamic between these two characters, who rarely dialogue in the play and, when they do, it is usually sparky. We now understood that the sparkiness could be based on a strange attraction. This imaginative understream – this secret – coursed beneath the little moments that we (as Arkadina and Shamrayev) did actually have in the text. From that moment on, the scene in Act 2 became particularly juicy, with a pleasurable sense of 'existence' on stage (Figure 7.2).

Weeks 2–7: The core of the rehearsal process: 'talking through'

Although the extended improvisations were one, very important strand of Kamotskaia's rehearsal process for developing levels of existence between characters, more conventional rehearsals of scenes also took place – although her rehearsal strategy was deceptively *un*conventional.

The background to Kamotskaia's directing is steeped in the practices of the Russian director Anatoli Vassiliev, in whose rehearsals Kamotskaia had spent many hours observing his techniques (see section 1). As she expressed it, Vassiliev takes psychological processes to a very deep and personal level with his actors: it is not about playing character, but about being yourself, and (in Kamotskaia's words):

> being the best of yourself, and opening and exploring yourself, and delivering your heart, blood and soul. And when the actors perform this way, it makes the audience connect with the play on such a deep level that every moment touches them.[12]

Figure 7.2 Bella Merlin as Arkadina and Brett Duggan as Shmarayev in Act 2 of *The Seagull*. Photograph: Kristine Slipson © University of California, Davis.

In discussing her experiences of Vassiliev's work, Kamotskaia stressed that he uses very simple words, to the extent that it is almost inappropriate to call *nagavor* (the phrase he uses to describe his rehearsal technique) 'terminology'. It simply means 'talking through'. He does not mention objectives or tasks; instead (as Kamotskaia observed and interpreted):

> He just talks and talks and talks to each actor, about their own personal world, as if he is urging each actor to dig into themselves and bring that personal quality to the story of the play. For Vassiliev, it seems that the words of the play are not information, but almost music for the theme of the play: he tells the story using what's *in* the script, rather than *using* the script. By which I mean the text is used nearly upside down – if I say I'm angry, I play not being angry: I constantly look for the counterpoint to the words, the undercurrent or 'understream' of the words.[13]

Subtly, this working against a literal interpretation of the lines frequently unlocks the real humanity and complexity of a text.

Indeed, this combination of talking, digging, and searching for the understream was the practice that Kamotskaia used for *The Seagull*, in a 'transmission' tracing Stanislavsky's later improvisations, Knebel's interpretation of Active Analysis, and Vassiliev's *nagovor*.[14]

During formative rehearsals of a scene, Kamotskaia talked to us almost constantly, usually remaining on stage with us and often enacting moments: 'At this point, you're thinking this and then this happens, and then you pick up the glass', and so on. Her suggestions featured thought processes, points of action and activities, and yet interestingly – like Vassiliev – there was very little talk of objectives. Often, however, her ideas involved emotional states, such as 'You're terrified, but you're trying to cover that fear'.

This was certainly the case with the scene in Act 3 between Arkadina and Sorin, which culminates in Sorin's asthma attack (Figure 7.3). Kamotskaia stressed that as Arkadina I am barely listening to Sorin, because my anxiety about Nina and Trigorin is too great (after all, only moments earlier I walked in on them being intimate together). Sorin has to fight hard to hook my attention, as my emotional energy constantly shoots elsewhere: from contemplating what might be going on in the corridors of the house, to pouring myself a drink, to putting on my make-up and repairing my 'mask' – while all the time Sorin is twittering away about my son, the horses, the farm.

As with all her rehearsals, Kamotskaia expressed with great specificity for this scene with Sorin (Brian Livingston) her insights into Arkadina's thought processes. Although I understood exactly where Kamotskaia's instinct was coming from – and as an actress I certainly liked the

Figure 7.3 Bella Merlin as Arkadina and Brian Livingston as Sorin in Act 3 of *The Seagull*. Photograph: Kristine Slipson © University of California, Davis.

imaginative provocations – it took me a while to truly understand the process of 'talking through'. Initially I thought I was to imitate and copy what she was suggesting. In fact, this was not the intention at all.[15] My task was provoke myself with my own inner monologue, and Kamotskaia was simply giving me examples, not prototypes, to stimulate the ideas that might inform that stream of consciousness. For example, my inner monologue during this scene with Sorin might be: 'Where's Trigorin? For God's sake not with Nina? Is she that interesting? Am I that old? We're about to leave – has he packed yet? What on earth is Sorin talking about now? My son? Yes, what about my son? Oh Lord, my son is a trial to me. The last thing I want to think about right now is why my son tried to shoot himself. (Where did I put my brandy glass?) Well, if he's got no money then why doesn't he get a job? Why is Sorin bothering with all this at the moment? All I really want to know is where is Trigorin? Where is Nina? Are they together? Am I too old for him now? Is that the problem? Where's my blusher? Where's my lipstick? Oh, for pity's sake, pour me another drink . . .'[16] While all this chaos is tumbling through Arkadina's head, she is continuing a dialogue with Sorin, though her answers to him are at the peripheries of her concentration, with her primary focus being somewhere else entirely. There are two different and (paradoxically) co-existing circles of attention – the bull's eye (Trigorin) and the outer radius of the target (Sorin), and Arkadina's attention expands and contracts momentarily between the two. Allied to which – as is often the case in real life – there are two contrapuntal melodies going on at the same time: the actual spoken text and the inner monologue, or the *main stream* and the *understream*.

At the heart of unlocking these textures of the characters' inner process lies Stanislavsky's notion of logic and sequence, which involves personalising every moment so that you own it as an actor and your performance does not belong to either the playwright (because you are bound to their stage directions) or the director (because you are shackled by their 'blocking'). As Kamotskaia explained:

> My process is about the logic of behaviour. That's why I usually ignore Chekhov's stage directions, as Chekhov is a genius playwright, but not a very good stage director. The stage directions are too primitive for the twenty-first century: we have a different behavioural aesthetic now. Instead, the logic comes from the spoken text. Your task is then to follow the logic physically, expressing that logic in a physical shape.
>
> Sometimes I do 'show' you as actors the precise moments of visual logic, because it's easier than putting it into words. (Don't forget English is my second language!) 'Showing' is just a short cut to what I mean,

it's not for you to repeat. If something doesn't work visually for you [i.e. you don't like the 'blocking'], it's because there's no logic in it for you. So find your own logic. If as actors you use the stage differently from what I've suggested, I won't notice, because I'm not looking for a particular picture, I'm just looking for the logic of the scene.[17]

Essentially, with this process of talking through the logic, we were like glass flasks: Kamotskaia was simply filling us up to the point where we were so full of thoughts about the character that there was no room for fear. This practice was a subtle – but highly significant – shift from working with those directors who do want you to do exactly what they have shown or asked you to do. Instead, Kamotskaia was feeding us with multiple prompts *in order for us to make them our own* until we were tumbling with the inner life of the character. If she talked about the emotions experienced by the characters, it was not that we should *play* or *indicate* those emotions. She was simply pointing out the emotional cartography inherent in Chekhov's play. It was then our job as actors to be sufficiently psychophysically co-ordinated that we could prepare our inner creative states appropriately – through the logic of the characters' thoughts and the line of physical activities – to stir our emotions organically.

Week 8: Eliminating gaps in the onstage existence

Once I understood it on a deep (non-intellectual) level, I loved the principles and practice of 'talking through'. However, a rather perturbing issue arose for me during the technical rehearsal, which showed that my inner process was not yet complete and the inner line was still broken. I began to find myself on the brink of losing my lines – lines that I had known perfectly well for weeks. The tectonic plates were shifting: my knowledge of the text was moving from mental memory to somewhere else that I could not quite fathom. I felt myself approaching a kind of acting that was much deeper and more dangerous than I had experienced before. For a moment, it felt like stage fright.

Thankfully, Kamotskaia had the answer for this: moments of stage fright are simply the result of not having the right line of logic and sequence. To that end, she asked me to look at the points in the script where I was forgetting my lines, as:

any doubts you have as an actor that don't belong to the character will appear as gaps in the sequence. If you fall into the abyss, it's because there are gaps in the logic. You just have to unlock the logic of the character's thoughts and actions.[18]

The problem area was (terrifyingly) much of Act 3 – which is really Arkadina's aria. So I went home that night and worked through my 'logic and sequence'. Although I had known and used this phrase frequently, I had never understood the idea of logic and sequence in quite the same depth before working with Kamotskaia on *The Seagull*. When I started to examine forensically my own logic and sequence for Arkadina in Act 3 and the seemingly broken line, it all boiled down to a very simple physical activity.

Early on in the rehearsal process, Kamotskaia had given me the idea that Arkadina regularly touches up her make-up to maintain her mask and keep looking fine. I liked the physical activity and subsequently sought to include it. During rehearsals, Stage Management had found me a prop compact and a prop brush, so each time it came to touching up the make-up, I simply applied more blusher, since those were the props I had. There were three times during Act 3 when I put on the make-up, and that night after the technical rehearsal it suddenly dawned on me why I felt so fake and why my inner process was screaming out illogic and non-sequiturs: 'That's not how you put on make-up. You don't endlessly apply blusher or you'd end up looking like a clown. If I'm really going to put on the mask, I need the blusher, the powder, the lipstick.'

It seemed embarrassingly obvious in retrospect but, until that moment, I had not made the sequence logical (ergo, credible) for myself. I simply

Figure 7.4 Bella Merlin as Arkadina and Brian Livingston as Sorin in Act 3 of *The Seagull*. Photograph: Kristine Slipson © University of California, Davis.

did not believe in my actions. Therefore, false notes were chiming in my subconscious every time I undertook the activity. Once I had sorted out the physical logic of my props (i.e. blusher, powder, lipstick), the psychological resonance of the physical activity also became more focused and, each time I/Arkadina put on the mask, the objective shifted. The first time it was to make sure she is looking young and colourful, as she prepares for hers and Trigorin's imminent departure from the estate into the outside world. Then she is plagued by thoughts of Nina, this attractive, carefree, young woman who is stealing her lover. Therefore, the second time Arkadina looks in the mirror, she wants to test her smile; yet, every time she smiles, she sees wrinkles all round her eyes. This prompts the thought, 'I'm trying to smile to be youthful and attractive, but by smiling, I'm revealing my age'. The third time occurs when Trigorin comes back into the room after Arkadina's argument with Konstantin and she needs to be absolutely sure she has conjured up the powerful, vivacious person she wants to be, not the crumbling wreck to which she has just been reduced by her son. On each occasion, the physical activity was layered *over* the spoken text and the psychological monologue coursed *under* the spoken word, the three strands braiding together to create the character's 'existence'. The density of this braid left no room for gaps in the logic into which my self-consciousness could spring.

From here on in, the various psychophysical textures of Act 3 made perfect sense. Each time I/Arkadina revivified the mask, a completely different logic and justification underpinned the activity, involving technically different props and psychologically different objectives. With these textures, my full comprehension fell into place of Kamotskaia's concepts of 'talking through', inner process, understream and logic.

Transmitting beyond the vocational

The Seagull production was the first time that I had focused so deeply and precisely on the detailed crafting of logic and sequence when building a character. The result was that Kamotskaia's recalibration of Stanislavsky's processes – evidently drawn from Vassiliev, Grotowski and a host of other influences, plus her own unique insights into acting – shifted my own acting processes considerably and re-aligned my application of Stanislavsky's 'system' for a contemporary, behaviourist aesthetic.

This re-alignment can be seen as part of a much wider refocusing of Stanislavsky's work currently percolating in the academy and the industry. There is certainly an increasing understanding of Knebel's contribution to Stanislavsky's legacy (Sharon M. Carnicke's work in this field is particularly valuable). As this lineage has passed through Vassiliev by way of his time at GITIS, and – in terms of this particular piece of practical research – through Kamotskaia and the evolution of her work at RSAMD, into my own experiences of and research into Active Analysis, it would seem that Stanislavsky's principles are undergoing active re-visioning as part of their transmission to new generations of actors and students.

Although much of the focus of this book is on the Russian impact in Britain, I am strongly aware that in the USA (where I work at the time of writing) a rather straitjacketed, dogmatic approach to Stanislavsky's teaching still persists in many quarters. The majority understanding of his 'system', it would seem, is clearly rooted in his early work, and is – to my mind – old-fashioned, if not obsolete. His later practices of Active Analysis, the holistic and playful elements of improvisation and the discovery of character through body, imagination, space, partner and emotions, are all vital aspects of Stanislavsky's own evolving theories that are slowly, but surely finding their way into European and American training grounds. Although it may take some time to dispel the belief that 'dry and boring' round-the-table analysis, affective memory and psychologically motivated objectives are the be-all and end-all of Stanislavsky, the future tendency towards embodied character research and the visceral sensations of inner process are promising and exciting. I sincerely believe there is profundity in the teaching of acting that goes beyond the vocational. The transferable skills inherent in actor training are vital, transformative and timely. Unquestionably, practitioners such as Kamotskaia and I will continue to transmute and transmit our personalised versions of Russo-British-American acting practices. In so doing, I hope that actor training – with its focus on integrating body, mind and spirit, and its synergising of psychology and physicality – will hold a significant place in the analysis, experience and empathic understanding of human behaviour. It is a place that reaches far beyond the theatre.

Notes

1 The contents of this chapter evolved from interviews, conversations, symposia and rehearsals involving two actors and trainers – Russian-born Katya Kamotskaia and British-born Bella Merlin – during a production of Chekhov's *The Seagull* at the University of California, Davis, Spring 2010. Kamotskaia and Merlin first met in 1993 at the State Institute of Cinematography, Moscow, where Kamotskaia was Merlin's acting 'master' (see Merlin 2001). Since that time, they have both taught extensively in the UK and around the world, bringing together Russian heritages and British practices, deeply informed by Stanislavsky. Indeed, Kamotskaia was the Russian language consultant to Jean Benedetti for his translation of Stanislavsky's *An Actor's Work* (Stanislavsky 2008).

2   My interpretation of Stanislavsky's 'inner creative state' involves knowing how to create individual inner process, and how to maintain it and develop it through (and within) the given circumstances of the character.

3   In *An Actor's Work*, ch. 13, 'Inner Psychological Drives in Action', is devoted to the unbroken line. In *An Actor Prepares*, the same ch. 13 is in fact titled 'The Unbroken Line'.

4   'Logic and sequence' are vital components in creating inner life. Again, Stanislavsky devotes a whole chapter to these in *An Actor's Work*: ch. 22, 'Logic and sequence'. 'Inner and outer logic and sequence are crucial for us as actors. That is why we base most of our technique on them' (Stanislavsky 2008: 507).

5   Interview with Mark Stevenson, Katya Kamotskaia and Bella Merlin, UC Davis, 12 March 2010.

6   Interestingly, Lisa Wolford writes of Grotowski's training, 'Ethics are what inform the use of technique' (Wolford in Hodge 2010: 202).

7   Curiously, the terms 'Ethics' and 'Aesthetics' were used constantly at the 'Acting with Facts' Conference (University of Reading, UK, September 2010), where the issue of constructing drama out of real people's lives – often involving traumatic experiences – was extremely current. Perhaps such currency will begin to transmute more overtly to fiction-based drama.

8   *The Seagull* rehearsal notes, Bella Merlin, 8 January 2010.

9   *An Actor Prepares* includes a chapter devoted to what Stanislavsky calls 'Communion' (translated as 'Communication' in Benedetti's 2008 *An Actor's Work*). 'Communion' is defined as the 'direct, personal intercourse with other human beings' that emanates from the 'many invisible, spiritual experiences' exchanged between faces, voices, eyes, speech and gestures (Stanislavsky 1980: 93–4). 'Grasp' (translated as 'grip' in *An Actor's Work*) sums up the powerful energy involved in engaging all the senses to communicate with other actors. It also refers to becoming 'absorbed in some interesting creative problem on the stage. If [the actor] can devote all his attention and creative faculties to that he will achieve true grasp' (Stanislavsky 1980: 218). Merlin maintains that when actors 'achieve true grasp', the audience may be magnetised towards – indeed, they themselves may be grasped by – the onstage action.

10 Cody Messick in conversation with Professor Jenny Kaminer at the *Idle Destruction* symposium, UC Davis Theatre and Dance Department, 12 March 2010.

11 Ibid.

12 Katya Kamotskaia in conversation with Bella Merlin, March 2010.

13 Ibid.

14 Vassiliev trained with Knebel's colleague Andrei Popov at GITIS, as well as adapting her writings on Active Analysis in the 2006 French translation.

15 It is not uncommon for directors to be active in their presence on the rehearsal room floor. Jane Baldwin describes Michel Saint-Denis as joining 'his actors on stage while developing the remaining blocking, explaining the motivation for each move, creating the feeling the director was part of the ensemble' (Baldwin in Hodge 2010: 95). Michael Chekhov himself thought that the best way for a director to communicate what is required from a scene is to act it. However, the process involves the actor not imitating the director externally, but 'grasping the essence' and making it their own (Chekhov 1991: 154).

16 This practice echoes Knebel's (1976) use of Nemirovich-Danchenko's 'inner monologue': 'A person's train of thought always depends on a whole series of

issues, each in its turn influencing physicality and behaviour' (cited by Carnicke in Hodge 2010: 109).
17 Kamotskaia in conversation with Bella Merlin, March 2010.
18 Ibid.

Bibliography

Carnicke, S. M. (2009) *Stanislavsky in Focus*, Abingdon: Routledge.

Chekhov, A. (1993) *Plays*, trans. Frayn, M., London: Methuen.

Chekhov, M. (1991) *On the Technique of Acting*, New York: Harper Paperbacks.

Ershov, P. M. (1992) *Teknologia Iskustvo Aktiorskovo*, Sochinenia Vol. 1, Moscow: Otkriti Universitat TOO, Gorbunok.

Hodge, A. (ed.) (2010) *Actor Training*, Oxon: Routledge.

Knebel, M. (1976) *Poeziia Pedogogiki* [Poetry of Pedagogy], Moscow: VTO.

Knebel, M. (2006) *L'Analyse-Action*, trans. Struve, N., Vladimirov, S., Poliakov, S. (adapted by Vassiliev, A.), Arles: Actes Sud-Papiers.

Merlin, B. (2001) *Beyond Stanislavsky: The Psycho-Physical Approach to Actor-Training*, London: Nick Hern Books.

Stanislavsky, K. (1953) *Acting: A Handbook of the Stanislavski Method*, ed. Cole, T., New York: Crown.

Stanislavsky, K. (1980) *An Actor Prepares*, trans. Hapgood, E. R., London: Methuen.

Stanislavsky, K. (1984) *Selected Works*, trans. Korneva, O., Moscow: Raduga.

Stanislavsky, K. (2008) *An Actor's Work*, trans. Benedetti, J., Abingdon: Routledge.

CONCLUSION

A common theatre history? The Russian tradition in Britain today: Declan Donnellan, Katie Mitchell and Michael Boyd

Jonathan Pitches

> I'm firmly convinced that Russian theatre is really closely linked with European theatre, and Russian theatre is a part of European theatre. I think that despite all our differences, a common theatre history is still there for Europe and Russia.
>
> (Lev Dodin in Lichtenfels 2010: 72)

If the individual chapters making up this book tell us just one thing it is that there is a significant and surprisingly continuous relationship between the actor-training traditions of twentieth-century Russia and the British theatre tradition. This may have been at times a latent, even unspoken, influence (consider Paul Rogers's reluctance to admit his relationship to Michael Chekhov, for instance) but it is one not to be discounted or overlooked or, worse still, conflated into a generalised and imprecise belief in British Stanislavskianism. On the contrary, this book indicates that there are various strands of Russian influence in Britain spreading far beyond the pages of *My Life in Art* or the contents of *An Actor's Work*. Each generation of Russian and Soviet acting practitioners, both contemporaries and disciples of Stanislavsky, seems to have found some route into the minds and behaviours of British actors and directors, like water seeping into the cracks and flaws of an old building. This may have occurred directly: Komisarjevsky bringing his own unique blend of romanticised truth and musicality to London and Stratford (Chapter 1), or Chekhov's work developing in Dartington, for a time simultaneously with Komis (Chapter 3). It may have happened indirectly, with the long-delayed introduction of Meyerhold's ideas, transmitted through the agency of second-generation biomechanics masters (Chapter 4), or it may have involved a process of further interpretation, at a distance: the processing of Stanislavsky through the curricula of British conservatoires in the 1960s, via the United States (Chapter 2). A further complexity is added to these transmission routes in the second phase of the book, when British-based practitioners have consciously integrated the ideas of the Russians into their own practices, often with some considerable eclecticism. Joan Littlewood is a particularly good example, drawing as she did on Meyerhold, Laban and Stanislavsky, not to mention Piscator and Brecht (Chapter 5); Alan Lyddiard's Dodin-inspired utopian experiment with the Northern Stage Ensemble was more philosophical than methodological but included moments of direct collaboration with the Maly Theatre (as is documented in Chapter 6); and the last chapter's detailed assessment of Active Analysis today develops a view of this complexity still further: an English actor, practitioner and academic, based in America and trained in Russia, collaborating with a native Russian director and teacher, who typically applies her skills in the conservatoire sector in Scotland!

For Dodin, quoted above, this process of transmission has been balanced and reciprocal, not one-way: the Russian theatre, he argues, has learnt as much from the British theatre in the same period. However, although there are clear reasons for seeing this development as a 'common theatre history', it has not been part of this book's aim or mission to chart this return passage of ideas – it would take another study as long as this to do so with any validity. Dodin's perspective does, however, raise questions that are pertinent in this concluding section, questions informed by the range of transmission routes identified above. How inter-related *are* the two traditions, today? What are the current developments? And what evidence is there for a common theatre future, if not history?

Before I attempt to answer these questions with reference to three contemporary practitioners based in Britain (though often working internationally), it may be instructive to analyse in abstract terms the various modes of exchange already encountered in the book and to examine whether there are patterns which work across the chapter examples. These routes might be summarised thus:

- direct, embodied, person-to-person transmission of an identifiable (and singular) training regime;
- direct, embodied, person-to-person transmission by a second- or third-generation trainee of an identifiable (and singular) training regime;
- direct, embodied, person-to-person transmission of a training regime which draws on two (or more) learnt practices;
- indirect appropriation (and reconstruction) of a singular training regime from alternative sources

- – books and written documents
- – photographs and moving footage
- – other research;
- • indirect appropriation (and reconstruction) of two (or more) training regimes from alternative sources;
- • principled borrowing from the spirit (not the letter) of the Russian tradition.

This is not offered as an exhaustive list and in practice there are many overlaps and alternative permutations possible. However, this arrangement does help bring into focus some of the debates encountered in the book and I would briefly like to pursue these here.

The first is the question of depth. Descending this list one gets further and further away from what is often called 'deep training'; that is, a longitudinal, immersive practice in a singular approach, passed on in the studio by a master or 'adept'. Deep training is the kind more often associated with ancient Asian traditions of training but in the current context might best be illustrated in the first category – singular transmission, person to person – and by the work that went on in the studios of Meyerhold in the 1920s and early 1930s: the early transmission of biomechanical études by Nikolai Kustov.

If this logic were followed the penultimate category of transmission – appropriation from alternative sources – would imply a more 'shallow' means of training. Yet this is almost precisely the approach Joan Littlewood took in developing her early training regime at Theatre Workshop before Jean Newlove joined from Laban with her own embodied learning to transmit. Littlewood's training was considered to be one of the most advanced of any company at the time; Robert Leach describes it as 'almost relentless' after 1930, leading to highly skilled demonstrations by company members (Leach 2006: 78).[1] It is clearly not enough to take physical access to the source as a benchmark of training validity, nor to consider depth simply as an indicator of commitment to one source.

This observation brings us onto the second question: purity and the myth of the original source. Although there is some comfort in arranging things causally, centring attention on a training progenitor and 'measuring' their impact on the receiver, in practice this is a problematic assumption. Granted, the structure of this book might imply such a taxonomy, with the first-generation practitioners (four big guns of the Russian theatre: Komisarjevsky, Stanislavsky, Meyerhold, Chekhov) cleanly informing those practising later in theatre history. However, the contents of these chapters do not support such a simplification: Komis practised first with Meyerhold and his own half-sister, Vera Komissarzhevskaya, taking his dose of Stanislavsky from books and production observations; Meyerhold's 'pure' biomechanics (as Gennady Bogdanov will have it) was in fact a heady mix of popular and contemporary theatre sources with a sprinkling of industrial theory; Chekhov's practice was similarly hybridised, even if it looked to a very different set of inspirational roots. Even the Stanislavsky System itself, which is so often considered to be at the root of all things Russian (a function of its later positioning as the Sovietised acting orthodoxy), was a product of mixed practical and theoretical sources and of course was never set in stone.

Such a picture suggests that it is perhaps even dangerous to use the term 'singular practice', as all these 'root' practices are themselves products of theatrical grafting and cross pollination. Indeed, in the latest edition of *Actor Training* Alison Hodge calls this process 'cross fertilisation' (Hodge 2010: xxiii–xxiv) and acknowledges the necessity for it in training regimes throughout the twentieth century. There is some virtue in defining what *kinds* of cross fertilisation have occurred in the period, however, to interrogate what has been identified in this book as the mechanics of transmission. There is benefit, too, in looking across practices to unpick what different understandings of the word 'influence' exist, something Hodge does not address directly in her introduction to *Actor Training*. This is the intention of the list of transmission possibilities above.

Questions of influence underpin much of this last chapter's examination of contemporary British theatre practice. Although Declan Donnellan, Katie Mitchell and Michael Boyd have all made their individual debts to Russia very well known, the manner and extent to which they have been influenced by the tradition are illuminatingly different, even if for each of them it is potent, serious and consistent. This is of course also true of the practitioners already examined in this book and a simple distinction might be observed: those who have drawn *methodologically* on the tradition of Russian training, and those who have been influenced by the *spirit* or *philosophy* of Russian practice. Again, there are nuances and gradations operating here, but such a distinction does bring to the fore the different kinds of responses evident in this book, which in turn are closely related to transmission routes. Lyddiard's influence, as noted, is clearly in the latter category, as Duška Radosavljević has shown: Dodin's model of the Maly Drama theatre and of the utopian, long-term ensemble was to provide inspiration for the working principles of Northern Stage but Lyddiard himself was not steeped in the practical demands of Lev Dodin's version of active analysis (although many of the Northern Stage Ensemble's actors were given a grounding). On the other hand, Katya Kamotskaia's contemporary take on Knebel is in the former category, as a Russian-trained actor and collaborator with Knebel's protégé, Anatoly Vassiliev. This is not to say that either category is hermetically sealed off from the other; Kamotskaia also talks of the ethical *spirit* of Stanislavsky, which she argues is often lost in the practical desire to engage with his exercises. However, it does help to identify the different knowledges created from the varying interactions with the Russian sources captured here, and to emphasise that the British theatre has benefited from the full range of interpretations.

What follows, then, is an epilogue to the narrative already developed on the Russians in Britain: a snapshot of the British scene today, focusing on three highly acclaimed directors. Much has already been written on Donnellan, Mitchell and Boyd, and two of them have published their own treatises on acting. However, drawing on new interview materials and with a specific focus on Russian training, which has not been highlighted before, this section aims to ground some of these examples and interpretations in contemporary, mainstream theatre practice. Thus it is to be read as a statement of the extent to which both the letter and the spirit of Russian training survive today in some of the most established cultural organisations.

Declan Donnellan and Cheek by Jowl

Cheek by Jowl was founded by Declan Donnellan and his partner Nick Ormerod in 1981. Since then they have developed an international reputation for sparse, intelligent productions of Shakespeare and lesser-known classics, with a strong emphasis on ensemble playing. Quickly developing notoriety as a national and international touring company, Donnellan and Ormerod met Lev Dodin from the Maly Theatre of St Petersburg five years later, in 1986, visiting his theatre at Dodin's invitation. By then, they had already developed a passion for touring work and they became firm friends with Dodin, constantly bumping into him on the international festival circuit. In 1997 Donnellan directed the Maly actors himself in a production of *A Winter's Tale* and this relationship culminated in a request from the Chekhov International Festival of Theatre for him and Ormerod to form their own permanent company of Russian actors, described on the Cheek by Jowl website as the 'sister company'.[2] This invitation was made in 1999. This parallel company now has four productions in its repertoire: *Boris Godunov, Three Sisters, Twelfth Night* and most recently *The Tempest* (premiering in 2011). In 2002 Donnellan published a book on acting, *The Actor and the Target* (originally published in Russia in 2000, revised edition 2005) and in 2008 he provided the introduction for Jean Benedetti's new translation of *An Actor's Work,* asking the pertinent question:

> Why does he [Stanislavsky] continue to inspire so many actors and theatre makers, including those who seem to be so far from his tradition?
>
> (Donnellan in Stanislavsky 2008: xiii)

Donnellan's interest in the Russian tradition dates from an early age:

> When I was about 13 or 14, I started to read about live theatre. I used to go to the public library in Ealing and read about people with names like Chekhov and Stanislavsky and Boleslavsky – all Slavic names. I didn't really understand it but it all sort of melted into a mist of snowflakes and the Russian Revolution and I thought it was just great. It was born in a kind of glamour, I suppose. When I subsequently went to Russia I found out that it was rather different from this fantasy that I had and that's one of things that very much interests me about our Western clichés about Russia in general (which we really need to shake ourselves out of or otherwise we're going to get a few surprises!). That's how my interest in Russian theatre started.[3]

The case of Donnellan, then, represents a multi-layered relationship to the Russian tradition of acting, based on a long-term intellectual enquiry, direct contact with Russian directors and actors, publication of his own methodologies, and his distinctly European style and experience as a director. Although he himself did not train in the Russian tradition,[4] his own company has been described as an 'unofficial acting academy' for British talent from Daniel Craig to Michael Sheen and Saskia Reeves (Sierz 2010: 146) and the central common reference point is what he calls the 'living experience':

> DD: I think everyone is looking at the same mountain from a different perspective.
> JP: And that mountain being the Stanislavsky tradition do you mean?
> DD: No, no, no! Absolutely not. I'm very suspicious of all traditions. No – I mean just the moment of living experience. That's the only thing that we should think about or really contemplate, as far as I'm concerned. There are many other different attitudes to theatre but I'm just very interested in having a living experience on stage. And I think that that is what Stanislavsky is also interested in.[5]

It is tempting at this stage to connect this well documented passion of Donnellan's for the living experience explicitly with Stanislavsky's life-long pursuit of the actor's e*xperiencing* of a role; in Russian the term is *perezhivanie*. Benedetti defines the word in his glossary for *An Actor's work*, comparing it with the previous translated term from Elizabeth Hapgood's version of *An Actor Prepares* (1936):

Russian	*An Actor's Work*	*An Actor Prepares*
Perezhivanie	Experiencing	Living

The process by which an actor experiences the character's emotions afresh in each performance.

(Stanislavsky 2008: 683)

Sharon Carnicke offers a more extended but similar definition in *Stanislavsky in Focus. Perezhivanie* is:

> The ideal kind of acting, nurtured by the System, in which the actor creates the role anew at every performance in full view of the audience . . . Such acting, however well planned and well rehearsed, remains essentially active and improvisatory.

(Carnicke 2009: 217)

Indeed, there is significant common ground here with Donnellan's practice – not least the idea that there are always discoveries to be had by the actor *in the moment* on stage and that some things need to be fluid and moveable each night.[6] 'Living experience', as an idea, peppers many of Donnellan's interviews and helps define his ultimate *raison d'être* as a director. However, he is careful not to attribute this solely to a Russian influence:

> It's rather more global than that. I think people are touched by Stanislavsky's extraordinary struggle to help life flow on stage. Very often people are much more inspired, I have to tell you, by *My Life in Art* which is, completely exercise free! It's more to do with the spirit. People often think of the tradition of Stanislavsky being expressed through the System but actually the important thing is his lifelong struggle to put life on stage and some of the very humble things he did – like to bring up the standard of acting to the highest – which we can so easily forget and instead freeze it off into something practical. It's the spirit of Stanislavsky: that's what's so important about him as far as I am concerned.[7]

Donnellan's suspicion of the idea of tradition comes through clearly in this statement. At one level he is simply expressing his own autonomy as a creative artist but he is clearly also wanting to generalise Stanislavsky's importance beyond the transmission of a *practice* (which might as a result end up 'frozen') to a wider, more philosophical kind of influence – what he calls the enduring *spirit* of Stanislavsky. For Donnellan, to borrow solely from Stanislavsky's practice is in some way to devalue his contribution.

What is more, such a pragmatic kind of borrowing makes him almost queasy:

> The idea of a theatre practitioner developing a theory coming from someone else makes me feel quite vertiginous . . . The exercises I have invented are inspired not by other theory. Any theory I have spun has been inspired by the living actor in front of me – and that's a terribly, terribly important point.[8]

Again, this is a constant theme in Donnellan's statements on acting – that in essence he does something very simple in the rehearsal room, observing the actions of his actors and waiting for something alive to emerge:

> Because basically the situation of every director is that you are watching some enactment in front of you . . . and you want it to be more alive. That's the absolute basis, the fundamental, the enormous first and last principle and it is so easily forgotten – you want it to be more alive. And consequently we invent things that will help life pass onstage. You cannot put life into something – you can only make sure you do not block life. So the whole thing is totally reactive. The director is absolutely reactive.[9]

It is interesting to reflect that for Donnellan a *practice* derived from another practitioner becomes, by definition, *theorised* and that that is the process he finds 'vertiginous'. For him, rather like his notion of 'the target' in his book of the same name, the inspiration for acting lies outside of the self – in the other actors in the room – and not in other acting pedagogies.

> The people who taught me are the actors who let me work with them, those are the people who have taught me. Those are my masters, those are my teachers. And what's collected in the *Actor and the Target* is a systematized series of advice for the actor when he feels lost. That doesn't come from me: that comes from the relationship I've had with actors within the bounds of the rehearsal room.[10]

Such a perspective on training and its transmission is perhaps hardly surprising for a director who sets so much store by nurturing living reactions in the rehearsal room but it points to a particular attitude to tradition which is worth noting. Donnellan's perspective on the Russian tradition is both reified and abstract (looking to the *spirit* of Stanislavsky) and pragmatic and actor-centred (responding to the momentary needs of the performer in the room). Such a dualism is articulated perfectly in his assessment of the challenges of working across cultures in his two companies:

> I think it's all to do with my response to work with actors. I don't really see in their essentials that actors are different in Russia or the English-speaking world. Or, indeed, in France. I think the challenges and the things I love to see in actors are actually identical. It's the systems that are very, very different. But it's not the people. Actual central issues in acting don't change in my opinion and are absolutely transcendent of culture.[11]

Katie Mitchell

As an Associate Director of the National Theatre, the Royal Court and the Royal Shakespeare Company (RSC), Mitchell is as much part of the mainstream British theatre scene as Declan Donnellan. However, even though they share a close relationship to Lev Dodin's work, Mitchell's route to this elevated place in British culture and her relationship to the Russian tradition are very different. Like Donnellan, she was educated at Oxbridge and developed her interest in theatre at university, becoming President of the Oxford University Drama Society. After graduating, she was awarded an Assistant Directorship with Paines Plough and then with the RSC, working alongside Di Trevis, Deborah Warner and Adrian Noble. She formed her own company, Classics on a Shoestring, and ran it from 1990 to 1993. As the name suggests, she too had a passion for the classics from the outset and this has continued over the last two decades with notable productions of Greek tragedy (Aeschylus, Euripides), and of classical European Naturalism and Symbolism (Strindberg, Ibsen, Chekhov). In addition to such established repertoire, Mitchell has staged several operas and has an ongoing creative relationship with Martin Crimp.[12] In 2009 she published a practically oriented book on directing, *The Director's Craft*, which in its final chapter, entitled 'How I Learnt the Skills the Book Describes', makes explicit her interest in eastern European practice; there she locates herself in what she calls a 'chain of practitioners' (Mitchell 2009: 230) leading back to Stanislavsky. The great stimulus for her productivity as a director goes right back to 1989 and her sense, articulated to Maria Shevtsova in an interview in *New Theatre Quarterly*, that the British theatre tradition lacked something at the time:

> There was something – and I couldn't put my finger on what it was – that was absent, if you like, here. And I had a hunch that I would find it in Eastern Europe.

(Shevtsova 2006: 4)

Her response to this perceived gap was to seek out the training of Russian and eastern European masters (Vassiliev, Dodin, Nekrosius, Tumanishvili, Staniewski), an urge which was facilitated by a Churchill fellowship awarded in 1989–90 to study how directors are trained in Russia, Poland, Lithuania and Georgia (Mitchell 2009: 227). In an interview conducted in 2011, I asked Mitchell to explain what this gap meant to her and to evaluate whether this well-publicised trip went any way towards filling it:

> It's difficult to track back and be the person I was then. I had a hunch, then; now I sort of know what it is. What I think I experienced then was that there was a great emphasis on speaking words clearly but there wasn't a great emphasis on constructing behaviour accurately and, if you're interested in constructing lifelike behaviour, language is only a small component of that. And I think it was the absence of everything else from life in the mix of how theatre was made. So, there would be all this emphasis going on with the production of sound and the articulation clearly of words but there would be no work on how those words would be modulated because of time, place, intention, obstacle – all the other components that create the lifelike sound of how we communicate.[12]

For Mitchell, looking back on the British theatre of the 1980s, there remained a perennial problem, so commonly associated with this tradition, of the work being text-bound and, by extension, *head*-bound. Her emphasis on motivated and contextualised *behaviour*, and its apparent absence from the work she had observed in the UK, indicates the kinds of practices she was exposed to in Russia. These are worth expanding on in the current context.

Mitchell's routes of transmission are again multi-layered but they are more heavily reliant on actual embodied learning than Donnellan's. Indeed, where the two part company in quite explicit terms is in their attitude to the place and status of the teacher. As we have seen, Donnellan's natural suspicion of tradition and his own deference to the actor-as-teacher lead him to generalise and universalise the influence of Russian practice. Mitchell, by contrast, seems to value highly the lineages of Russian actor training and the attendant master–teacher relationship that often underpins such histories:

> Bit by bit, it's like I homed in and refined my own of practice in response to what people who have direct contact with Russian practice were teaching me and then I constructed my own efficient way of doing it that suited me and then I wrote a book about the tools that I had taken from Russian practice that were very useful for making theatre.

Because I felt, and I still feel really strongly, that they are very old tried and tested tools that can raise people's craft. That's all clear: that's all said in the book. But I really haven't stopped that contact – even today it's there. Even when I finished the book and I went into multimedia work and other forms of expression it was still underpinned by that [practice].[13]

During her Churchill fellowship she observed productions, including Yefremov's work at the Moscow Arts Theatre, sat in on directors being trained by Vassiliev at the Russian University of Theatre Arts (GITIS) in Moscow, did the same with Dodin in the then Leningrad State Institute of Theatre, Music and Cinematography (LGITMiK) and watched both directors working with their own actors in rehearsal. She followed that experience with a month's embedded training at Gardzienice in Poland, which very much influenced the work of Classics on a Shoestring (Rebellato 2010: 324). Her link with Dodin – a practice she celebrates in *The Director's Craft* – was forged more deeply by her ongoing relationship with one member of his ensemble, Tatiana Olear, who was critical of her otherwise much lauded production in Milan of *Attempts on Her Life* (1999):

She said: 'You're not very good at directing Stanislavsky.' And I said: 'What is Stanislavsky, then – from your point of view?' And she then said: 'Invite me over to the UK and I'll show you what it is – what Stanislavsky's actual practice is.' So she came over and did a series of workshops, she came and saw my work, gave me feedback. So all the time my career is going along in the UK but all the time these people are coming in and out of my life, scrutinising it.[14]

This observation evidences the extent to which the Russian tradition of training is valued by Mitchell, first because she is clearly keen to understand, from within, how the ideas work in practice in order to utilise them in the rehearsal room and second because this curiosity has remained throughout her career so far – it is a constant in her own development as an artist. On this point she is unequivocal:

That trip that I then made in 1989 into '90 underpins everything I do today [laughs]. *Everything*. I was uniquely shaped by my exposure on that trip to those practitioners in Stanislavsky.[15]

In addition to her exposure to Dodin through Olear, two other figures loom large: Professor Soloviova, head of Dramaturgy at GITIS and an early critic of Mitchell's 'superficial' directing,[16] and Elen Bowman, a freelance acting teacher, trained at Sam Kogan's School of the Science of Acting. Bowman, described by Mitchell as 'an enormous cultural influence, secret, quiet . . . but tough', worked with Mitchell in one-to-one sessions for two years, developing the Active Analysis side of Kogan's practice (originally introduced by Maria Knebel when she taught Kogan at GITIS). Again, this commitment to a long-standing training practice, as a *director*, is worth noting and in itself is peculiarly Russian: there is as much weight placed on training directors in Russia as there is on training actors, even if there is not always a clear distinction made between the two. When Alexei Levinsky taught biomechanics for the first time in the UK in 1995 he led two classes, one for directors and one for actors. When the two groups shared their experiences out of the sessions, it became clear that exactly the same material was being taught to both groups!

There is evidence of the connection between Bowman/Kogan's methodology and Mitchell's in their mutual commitment to the finding of facts (Kogan 2010: 188–90; Mitchell 2009: 11–12) and more widely, as Rebellato notes, in the clear understanding that 'a director's role is to make some fundamental decisions before the rehearsal process has begun that will provide a concrete and precise starting point' (Rebellato 2010: 327). However, Mitchell does not by any means embrace all of the Science of Acting:

> Obviously with Kogan it's a mixture of 'clean' Stanislavsky with his own work as a psychiatric nurse – so it has other components, some of which are useful, some are not.[17]

In fact in this pursuit of a clean Stanislavsky Mitchell betrays her own transmission bias: a distinctly Russian 'line' from Stanislavsky, through Knebel, to Vassiliev or a similar line from Stanislavsky to Boris Zon and thence to Dodin. As a late behaviourist, there is no space in her thinking for an alternative route back to Stanislavsky via Boleslavsky and Strasberg:

> That does not influence me. I *reject* what happened in America because Stanislavsky moved on in his mature years into a much more profound practice. That's the bit of it that I really like. When it comes back, the American interpretation of it, it doesn't seem to be very useful.[18]

In effect, Katie Mitchell is an excellent example of a practitioner who has researched, sought out and embraced the *methodology* of the Russian tradition and, in doing so, has achieved a kind of affinity, or proximity to the practice, redolent of the direct, embodied person-to-person transmission identified above. Again there is little space for doubt in her mind on this point:

I am very, very close: you can track back what I do to Dodin and then behind him to other practitioners that go back. And in my interpretation and application of it, I am closer I think than Declan. I am closer because I'm slightly more practically [embedded]. I don't say that in a competitive way. I just think it's really important. I'm not influenced by much in this culture. I really am not. My bars are all set completely out of the culture, particularly by those shows. With Nekrosius and Vassiliev the bar is set so high. I'm so grateful to them.[19]

Michael Boyd

There is no concealing the emphasis Michael Boyd has brought to the Royal Shakespeare Company since being appointed as Artistic Director in 2003, nor any attempt to hide its history. As he says in a video interview on the new RSC website:

> The Royal Shakespeare Company was founded as an ensemble company on the inspiration really of the great eastern European ensembles of the late fifties, early sixties, that Peter Hall saw come to London or on his travels. One of the virtues of the European model of companies coming together over a long period of time is their ability to build rapport, trust, their skills.[20]

Boyd has clearly modelled his approach on the principles Peter Hall tried to establish at the RSC when he founded the company in 1961 and steered its transformation from the Shakespeare Memorial Theatre, where Komisarjevsky had worked in the 1930s. Fittingly, these principles were established between Hall and the then Chairman of Governors, Fordham Flower, in Leningrad in 1958, in a discussion which bore an uncanny resemblance to the Slavyansky Bazaar meeting between Stanislavsky and Nemirovich-Danchenko when the remit of the Moscow Arts Theatre was decided in 1897:

> There, in the Hotel Astoria, in a room . . . that resembled a set for *The Cherry Orchard*, talking late into the early hours of the next morning, Fordham and Hall finally thrashed out what was to become the blueprint for the Memorial's future.
>
> (Beauman 1982: 234)

Chief amongst these principles was to establish a company ethos with three-year contracts for the actors, something 'never attempted before in English theatre' (Beauman 1982: 240). It is a development Michael Boyd has reinstated with RSC performers now (in 2011) signing up for two and a half years' work to contribute to an ensemble made up of some 44 actors. Whereas Peter Hall was inspired at a distance by companies such as the Berliner Ensemble, Boyd's starting point, like Mitchell's, was a training for directors in Russia (a decade earlier in 1979). Here, in his own words, he was 'profoundly sheep-dipped . . . at the Malaya Bronnaya' under Anatoly Efros (Boyd 2004). Following this, he served his apprenticeship at the Coventry Belgrade and then the Sheffield Crucible, before becoming the founding Artistic Director of the Tron Theatre in Glasgow (1984–96). He joined the RSC as Associate Director in 1996.

In an interview for *What's On Stage* Boyd identified precisely the influence of Efros on his future practice:

> At the Malaya Bronnaya Theatre under Antolii Efros, I witnessed theatre making that was not afraid of being bold, expressive and challenging, or of its deep duty to tell the truth. I saw a theatre director given responsibility to be an artist in his own right and big enough to embrace that responsibility in a world where theatre was the most important art form. Poetry, film and the novel were easily censored, and music and art were less dangerous. I saw how Efros and his actors benefitted from working as an ensemble, refining their working practices over decades together. They achieved trust, an intimacy and a playful nature hard to sustain while in the hire and fire culture of British theatre. I witnessed the rigour of artist's training, which was longer and tougher than in Britain.[21]

The lack of *developmental* training delivered within a theatre company, as opposed to the formative training of a conservatoire, is a common theme in Boyd's thinking and this may also be part of his affinity with Russia, where, he says, 'no self-respecting major company in Moscow is without its own theatre school'.[22] Without a separate teaching institution there are limitations to what can be achieved. However, Boyd has developed several strategies at the RSC for addressing the training gap forged in a sector which still focuses on essentially naturalistic skills for small theatre spaces, film and TV. At the time of writing these include an Artist's Development Programme, company-wide skills sharing, and a reinvigorated movement direction programme, which recently has drawn on Meyerhold's biomechanics as one practice to counter a naturalistic diminutive tendency.[23] As Boyd asserted at the 2004 Ensemble Theatre conference at the Barbican: 'those non-naturalistic skills allow theatre to speak with a confident voice . . . we have begun at the RSC to encourage actors to look at their work as if they were dancers or musicians' (Boyd 2004).

At one level, Michael Boyd is moving the training at the RSC beyond the tradition of voice work, embodied in Cicely Berry, and 'downwards' to the rest of the body. However, he is also recognising a softer, more organic skills development that comes with a longer-term gathering of artists working together. Younger actors, particularly, can learn technique from the more experienced members of the company over an extended period of time, a process redolent of the repertory theatre culture of the earlier twentieth century.[24]

These developments in training evidence Boyd's canny recognition of the benefits of ensemble culture beyond the purely artistic domain and it is the organisational aspect of Boyd's Russian-inspired experiment which is arguably of most interest for us here. For beyond the rehearsal room and the stage, a similar ethos of ensemble has been promoted since his tenure as Artistic Director began, an ethos that is designed to permeate right across the organisation. The 2010 DEMOS report commissioned to measure the success of the project captures the idea:

> Ensemble should be thought of not only as a management tool, but as a set of moral principles that remains constant as a guide to leadership decisions and administrative actions. Ensemble is a value, as well as a description of a particular way of organising people: a way of being as much as a way of doing. It is also a moving target in that it can be rearticulated to meet changing needs and circumstances.
> (Hewison, Holden and Jones 2010: 17–18)

The DEMOS report chronicles a pivotal period in the RSC's history and relates the details of a profound shift in leadership style and organisational approach from Adrian Noble's tenure to the joint leadership of Boyd and the Executive Director Vicki Heywood. In short this was an abandonment of 'Project Fleet', a remedy for the organisation's 1999 financial crisis, which proposed several redundancies, a departure from a permanent home in London and a 'weaken[ing of] the ensemble principle in the acting company, with actors' contracts limited to six to nine months at most' (Hewison, Holden and Jones 2010: 34–5). The move away from Project Fleet was not an out-and-out *volte-face*, as the plan to leave the Barbican in London was carried through and the rebuilding of the Royal Shakespeare Theatre (RST) was originally part of Project Fleet and has just been completed, at the time of writing. However, on all other counts it did represent a significant change of culture and for the purposes of this concluding view it is this culture shift that is interesting.

Consider the RSC's revised statement of Purpose and Values: the corporate vehicle for communicating (and sharing) organisational culture. It is written in strikingly similar terms to the passage quoted above by Boyd on Efros:

> To create our work through the ensemble principles of collaboration, trust, mutual respect, and a belief that the whole is greater than the sum of its parts.
>
> (Hewison, Holden and Jones 2010: 45)

These core egalitarian principles, shot through with a theatrical sensibility, are now in evidence throughout the company – from the organisation of the executive office to the networking opportunities set up across departments – and the report is happy to recommend the application of this model to other organisations, which may be outside the cultural sector. That said, the report evidences examples of 'ensemble fatigue' in some sections of the RSC and a sense that, after a concerted 'push' since 2003 for change based on its principles, there is now limited currency left in the *word*, even if the associated behaviours and actions should remain.

It is of course recognised that change and flexibility are an essential part of any working environment, particularly in the creative industries, but there is a clarity of message evident in this report and in Boyd's consistent theme in the many interviews he has offered since taking on his role, which signals a new confidence at the heart of mainstream British theatre practice, one that does not see the ensemble as something peculiarly foreign or eastern European. In 2004, Boyd listed the main contenders for such a crown – including Mitchell and Donnellan – but he also cited a series of less obvious contributors to this twenty-first-century burgeoning of the theatre collective (Shunt, Told by an Idiot, Forced Entertainment) (Boyd 2004), suggesting that these informal ensembles may not have taken *their* inspiration from eastern Europe and Russia but may nevertheless be pursuing a cognate urge.

Of course there are other factors influencing the move (back) to ensemble values at the RSC – not least a much older Shakespearean tradition and its use of the thrust stage. This redesign of the RST now extends the notion of the ensemble to embrace the audience, a point made repeatedly by Boyd as the new space neared completion. Boyd's debt to Russia in fact lies somewhere between the two poles identified above. Like Mitchell, he was inspired to visit Russia to fill the gap in directors' training in the UK. With a few exceptions, this gap continues more than thirty years later in Britain. However, the impact of his immersion in Efros's theatre culture at the Malaya Bronnaya is less methodological than Mitchell's uncomplicated indebtedness to Dodin, Olear and Kogan. Boyd's vision is in some way grander: to establish a principle of thinking in one of the best known theatre organisations in the world that draws quite fundamentally on a practice which was alien to British theatre when Komisarjevsky arrived in Britain in 1919 – a practice which values long-term, collective interrogation of the play text, deep and developmental training and organic, evolving productions which can develop a life of their own during a long run.[25] There were factors in inter-war Britain when Komisarjevsky was struggling to establish a respect for the ensemble that made this impossible to achieve, and there are factors today which clearly militate against a wholesale adoption of Boyd's economic and artistic model. These might cynically be summarised as a powerful force for quick-fix short-termism fuelled by a fascination with immediacy and celebrity. However, the fact that such a counter-urge to emulate the spirit of Russian theatre is being led by all three of these respected practitioners, operating in the heartlands of the British theatre tradition, gives at least some cause for optimism and, in putting history to bed, offers several options for a shared theatre future.

Notes

1 Leach (2006: 78) quotes Rosalie Williams: 'The range and intensity of the training programme that Joan and Ewan had worked out, and the combination of their unique talents seemed quite extraordinary . . . We started each evening with relaxation exercises, lying on the floor. Then voice production, Stanislavsky, ballet, movement and mime'.
2 http://www.cheekbyjowl.com/history.php (accessed 4 April 2011).
3 Interview with the author, 14 October 2009. An edited version of this part of the interview has been published in 2010 in the Training Grounds section of *Theatre, Dance and Performance Training*, 1.1: 125.
4 'I never received a formal training in the theatre' Donnellan stated. 'But everybody is self-taught and nobody is self-taught, I think. But I was very influenced by teachers at school – the guys who taught me for A level were the most fantastic people and took me individually to see plays' (interview with the author, 14 October 2009).
5 Interview with the author, 14 October 2009.
6 'Some things must be the same each night, but many things must change' (Donnellan in Sierz 2010: 153).
7 Interview with the author, 14 October 2009.
8 Interview with the author, 14 October 2009.
9 Interview with the author, 14 October 2009.
10 Interview with the author, 14 October 2009.
11 Interview with the author, 14 October 2009.
12 There are three collaborations between Mitchell and Crimp to date: *Attempts on Her Life*, *The City* and Crimp's version of Chekhov's *Seagull*. She and Crimp 'work together "hand in glove"', according to Mitchell in an interview for *The Independent*, 17 April 2008, http://www.independent.co.uk/arts-entertainment/theatre-dance/features/katie-mitchell-id-hate-to-hang-around-making-theatre-when-theyre-tired-of-it-810224.html (accessed 7 April 2011).
13 Interview with the author, 11 January 2011.
14 Interview with the author, 11 January 2011.

15 Interview with the author, 11 January 2011.

16 Interview with the author, 11 January 2011.

17 Cf. Laura Barnett's interview with Mitchell in *The Guardian*, 15 July 2008: 'Q: What's the best advice you've had? A: A Russian woman called Professor Soloviova once saw a hit show of mine and said: "It looks very beautiful, but there's absolutely nothing going on between the actors." It set me up to ensure that was never the case again' (http://www.guardian.co.uk/stage/2008/jul/15/ theatre.culture, accessed 7 April 2011). In my interview with Mitchell she reiterated the point: '[Soloviova] became an important figure in the first few years of my directing life in the UK' (11 January 2011).

18 Interview with the author, 11 January 2011.

19 Interview with the author, 11 January 2011.

20 Interview with the author, 11 January 2011.

21 'Michael Boyd on Ensemble', a video interview from the RSC website: http:// www.rsc.org.uk/about-us/ensemble/michael-boyd-ensemble-interview.aspx (accessed 11 April 2011).

22 'Michael Boyd On . . . Russian Revolutions & the RSC', http://www.what-sonstage.com/interviews/theatre/london/E8831253193874/index.php?pg=234 (accessed 11 April 2011).

23 'Michael Boyd on Ensemble', a video interview from the RSC website: http:// www.rsc.org.uk/about-us/ensemble/michael-boyd-ensemble-interview.aspx (accessed 11 April 2011).

24 *The South Bank Show*, 28 December 2009. In addition, two symposia have been held at the RSC in 2009 and 2010. The first was designed to complement the commissioned productions of *The Grain Store* and *The Drunks*, and the author and Robert Leach led workshops on Russian actor training. The second, led by Struhan Leslie, focused on movement direction and had input from Andrei Droznin and Natasha Federova.

25 Boyd cites the example of Dharmesh Patel, who was relatively new to Shakespeare, being prepared by his experience of working for a year with the ensemble, to take on the part of Hamlet a year later (http://www.rsc.org.uk/ about-us/ensemble/michael-boyd-ensemble-interview.aspx, accessed 11 April 2011).

26 In an unpublished interview with Rob Elkington, Head of School Partnerships at the RSC (8 June 2009), Boyd identified three formative influences: his Scottish background, Coventry Belgrade and his 'experience in Russia'. The last is described in the following revealing terms: '[It was] where I witnessed the depth and richness of work that was possible when a community of artists work together for a very long period time, in some cases over 20 years, and then on any given project much more time was given than was the norm in British theatre or indeed at the RSC at the time. And I felt that there was fertile ground at the RSC for working towards the conditions of work that I wanted as theatre director, i.e. continuity of relationship, with a shared community of artists and time to devote to the work to give a depth of inquiry into the work and also time to develop a skill base I witnessed vividly in Russia, and very rarely witnessed in Britain'.

Bibliography

Beauman, S. (1982) *The Royal Shakespeare Company: A History of Ten Decades*, Oxford: Oxford University Press.

Boyd, M. (2004) Speech at Ensemble Theatre Conference, The Barbican, London, 23 November.

Carnicke, S. M. (2009) *Stanislavsky in Focus*, 2nd edn, Oxon: Routledge

Delgado, M. and Rebellato, D. (eds) (2010) *Contemporary European Theatre Directors*, Oxon: Routledge.

Donnellan, D. (2005) *The Actor and the Target,* London: Nick Hern.

Hewison, R., Holden, J. and Jones, S. (2010) *All Together: A Creative Approach to Organisational Change*, London: DEMOS.

Hodge, A. (ed.) (2010) *Actor Training*, 2nd edn, Oxon: Routledge.

Kogan, S. (2010) *The Science of Acting*, Oxon: Routledge.

Leach, R. (2006) *Theatre Workshop: Joan Littlewood and the Making of Modern British Theatre*, Exeter: Exeter University Press.

Lichtenfels, P. (2010) 'Lev Dodin: The Director and Cultural Memory', in Delgado, M. and Rebellato, D. (eds), *Contemporary European Theatre Directors*, Oxon: Routledge, pp. 69–86.

Mitchell, K. (2009) *The Director's Craft*, Oxon: Routledge

Rebellato, D. (2010) 'Katie Mitchell: Learning from Europe', in Delgado, M. and Rebellato, D. (eds), *Contemporary European Theatre Directors*, Oxon: Routledge, pp. 317–38.

Shevtsova, M. (2006) 'On Directing: A Conversation with Katie Mitchell', *NTQ*, 22:1 (February), 3–18.

Sierz, A. (2010) 'Declan Donnellan and Cheek by Jowl: To Protect the Acting', in Delgado, M. and Rebellato, D. (eds), *Contemporary European Theatre Directors*, Oxon: Routledge, pp. 145–64.

Smeliansky, A. (1999) *The Russian Theatre after Stalin,* Cambridge: Cambridge University Press.

Stanislavsky, K. (2008) *An Actor's Work*, trans. Benedetti, J., Oxon: Routledge.

INDEX